EUCHARISTIC
PRESENCE

Robert Sokolowski

EUCHARISTIC PRESENCE

A Study in the Theology
of Disclosure

The Catholic University of America Press
Washington, D.C.

Nihil Obstat:
Rev. Isidore Dixon
Censor Deputatus

Imprimatur:
Reverend Msgr. William J. Kane
Vicar General for the Archdiocese of Washington

September 30, 1993

The paper used in this publication meets the minimum requirements of
American National Standards for Information Science—Permanence of
Paper for Printed Library materials, ANSI z39.48-1984
∞

LIBRARY OF CONGRESS
CATALOGING-IN-PUBLICATION DATA
Sokolowski, Robert.
    Eucharistic presence : a study in the theology of disclosure / by
Robert Sokolowski.
        p.   cm.
    Includes bibliographical references and index.
    1. Lord's Supper—Catholic Church. 2. Lord's Supper—Real pres-
ence. 3. Mass. 4. Phenomenological theology. 5. Catholic Church—
Doctrines. 6. Catholic Church—Liturgy. I. Title.
BX2220.S64. 1994
264' .30—dc20
93-25826

            ISBN 0-8132-0788-6 (alk. paper)
            ISBN 0-8132-0789-4 (pbk. : alk. paper)

CONTENTS

ACKNOWLEDGMENTS

I am grateful to many people who have helped me in the preparation of this book. I wish especially to thank Gerard Austin, O.P., Christopher Begg, Romanus Cessario, O.P., Bishop Francis E. George, O.M.I., James T. O'Connor, Kenneth Schmitz, and Francis X. Slade. Jude P. Dougherty was an unfailing source of encouragement and good advice, in both the theoretical and practical orders. Finally, I wish to express my thanks to Paul J. Chiapparone and Criton Zoakos for the generous support they provided for the production of this volume.

I worked closely with Thomas Prufer throughout the years during which this book was written, and the thoughts expressed in it reflect our conversations over some three decades. Thomas Prufer died in March 1993; his death was a great loss to me and to the faculty, students, and staff of the School of Philosophy at The Catholic University of America. It is fitting that the mystery of the Eucharist should have been the theme of the last book on which we were able to collaborate.

To Joanna and Bill
my sister and brother

INTRODUCTION

I WISH to do two things in this book. One is to discuss a type of theological thinking that draws on philosophical resources provided by phenomenology. The other is to carry out some theological reflections on the mystery of the Eucharist. The thoughts about the Eucharist will be offered both as ends in themselves and as illustrations of the theological style I wish to describe.

Before addressing these two issues, let us review the articles of Christian faith that will be especially significant for our study. As Christians we believe that God has acted within the world and within human affairs. We believe that the central action God has performed occurred in the life of Jesus of Nazareth, who was not simply man but the incarnate Son of God. The culminating action in the life of Christ was his death on the cross, which redeemed mankind from sin and made it possible for man to participate in God's own life. The death and burial of Jesus were followed by his Resurrection from the dead, in which he entered, body and spirit, into a new, glorified form of being; his Resurrection revealed, confirmed, and completed what his sacrificial death had achieved.

The action that God performed in the life, death, and Resurrection of Jesus had been preceded by the actions he accomplished in the history of the Jewish people, especially in their liberation from slavery in Egypt; the Exodus not only freed the Jews from oppression but also established them as a special community within which God's glory, love, and justice were to be revealed: "In Judah God is known, his name is great in Israel" (Psalm 75:1). The ritual of the Jewish Passover, celebrated once a year, commemorated this liberation and establishment. Other Jewish meals, with their prayers and blessings, also proclaimed God's saving actions, especially his deliverance of his people.

The death and Resurrection of Jesus were a completion of the deliverance of the Jews. It was a new Exodus, leading not only a single nation but members of the whole human race from the bondage of sin into the life of adopted children of God. Christ in his death was compared to the lamb slain at the Passover: "For our Paschal lamb, Christ, has been sacrificed" (I Corinthians 5:7). And just as the Passover reenacted the first Exodus, so the Christian Eucharist reenacts the death and Resurrection of Christ.

Jesus established the Eucharist during the meal he had with his disciples on the night before he suffered. The Last Supper took place during the time of Passover and is presented as a Passover meal by the synoptic Gospels. It may in fact not have been a Passover meal, but it did take on the significance of the feast.[1] At that supper, Jesus transformed the bread and wine that were part of the ritual of the meal into an expression of himself in his death and Resurrection. In doing this, he indicated that what he was about to undergo would fulfill the action that God accomplished in the Exodus. It would be the completed form of the

---

1. See Bouyer, *Eucharist*, 99: "Paschal references were present not only in the prayers of this one night [Passover] but in all the meal prayers. And in fact, whether the Supper was this special meal or another, there is no doubt that Jesus did not connect the eucharistic institution of the New Covenant to any of the details that are proper to the Passover meal alone. The connection is solely with what the Passover meal had in common with every meal." See also Haag, *Vom alten zum neuen Pascha*, 136: "The Eucharist can rightly be called the Passover not because it continues and fulfills the Old Testament Paschal *meal*, but because in it the perfected Paschal *mystery* is celebrated sacramentally." On the scriptural and chronological problems concerned with taking the Last Supper as a Passover meal, see Haag, 121–36. For further discussion of the scriptural accounts of the Last Supper and a survey of recent scholarship concerning them, see Kodell, *The Eucharist in the New Testament*, 22–67.

Old Testament action, which was now to be seen as an anticipation of what occurred in Christ.

Jesus instructed his disciples to repeat what he did at the Last
Supper. The Eucharist, in its countless celebrations, was to allow
the divine action of Christ's death and Resurrection to be reenacted throughout the world. The Eucharist was to allow the act
of our Redemption to exercise its effect sacramentally, but still
visibly and audibly and palpably, throughout the human race, to
bring together before God the lives and the suffering of all who
believe: "The Spirit himself bears witness with our spirit that we
are children of God, and if children, then heirs, heirs of God
and joint heirs with Christ, if only we suffer with him so that we
may also be glorified with him" (Romans 8:16–17). Through the
Eucharist, the one action of God in Christ can be reenacted in
all places and times. The one action is made able to spread
sacramentally throughout the human race and we are enabled to
participate in it.

The Eucharist looks backward in time to the Last Supper and
the death and Resurrection of the Lord, and, more remotely, to
the Passover and the Exodus. It also looks forward to the eternal
life that was won for us by Christ on the cross: "*et futurae gloriae
nobis pignus datur*; the promise of future glory is given to us."
The Eucharist images the eternal banquet that is the fruit of our
Redemption.

These elements of Christian belief will be the subject of our
theological reflection. Before beginning our study, let us discuss
what kind of thinking our reflection will be.

꧁ꕥ꧂

THREE FORMS OF THEOLOGY

CHRISTIAN THEOLOGY has traditionally been distinguished into the positive and the speculative. It would be helpful to introduce a type of theological thinking that comes between these two. I would like to call this intermediate form of reflective thought the "theology of disclosure" or "theology of manifestation." We can describe the theology of disclosure by contrasting it with both positive and speculative theology.

Positive and speculative theology exemplify two ways in which faith seeks understanding. In pursuing their understanding, both forms of theology make use of human reason, but each does so in a different way: positive theology draws especially on the art and science of history, while speculative theology draws primarily on philosophy and the philosophical aspects of other sciences. Both forms of theology are critical sciences conscious of their methods; positive theology began in the Renaissance and speculative theology was most fully developed in the Scholasticism of the Middle Ages.

Positive theology attempts to show how the articles of faith are found and developed in Scripture and Tradition; it also attempts to formulate the truths of revelation in contemporary terms.[1] Biblical studies are the primary part of positive theology, but other parts examine the Fathers of the Church, the Papacy, the Councils, the liturgy, and the general history of the Church as it is related to the articles of faith. Positive theology discusses the historical settings in which the truths of faith have been revealed, confirmed, and transmitted; it tries to shed light on these truths by discussing the historical contexts in which they have been presented to us, and it also tries to formulate them again in terms appropriate to our own context.

Speculative theology attempts to do more than restate the truths of faith in a contemporary manner; it attempts to provide an ordered and comprehensive understanding of these truths, using distinctions, definitions, causal explanations, and analogies. Speculative theology is concerned with what we might call Christian realities or Christian "things," the things that have been presented to us in biblical and Christian revelation. Its primary task is to reflect on God, his divine nature and attributes, and his actions in the world. It also studies things such as human being, human responsibility, language, society, even things like time, matter, and life, but it studies them specifically in their relation to the God who has revealed himself to us. Speculative theology attempts to bring out more clearly the meaning of what has been revealed; it tries to explain some truths by showing how they can be derived from, clarified, or supported by others; and it draws analogies between various things that are known or believed. Its explanations work, of course, within the domain of faith; the reasons and causes it appeals to come from revelation. It is not the case that speculative theological arguments would "explain away" an article of faith by making it rest simply on natural truths.[2]

1. We cannot repeat something from the past or from another context without reformulating it to some extent in contemporary terms, particularly when the belief in question is one that we share. We cannot really say what *they* said unless we are able to express for ourselves *what it was* that they said. Stating something in contemporary terms is the reverse side of stating what was said in another context.

2. Thus, St. Thomas Aquinas considers theology (which he calls *sacra doctrina*) to be a demonstrative science whose principles are given in revelation. See, for example, *Summa theologiae* I 1 2 and I 1 8 ad 2.

Both positive and speculative theology must be distinguished from the teaching of the Church, which receives and hands on the elements of faith, the things that are believed. The Church conveys these things both in its ordinary life and instruction and in the particularly solemn pronouncements that it must formulate from time to time. Both positive and speculative theology are reflective; those who pursue these sciences presuppose the treasury of faith and go on to think about it according to the ways of thinking proper to their disciplines. The work of positive and speculative theologians is important for the preservation of faith, because by their questioning and investigation they help deepen the Church's possession of what it believes, and they are often able to help the Church draw distinctions between what is essential and what is coincidental in its practice and its revealed beliefs.

Normally the relationship between both forms of theology and the teaching Church is cooperative, but on occasion tensions may arise. It may sometimes appear that speculative theology puts its own reasoning in the place of the articles of faith, and it may at times seem that positive theology reduces the articles of faith to opinions prevailing in certain historical circumstances. The first error is called "rationalism" and the second "historicism"; they are the pitfalls that the two forms of theology must avoid. Theology may be tempted to fall into either rationalism or historicism because the truths of faith so greatly transcend human reason; the truths of faith are highly intelligible in themselves but only slightly intelligible to us, and so we may be inclined to allow the instruments used in theology (philosophy and history, with their more accessible intelligibility) to overshadow what has been revealed to us and what is believed.

There is room for another form of reflective theological thinking. This third form, which I will call the theology of disclosure, would have the task of describing how the Christian things taught by the Church and studied by speculative theology come to light. It is to examine how they appear. If speculative theology, with its focus on Christian things or Christian realities, were to be considered an "ontological" investigation, the theology of disclosure could be called "phenomenological."

At first glance it might seem that such a study of the appearance of Christian things resembles the work done by positive theology, which examines how the elements of faith have been made manifest in certain historical events, statements, and texts; but the approach followed by the two theologies is not the same. While historical theology examines facts, the theology of disclosure examines structures of disclosure; it describes the forms of manifestation proper to Christian things. It tries to describe how Christian things must display themselves, in keeping with what they are, and how they must distinguish themselves from things that resemble them and with which they may be confused. Thus, the theology of disclosure differs from speculative theology because it examines the manifestation of Christian things and not, primarily, their nature, definition, and causes; and it differs from positive theology because it is concerned with essential structures of disclosure, which would hold in all times and places, and not with matters of historical fact. Although it differs from these two theologies, it is obviously closely related to them and does not contradict anything they establish as true.

When we say that the theology of disclosure is supposed to examine the way of appearing of Christian things, many readers will immediately conclude that this theology is a type of psychology. But the theology of disclosure is not a form of psychology. It is not meant to be a psychology of religious experience, nor a psychology of Christian religious experience. If it were to be done as a kind of psychology, it would almost certainly become reductionist. It would fall into an error analogous to the historicism that positive theology can fall into when it is not done properly. The error into which the theology of disclosure would fall is called "psychologism," the reduction of things and objects into human projections, mental acts, or mere appearances in the human mind and sensibility. To interpret the theology of disclosure psychologistically would imply that this form of theology had nothing to do with Christian things themselves but only with certain subjective, psychological states. But this would be a misconception of the theology of disclosure, and it would also betray a misunderstanding of the being of appearances: it would misconceive the display of being. Thus, just as speculative theology must be distinguished from rationalism and positive theology from historicism, so must the theology of disclosure be distinguished from psychologism. I hope to elaborate and illustrate this distinction in the course of this book.

The hostile reaction we have described, which equates the theology of disclosure with psychology and which is highly suspicious of any study of appearances, is a response that one quite commonly encounters on the philosophical level when one tries to explain what phenomenology is. Phenomenology is often taken as a kind of psychology, and what it studies is often taken to be mere subjective experience. The reason why people frequently interpret phenomenology in this way is that in our cultural tradition, since the late Middle Ages and the early modern period, appearances have been badly misunderstood. Appearances have been turned into mere ideas, into subjective impacts that at best only hint at what things in themselves really are and at worst prevent us from ever reaching things at all; sometimes appearances are even said to be all that there is, with no "things" behind them whatsoever. Thus, when we begin to speak about a theology that investigates appearances, the average listener will immediately suppose that we intend to examine "merely" the way things appear, not the way they are. When one tries to describe and carry out the theology of disclosure, one is obliged to work against deeply ingrained prejudices that distort both our religious and our cultural understanding. A successful formulation of such a theology may be of benefit not only for religious thought but also for our general comprehension of how things come to light.

It is my conviction that Edmund Husserl has accomplished in principle a more adequate understanding of the relationships among things, displays, and ourselves as datives of display, but his achievement still needs to be adapted to various intellectual disciplines and still needs to be made better known. Husserl (1859–1938) was the founder of phenomenology, the philosophical movement that set the tone for Continental European philosophy in the twentieth century. Although his influence has already been very great, it seems to me that there are aspects of his thought that deserve further development and application, particularly in overcoming the limitations of modernity. I will discuss these possibilities more extensively in Chapter 13.

The three scientific forms of theology that we have distinguished—the speculative, positive, and phenomenological—have arisen within the cultural developments of the past thousand years. The first millennium of Christian thought was dominated by "Patristic" theology, which is named after the writers who practiced it and not the methods that it used. Patristic theology was a more immediate reflection on faith. The historical and the speculative were not yet clearly distinguished, and appearances were not subject to the suspicion that would later be raised against them. The second millennium of Christian thought introduced specialization and a self-conscious use of methods, but so long as the speculative and the positive were the sole major forms of theology, the wholeness of Patristic thought could not be critically restored. The Fathers, in their Neoplatonic style, accepted the display of Christian things as part of the subject of their theology. Emanation, splendor, presence, concealment, and imaging were spontaneously accepted and vividly described. It is this aspect of Christian reflection that the theology of manifestation is to recover, but in a manner appropriate to our day and age and with recognition of the contributions of both speculative and positive theology.

In recent years many theologians have discussed the issue of the appearance of Christian things; in this book we will draw especially on the writings of Hans Urs von Balthasar and Dom Anscar Vonier, O.S.B.[3] We will try to offer a philosophical in-

3. James T. O'Connor lists Vonier as one of the representatives of an interpretation of the Eucharist that he calls "the approach favored by almost all recent Catholic theologians." *The Hidden Manna*, 240; see 240–45. Masure, *The Christian Sacri-*

strumentality for the work of such theologians. The term "philosophical instrumentality" may at first seem to be an oxymoron, since it suggests that philosophy, which in the natural order is an end in itself, can become a means and an instrument for purposes beyond itself. But part of the sense of Christian belief is that everything natural is understood to have been created, so the theological context of Creation allows even what is ultimate in the human order to become subordinated to the theological. The manner of subordination, however, is distinctive: philosophy is *ancilla theologiae* in a way different from the manner in which things function as instruments for ends and purposes in the natural order. The service that philosophy provides in theology is not like the service it might be called upon to provide, say, for a particular political society, a task that would turn philosophy into an ideology.[4] Philosophy does not become ideological in Christian theology; it continues to function as a contemplative activity. It is not meant to establish Christian belief but to be involved in its understanding.

Philosophy can be elevated into this theological service without losing its integrity because of the unique new setting that is introduced through the Christian distinction between the world and God; this distinction is not like any of the distinctions that are drawn within the world. The Christian distinction opens up an entirely new understanding of the whole. It permits a transposition of senses in which some claims that might seem contradictory in the natural order can be understood as coherent and consistent in the theological; mysteries like those of the Incarnation and grace can be accepted as mys-

---

fice, and Journet, *La Messe*, are two other examples of this interpretation, which is a variation of that given by Dom Odo Casel, O.S.B.; see O'Connor, p. 243.

4. The prepolitical communities described by Aristotle are not based on argument or *logos*; the relationships between husband and wife, parents and children, and master and slave do not need justification by speech. Political society is based on argument; those who rule over others in the political order have to give a justification for their claim to rule. If philosophy were to become involved in providing this justification (as it does in Hobbes), it would cease to be contemplative and would become instrumental and ideological. The distinction between political and prepolitical society as regards the need for justification was made for me by Francis Slade.

teries and not as contradictions when they are understood within the setting of the Christian distinction. Likewise, the subordination of philosophy to biblical revelation does not destroy the preeminence and ultimacy of philosophy in the natural order.[5] Indeed, philosophy can flourish as a human activity in this new religious setting.

I have discussed the Christian distinction in a book entitled *The God of Faith and Reason*. That book deals with the widest and ultimate context of Christian belief, the context of Creation and the dependence of the world on God's creative choice. It also treats more particular issues, such as the sacraments and the Christian moral life, but it treats them in a derivative way. In the present volume, I will try to develop the same themes but will approach them from the other extreme. Instead of beginning with what is first in itself, I begin with what is first for us: the eucharistic action and eucharistic devotion that are a tangible part of the ordinary Catholic life, part of the things we encounter daily. We will explore how the Eucharist appears, the presentational forms through which it is given. But we will also explore the deeper levels revealed in sacramental life: the mysteries of the Incarnation and Redemption, the mystery of the God who creates out of freedom, wisdom, and love, and the mystery of the Holy Trinity. These dimensions are refracted and disclosed to us in the Eucharist, and exploring them is not tangential but essential to the study of eucharistic presence.

Our theological reflection will focus on the appearance of Christian things. Before speaking further about the theology of disclosure, let us develop some thoughts concerning the Eucharist. The issue of appearance is obviously essential to this Christian mystery. We will return intermittently to the theology of disclosure to explain more fully how it is to be understood, and we will discuss it again systematically in Chapter 13.

5. This is why Averroes' subordination of religious understanding to philosophy does not apply in the case of Christian belief. See Chapter 10 (d) and Chapter 14 (c)–(d).

2

❧

EUCHARISTIC PERSPECTIVES

THOMAS AQUINAS says that the Eucharist is both a sacrament and a sacrifice.[1] It is a sacrament insofar as it spiritually nourishes us, a sacrifice insofar as it is offered by the Church to God. Let us dwell on the Eucharist as a sacrifice, and let us develop two lines of thought.

First, the Eucharist is the same sacrifice as the one offered by Jesus on the cross, and yet the eucharistic celebration and the death of Christ on Calvary are two different historical events. How can the same redemptive action be achieved at different times and places? Clearly, a special sense of sameness and otherness is at issue in the Eucharist, one quite different from the identities and differences we encounter in our ordinary worldly experiences. The new sense of sameness and otherness needs to be clarified theologically.

Some light may be shed on this question by our second line of thought, in which we examine the perspectives from which the eucharistic celebration presents the sacrifice of Christ. Most of the prayers said by the priest during the Mass are stated in the first person plural. The priest says that "we" come before God

1. *Summa theologiae* III 79 5 c. See also Vonier, A *Key to the Doctrine of the Eucharist*, 82–83.

and pray, and he asks for blessings and forgiveness for "us." He prays in the name of the congregation and the whole Church. In particular, all the prayers in the eucharistic prayer are expressed in the first person plural. From the prayer of thanksgiving in the Preface, through the invocation of the Holy Spirit, through the memorial and offering that follow the institutional narrative, through the intercessions and final doxology, the priest addresses God the Father by expressing "our" thanks, praise, and petition.[2] At the central point of the Canon, however, within the context set by the prayers spoken by "us," and within the narrative describing the Last Supper, which is also stated by "us," the celebrant begins to quote the words of Jesus at the Last Supper and, within this quotation, he speaks in the first person singular: "This is my body. . . . This is the cup of my blood." Correlated with this quotational use of the first person singular is a citational use of the second person plural, referring to those whom Christ addressed: "Take this, all of you, and eat it. . . . Take this, all of you, and drink from it." The same form is used when the priest, speaking in the voice of Christ, says that his body "will be given up for you," and that his blood "will be shed for you and for all."

This change of person, even within a quotation, is dramatic and profound. It is not merely a grammatical change. The words express a change of perspective, a difference in intentionality and disclosure. We as a group of Christians at worship, we as addressing the Father, living in our own present time and place, scattered into countless celebrations of the Eucharist all over the earth, "we" are now all brought together to the single time, place, and perspective from which Jesus, at the Passover he celebrated with his disciples, anticipates his own sacrificial death. The one event on Calvary that we commemorate and reenact was first anticipated, before it occurred, by Jesus. It was anticipated and accepted by him as the will of the Father. In our eucharistic liturgy, through our quotation, we join in the per-

2. For these structural elements of the eucharistic prayer, see the "General Instruction of the Roman Missal," §55.

spective he had on the event that was to take place, that has taken place.

St. Thomas observes that the use of the first person singular in the eucharistic consecration is different from its usage in the other sacraments. In the cases of baptism and penance, for example, when the minister of the sacrament says, "I baptize you," or "I absolve you from your sins," he speaks in his own voice. Aquinas says that the "form" or verbal expression of such sacraments is stated "by the minister speaking in his own person."[3] The minister, speaking as a minister of the Church, expresses himself as the one doing the baptizing and the one forgiving sins. In the Eucharist, however, the "my" stated in the words of consecration is the first person singular uttered by Christ and only quoted by the priest. St. Thomas says that the words expressed in this sacrament are now spoken as though spoken by Christ himself: "The minister who accomplishes this sacrament does nothing except to state the words of Christ."[4] In the words used by the encyclical Mediator Dei and taken from St. John Chrysostom, the priest "lends his tongue and gives his hand" to Christ: his tongue allows Christ's words to be stated again, and his hand allows Christ's gesture of taking the bread and the wine to be carried out again.[5] The priest's gesture is an analogue to the verbal citation; it is a kind of quotation of the bodily movement. The citation of the words and the quotation of the gesture allow the things taken up and spoken about—the bread and the wine—to become the same in substance as those that were taken up by the Lord.

3. St. Thomas Aquinas, *Summa theologiae* III 78 1 c. Translations from the *Summa* are taken from the Blackfriars edition except when noted. St. Thomas explicitly distinguishes between the consecration, which is carried out by the priest *in persona Christi*, and the prayers of the Mass, which the priest says *in persona ecclesiae*; see *Summa theologiae* III 82, articles 1 and 6. On the history of the use of the term "in the person of," see Marliangeas, *Clés pour une théologie du ministère. In persona Christi, in persona ecclesiae*. See also his short essay, "'In persona Christi,' 'In persona ecclesiae'. Notes sur les origines et le développement de l'usage de ces expressions dans la théologie latine."

4. St. Thomas Aquinas, *Summa theologiae* III 78 1 c; my translation.

5. *Mediator Dei. Encyclical Letter of Pope Pius XII on the Sacred Liturgy*, §69. The citation is from Chrysostom's Homilies on St. John's Gospel, 86 §4.

It is true, of course, that Christ is the ultimate agent in all the sacraments, but the presentational form in which his agency is carried out is distinctive in the Eucharist; the words used in baptism and in absolution, for example, are not the quoted words of Christ. When Christ told his apostles to "make disciples of all nations, baptizing them in the name of the Father, and of the Son, and of the Holy Spirit" (Matthew 28:19), he was not at that moment performing what his words described; he was not baptizing. When he said to his disciples, "Receive the Holy Spirit. Whose sins you forgive are forgiven them, and whose sins you retain are retained" (John 20:22–23), he was not at that moment forgiving sins. Baptism and absolution are not the reenactment of any particular action of either baptizing or absolving carried out by Christ. But when Jesus told the apostles to "do this in memory of me" (Luke 22:19), he referred not just to something they should do but to what he himself was doing.[6] Whenever they would do it, they would reenact the same thing he accomplished when he spoke the words.

The interplay of the first-person plural ("we") and the first-person singular ("I") occurs within the wider context of the liturgical celebration of the Eucharist, which develops in a beautiful progression of stages. First, there are the introductory greetings, prayers, and rituals, in which the local community is assembled: the Church is actualized into this time and place, into this particular church, this particular manifestation of the Body of Christ. Second, once assembled, the community listens and responds to the word of God in the scriptural readings and responsorial psalm, as well as in the application made to the present in the homily and the prayer of the faithful. Third, having assembled and heard God's word, the community, now acting even more explicitly through the priest, carries out its eucharistic action, which ends in the "application" that occurs

6. According to Léon-Dufour, the *this* that the apostles are to do "refers to the total action Jesus has just performed over the bread. . . . The *this* refers not to the entire meal taken at the Supper, but specifically to the actions and words over the bread and the cup." *Sharing the Eucharistic Bread*, 109.

in communion, as the altar becomes the table of the eucharistic meal. The eucharistic action can be carried out only by the baptized; although catechumens can share in the initial assembly and in hearing the word of God, they cannot, in principle, participate in the offering of the eucharistic sacrifice and the reception of the eucharistic meal; only those who are formally members of the Body of Christ can do so. Eucharistically the catechumens can listen but they cannot yet act.

The three stages of the Mass involve many presences of Christ in his Church: the community itself establishes a particular presence of the Body of Christ, Christ is present in the minister who celebrates the Eucharist, he is present in the Scriptures read during the liturgy of the Word, and he becomes sacramentally present as he is both offered in sacrifice and received in communion during the liturgy of the Eucharist.[7] These presences are graded in intensity, leading up to the real presence of Christ that occurs when the bread and wine are changed in their substance into the Body and Blood of the Lord: "The Word assembles the Church for his incarnation in her."[8] Moreover, there is a graded order among those who participate in the Eucharist, particularly between the priest and the congregation. This order emerges not because of any personal qualities of the individual celebrant, but because the ordained celebrant represents Christ the Lord. The liturgy culminates in the assumption of the voice of the celebrant by the quoted words and voice of Christ. In a sacramentally and grammatically perceptible way, Christ becomes the speaker of the words of institution and the doer of the gestures associated with them. The appearances of the words and gestures of institution become, through quotation, those of Christ, as the "we" of the community, the Body of Christ, becomes the "I" of Christ the Head of his Body the Church (Ephesians 1:22–23).

The distinctive role of the priest in the Eucharist has been ex-

---

7. See "Constitution on the Sacred Liturgy," §7.
8. Schmemann, *The Eucharist*, 68.

plained in various ways. He is a representative of the bishop and hence a link between the particular community and the universal Church. He does not only come from and represent the local community, but has been sent to it: first by the bishop, more remotely by the apostles, and ultimately by Christ; in this sense his presence is apostolic, the presence of someone who has been sent. But the deepest reason for the distinctive role of the priest in the Eucharist lies in the fact that only God can offer worthy sacrifice to God: the Christian God is so transcendent to the world, so holy, that no act of human religion is adequate in his presence. Only the incarnate Son of God can make the suitable offering and exchange.[9] The priest must speak and act *in persona Christi*, because only Christ can act in the appropriate way in the presence of the Father; in what other name could the Church speak and act? This offering of the Son of God is not just mentioned or remembered in the Eucharist but expressed and actualized in the Son's own words. The community, in adoration and thanks, joins in this offering, but the offering is first there through the action of Christ, who uses the words and actions of the priest to reenact his perfect offering sacramentally. In speaking of the role of the priest in the Mass, Pope John Paul II says, "The sacrifice is offered 'in the person of Christ' because the celebrant is, in a special sacramental way, identified with the 'eternal high priest' who is the author and primary agent of his own sacrifice. . . . His sacrifice—and it alone—could and can have expiatory value in the eyes of God, of the Trinity, of the all-transcendent holiness."[10] The priest represents the community before the Father as he says the prayers in the first-person plural, but he represents Christ to the Father and to the community as he speaks in the first-person singular. As Josef Jungmann says, "The rite makes it clear that the priest, when he

9. See Bouyer, *Rite and Man*, 92: "In Christianity, not only will the sacrifice offered by man appear as an act of faith and obedience to the free and sovereign Word of the God of the alliance, but it is this God who becomes in the most explicit fashion the offerer, the priest, and the victim."

10. Pope John Paul II, "The Lord's Supper (*Dominicae Coenae*)," 150.

begins the words of consecration, is no longer merely the representative of the assembled congregation, but that he represents
now the person of Christ, because he does what Christ did." [11]

The Christian eucharistic prayer was developed from Jewish
prayers of proclamation, thanksgiving, and blessing for the
great works of God, prayers that were part of the ritual of Jewish meals. [12] However, the eucharistic prayer was not a simple

11. Jungmann, *The Eucharistic Prayer*, 16. In speaking about the sacrament of offering in the Eastern liturgy, Schmemann states that the ritual offering is the same as
the offering made by Christ, and he continues, "It is only the priest who is called and
ordained to affirm this identity, to manifest and fulfill it in the mystery of the Eucharist" (*The Eucharist*, 115). He adds that this distinction does not separate the priest
from the community: "Not only does the priest not separate himself from the gather-
ing, but, on the contrary, he manifests his unity with it as the unity of the head with
the body."
There has been considerable emphasis in recent years on the role of the local
community as the subject of eucharistic celebration. An important stimulus to this
discussion was the article by Congar, "L'ecclesia' ou communauté chrétienne, sujet
intégral de l'action liturgique." See also Jungmann, *The Eucharistic Prayer*, 30; Austin, "Is an Ecumenical Understanding of Eucharist Possible Today?"; and Power, *The
Sacrifice We Offer*, 156. The recognition of the role of the community need not di-
minish the distinctive function of the ordained celebrant in linking the local
community to the universal Church and in representing Christ, the one whose
action the Eucharist ultimately is. The roles of the community and of the celebrant,
as we have noted in the text, can be different, and the one role or voice is made
more distinct by its contrast with the other; see Congar, "L'ecclesia' ou communauté
chrétienne, sujet intégral de l'action liturgique," p. 270 and p. 280: "We must say
that if the whole Church is priestly, and if it is so ontologically, prior to the distinction between the simple faithful and the ordained ministers, the Church is, however,
not fully sacerdotal except through these ordained ministers, who alone can perform
the Eucharist and transmit the priesthood."
12. Thus Bouyer, in *Eucharist*, has a section entitled "From the Jewish *berakah* to
the Christian Eucharist," 91–135. In *Rite and Man*, p. 116, Bouyer describes the *berakah* as the summit of the religious sensibility of the Old Testament and the predecessor of the Christian Eucharist. See also Léon-Dufour, *Sharing the Eucharistic Bread*,
44–45: "Thus the 'blessing' or *berakah* was the context in which the Eucharist took
shape; in all probability the liturgical meal, accompanied as it was by words of praise
and proclamation, had its prototype in the Israelite *toda*." Discussion continues
about which Jewish prayers formed the background and origin of the eucharistic
prayer and how they did so. See Talley, "From *Berakah* to *Eucharistia*: A Reopening
Question," and "The Literary Structure of the Eucharistic Prayer"; Giraudo, *La struttura letteraria della preghiera eucaristica*; Ligier, "From the Last Supper to the Eucharist," and "The Origins of the Eucharistic Prayer: From the Last Supper to the
Eucharist." O'Connor, however, mentions some reservations that have been expressed "concerning the relationship between the berakoth prayers and the Christian Eucharist" (*The Hidden Manna*, 7 n. 6).

transposition of Jewish prayers; folded into the prayer of praise and thanksgiving was the institutional narrative, together with the words of institution included in the narrative. This blending of old and new is appropriate. What "work of God" could, for the Christian, be more deserving of proclamation, thanks, and praise than the Redemption achieved in the death and Resurrection of Christ?[13] And what more intense way could there be of proclaiming this action than to quote the words used by the priest and victim when he anticipated the sacrifice? The eucharistic prayer fulfills the Jewish prayer of thanks and praise in the way that the New Testament fulfills the Old, and also in the way the Christian tabernacle differs from the Jewish: in the Jewish synagogue the tabernacle contains the Torah, but in the tabernacles of Christian churches the Word of God dwells not as the Law, not as the inspired written word, but as the incarnate Son of God in his eucharistic presence.

In the sacred liturgy the Christian community is brought into the offering of the Son to the Father, an action that was once achieved in the past but endures as an eternal offering in heaven (Hebrews 8:1–3, 9:23–26). The Eucharist is our participation, even now, in the celestial liturgy. Alexander Schmemann describes the divine liturgy as "the continual ascent, the lifting up of the Church to heaven, to the throne of glory, to the unfading light and joy of the kingdom of God."[14] In accomplishing the center of its liturgy, the Church forgoes any verbal initiative of its own and simply quotes the words and gestures of Christ, using the ordained priest as the instrument for this quotation. The Church thus expresses itself through the interaction of the pronouns "we" and "I," and the use of these pronouns expresses a shift of perspective between two points of view, that of the Christian community at worship and that of Christ at the

13. The combination of the old and the new prompts Schmemann to speak of a "liturgical dualism" in the early Church; see *Introduction to Liturgical Theology*, 45–51.

14. Schmemann, *The Eucharist*, 165. One might ask whether this exalted aspect of the eucharistic ritual is not sometimes neglected in practice in the current Western liturgy.

Last Supper. The two perspectives, as well as the transition between them, deserve fuller theological exploration. The two points of view manifest one and the same event, the sacrificial death of Jesus, and the way in which the "two" bring the "one" to light calls for further discussion. Before pursuing this theological issue, let us make some philosophical remarks about identity and recognition, and about the appearances through which they are achieved.

3

❧

IDENTITY IN APPEARANCES

ONE OF THE themes that run through Husserl's philosophy is that of the identity of objects as given through a manifold of appearances. Every object of experience is presented through a series of appearances that are proper to that sort of thing.[1] A material object, a cube, for example, presents spatial profiles and sides to one point of view, but it presents other sides and profiles as we change our point of view by walking around the cube, by turning it, or by cutting it open and letting its internal sides and profiles become visible. Moreover, even while we are examining the cube from one particular angle, it presents itself as also having other sides and other profiles that we *would* see if we were to move around the cube, rotate it, or cut it open. The absent sides and profiles are cointended as absent while we directly see the sides and profiles facing us or faced by us. Our seeing is accompanied by a halo of what Husserl calls empty intentions, those that anticipate the absent parts. Now the cube itself is not to be understood as the sum of these profiles and sides, nor is it to be completely separated from them; rather, the cube is the identical thing that appears as one and the same while the vari-

1. See Sokolowski, *Husserlian Meditations*, chapter 4, "Identity in Manifolds," 86–110.

ous profiles and sides are presented and cointended in the course of perception. The cube is an identity in and through a manifold of manifestation or display or disclosure.

Besides appearing to perception in a mixture of presences and absences, the cube can also be remembered (as having been seen from a particular point of view at a certain moment), it can be imagined (again, from some particular angle and in some particular context), and it can be merely named and talked about. We can articulate it in speech, bringing out various features and relationships. We can also intend it as being intended by other persons, by other minds, whether as perceived, remembered, imagined, anticipated, named, or articulated by them. The cube presents itself not only as given to us but as also given or emptily intended by others; the intersubjective dimension is one of the levels or patterns among the modes of appearance enjoyed by bodily things.

Each mode of intending that we accomplish, each of the modes of presentation the thing offers, allows the thing to be identified and recognized as one and the same in all this diversity of appearance. Furthermore, each level of manifestation intensifies the identity of the thing. The thing can be itself in more ways when it has aspects beyond those that I see or touch now, and it can be itself in still more ways when it has profiles that can be given to others and not only to me; and when the thing can be itself in a greater variety of presentations, then there is, so to speak, more "itself," more identity in the displays of the thing in question. The greater the being of the thing, the greater its powers of display, the greater its *eidos*.[2]

We have used a simple bodily object, the cube, as an initial example. Other kinds of objects have other kinds of manifolds. An embarrassing situation, for example, has a flow of displays differ-

2. Thus Gadamer speaks of an "increase in being (*Seinszuwachs*)" when an object is presented in a new light. Such an increase occurs, for example, when a theme is presented anew in a literary work or a painting. See *Wahrheit und Methode*, 133, 141. Karl Rahner also discusses how a being manifests or expresses itself through a manifold of appearances; see his essay, "The Theology of the Symbol," 222–35.

ent from that of a cube, but it is formally similar in being one "object" identifiable in a complex series of appearances. One of the prominent features in the presentation of embarrassment is the force of the perspectives of other persons. There could not be embarrassment unless the perspectives of others, indeed of particular other persons, were copresent to the one who is embarrassed. An event was embarrassing to me because what I did was also seen or known by others, and their points of view had to be cointended by me as I experienced the action from my own point of view. To be embarrassed, I must have known that what I was doing was also seen or known by those other persons. Furthermore, I appreciate their perspectives on my embarrassment as a different kind of presentation from the perspectives they have on the cube that I see from this side; they see the event as something being done by someone, not as a mere object that is presented to them. The mixtures of presence and absence, the kinds of appearances involved in the manifold of each, are different.

Still other kinds of objects have still other kinds of manifolds. The identity of a word or a sentence is different from that of a sports event; the identity of a tree is recognized in a manifold different from that of a railroad station; a cat presents a different mixture of presences and absences than does a human being; an artifact presents itself differently than does a thunderstorm; a picture has a manifold different from that of a fossil. Some differences can be rather subtle: is the mode of appearance of a decoy, for example, different from that of a statue? Is a carved duck-decoy a decoy or a statue when it is place on a mantlepiece? Each kind of thing prescribes its own particular series of appearances within which it can be identified as itself; Husserl says that each kind of thing is a rule for a certain sequence of ordered appearances.[3] The thing itself governs its own appearances, within which it is recognizable for what it itself is.

One of the tasks of phenomenology is to explore the manifolds of appearance through which different things become

---

3. See Husserl, *Ideen*, Book 3:33. Also, *Ideas*, Book 1:357–58.

identified. Such exploration is what is meant by phenomenological description. Phenomenology is not supposed to describe
"how things happen to look to me," "how I feel when I'm tired,"
"how I feel when I get mad," and the like. Its task is more formal and more objective. Things by their nature have a certain
style of appearing, and if we are to recognize those things, we
have to respond to them by carrying out certain appropriate
kinds of intending, certain cognitive achievements. Without our
involvement, things will not appear for what they are. We have
to move spatially, bring into focus, articulate thoughtfully, remember, imagine, anticipate, sympathize, intend emptily in
many diverse ways, return and recognize the same thing again,
and so on, and the activities we have to carry out are prescribed
by the nature of the thing we are trying to identify. Both the objective presences and absences and the subjective intuitions and
empty intendings, both the "noematic" and the "noetic" factors,
as Husserl calls them, have essential and necessary structures,
and these patterns are to be brought to light in a phenomenological analysis.

In carrying out such analyses, phenomenology takes appearances seriously and gives them their proper philosophical
formulation. Displays are distinguished from things; displays are
the ways things can be presented and intended, but the thing
itself—the cube, the word, the tree, the man—is the identity
that presents itself and is recognized in the displays.

Appearances are not merely psychological impacts. They are
not things, but they are *of* things, and they have their own way
of being and their own necessity and essential structure. Appearances are worthy of philosophical recognition. For example, if I
say to you, "Come and see how this building looks from this
angle," and if you come and take a look, you will have the same
view I just had. It is not just the building that is the same; the
view or the look—the look you came to take—is also the same.
The view is "out there" and not just in my mind or in your
mind. The view belongs to the building, even though it must be
distinguished from the building. The building itself is an identity

that discloses itself through many such views and looks, which have their own mode of being as forms of presentation, disclosure, display, manifestation, appearance.

Of course, we must distinguish the appearance at one moment from the appearance at another: Husserl would call such momentary views the "profiles," the *Abschattungen*, of the building.[4] These do change from moment to moment and from viewer to viewer; you could not enjoy the very same profile I had of the building. But within these profiles, a common view or a common look can be had. Often the objectivity of a view is unnoticed philosophically because the difference between a view and a profile is not recognized; all appearances are mistakenly reduced to profiles, to momentary views.

The reason we tend to dismiss appearances as merely subjective and accidental is that we remain caught in the prejudices of our modern age, which devalues appearances to "mere" appearances and also devalues the direct experience we have of things, giving preference to the scientific knowledge of the "thing in itself" as the only reliable access to truth. Appearances are taken as "mere" appearances; perception is taken as a form of imagination. These prejudices can be overcome, and in principle they have been overcome through Husserl's thought, but they remain premises that underlie most of our cultural expressions, controversies, and convictions.

4. On the differences among sides, views (or aspects), and profiles, see Sokolowski, *Husserlian Meditations*, 87–89.

4

❦

THE ONE SACRIFICE OF CHRIST

LET US NOW return to our theological reflections on the Eucharist. The two perspectives that are expressed in the eucharistic prayer, that of Jesus at the Last Supper and that of the congregation at worship, are two perspectives on one and the same event. On the night before he suffered, Jesus anticipated his passion and death. He interpreted what he was about to undergo in terms of the Jewish Paschal sacrifice; the words "which will be given up" and "which will be shed" recall the sacrifice of the Passover lamb. But Jesus did not just think and speak about his coming death: he enacted it in the first Eucharist. Stated more precisely, he preenacted what was about to occur. Jesus said that his disciples should do *this* in memory of him, but what he did was not a memorial but an anticipation.

There is only one central sacrifice, the one that was offered by Christ as a bloody sacrifice on the cross, for the Redemption of mankind and the glory of God. It is not the case that one sacrifice was offered at the Last Supper and another on Good Friday. It is also not the case that the first Eucharist was merely the beginning of what occurred on Good Friday; as Dom Anscar Vonier says, the first Eucharist *was* what occurred on Good

Friday. But the event at the Last Supper was indeed a sacrifice, precisely because it preenacted the sacrifice on Calvary. Jesus did not merely intend an idea of his death; he intended his actual sacrificial death and identified it as the thing that was happening as he took the bread and wine, said the words of institution, recalled the sense of the Passover sacrifice, and told his disciples to do as he had done. He did not tell them just to say what he said but to do as he did. In his action, Jesus achieved not only the sacrament of the Eucharist, by which he spiritually nourished his apostles, but also the sacrifice of the Eucharist, because what he did at the Last Supper embodied what he would do when he gave himself up for sinners. Jesus identified his own sacrificial death in the appearances of the action he performed at the Last Supper.

And when we Christians now—wherever or whenever we may be, wherever the "now" is stated—when we Christians celebrate the Eucharist, we do not, as it were, have a simple, immediate contact with the sacrifice of Jesus on the cross. The Eucharist is not a ritualized Passion Play. Our celebration does reenact the sacrifice of the cross, but it does so only through the perspective on that sacrifice that was held by Jesus at the Last Supper. As Léon-Dufour says, "The Supper symbolizes the sacrifice of Christ on the cross. The Mass likewise symbolizes the sacrifice of Christ on the cross, but it does so by way of the Supper."[2] In the Eucharist we look back at the death of Jesus, but we look back at it as profiled through the Passover anticipation by Christ. Only because the sacrifice of the cross was embodied and preenacted at the Last Supper can it be reenacted and sacramentally embodied now. This complex relationship of manifestation is expressed by the dramatic shift from the first-person plural to the quoted first-person singular during the prayer of consecration.

1. See Vonier, A Key to the Doctrine of the Eucharist, 94–95. Also Journet, La Messe, 10: "The words of transubstantiation at the Last Supper bring about not another sacrifice, but another presence of the same sacrifice."
2. Léon-Dufour, Sharing the Eucharistic Bread, 287.

Earlier we said that the Eucharist seems to require that two different historical events, the liturgical action and the death of Jesus, must somehow become one. But strictly speaking, the theological issue requires that not two but three events become somehow one and the same: the action at the Last Supper must be added to the events of Calvary and the altar. But the Last Supper and the Eucharist are not only events; they are also representations, and each offers a perspective on something beyond itself, on the sacrifice of Calvary. The matter is even more complex, however, because one of these two perspectives, that provided by the altar, not only is directed to the cross, but also includes the perspective on the cross provided by the Last Supper. The altar represents the Supper, which in turn presents the death and Resurrection of the Lord.

This set of perspectives is part of the manifold of appearances through which the redemptive sacrifice of the cross is presented to us, to be identified as one and the same. Let us remind ourselves that the sacrificial death of Jesus, besides having been anticipated at the Last Supper, besides having taken place and been experienced by many witnesses on Calvary, and besides being reenacted in the Eucharist, is also made manifest to those who read the narrations of the passion in the Gospels; it was named and articulated by St. Paul and other New Testament writers; it is intended in the prayers and meditations of Christians; it is made manifest in the preaching of the Church. In still another way it is represented in the suffering of martyrs and the lives of confessors. The martyrdom of St. Stephen, for example, is presented as an imitation of the death of Christ. Through the power of the Holy Spirit, Stephen was, in his death, configured to Christ: he said he "saw Jesus standing at the right hand of God," and he spoke words that echoed the words of the crucified Christ (Acts 7:54–60, Luke 24:33–46).[3] Stephen imitates Christ by asking forgiveness for those who kill him, and whereas Christ commends his spirit to the Father, Stephen prays that his spirit

---

3. See von Balthasar, *Licht des Wortes*, 235.

be received by the Lord Jesus. The death of Stephen draws its meaning from the death of Jesus, but it also in its turn sheds light on the crucifixion of the Lord; it is a new profile on his redemptive death. It was one of the appearances through which St. Paul was enabled to recognize the identity of Christ: Paul's conversion took place shortly after his participation in the martyrdom of Stephen (Acts 9:1–9).[4]

All these forms of disclosure are part of the way the one event of our Redemption is presented and identified for what it is. Each form is a different manner of presentation and adds a new dimension to the event. The identity of the sacrifice of the cross, although it was achieved on Calvary, was not fully manifested on Calvary. All that it is was not revealed to the onlookers there. Only as anticipated and accepted by Christ, and only as reenacted in the Church's Eucharist, at Emmaus and Corinth and Rome and at all the places where it has since been and will continue to be reenacted, only as presented in the Scriptures and the life of the Church, and only as mirrored in the suffering of martyrs and the virtues of confessors, is its identity made recognizable to us in our present state, and even in our present state we anticipate looking back at our Redemption from the eschaton, through the Paschal appearance of the "Lamb that seemed to have been slain" (Revelation 5:6). The redemptive sacrifice of the cross prescribes these appearances and all of them are important; the identity of the central sacrifice appears in the continuation of Christ, in the life of the Church, in a way in which it did not yet appear at the moment of its consummation.

A simply ontological theology would tend to look through these many appearances of the death of Jesus and would concentrate on the fact that his death was a sacrifice and that it redeemed all men. But a theology of disclosure, without denying the outcome of such an ontological analysis, would show the relevance of the further appearances of Christ, in his Resurrec-

4. See von Balthasar, *Theodramatik*, 3:385.

tion and in his sacramental presence, in the Scriptures and even in prayer, preaching, and the Christian life, as further irreducible manifestations of the identity of the sacrifice of the cross. In regard to the Eucharist, an ontological theology emphasizes the sacrificial character of the Eucharist and the real presence of Christ within the sacrament, and it discusses the forms of causality by which the sacramental presence occurs.[5] A theology of disclosure, however, brings out the perspectives of anticipation and commemoration, and their interweaving in the Eucharist, as part of the manifold of appearances proper to this reenactment of the action by which we were redeemed.[6]

After all, besides being a true sacrifice, the Eucharist is also essentially a sign. As Vonier says, the Eucharist is a sacramental sacrifice and not a natural one.[7] It involves a representation. While it would be theologically incorrect to deny the sacrificial character of the Eucharist and the real presence of Christ in the sacrament, it would be no less incorrect to deny its character as a sign. Indeed, if the Eucharist were simply a new natural sacrifice and not a sacramental one, the altar would become a rival to the cross.[8] The Eucharist accomplishes what it signifies, but this accomplishment does not eliminate its being as a sign; the Eucharist continues to signify. Since it is a sign, its distinctive mode of appearing becomes part of what it is; even an ontological reflection on the Eucharist would have to take into account its mode of presentation. Being a sign is not a matter of just psychological interpretation or of something that occurs "only" in our minds.

5. For an excellent example of a theological discussion of instrumental causality, see Barden, "The Metaphysics of the Eucharist."

6. Karl Rahner says that the word of God in the sacrament "accomplishes what it signifies and makes present what it proclaims" ("The Word and the Eucharist," 315, translation modified). If an ontological theology emphasizes the accomplishment of the sacrament, a theology of disclosure focuses on how the sacrament presents what it declares. Rahner, in this essay, calls for a deeper theology of God's word in the sacraments, a theme that could well be explored in a study of manifestation. The role of words in natural disclosure would be contrasted with their role in sacramental proclamation.

7. Vonier, A Key to the Doctrine of the Eucharist, 86–91, 110, 141.

8. Ibid., 135.

We can react to the Eucharist as a sacramental sign only because it *is* such a sign.

The fact of being a sign takes on particular importance in the Eucharist, because the Mass can be considered a true and proper sacrifice each time it is offered only if the sacramental appearance brings an increase in identity and being. If the new appearance did not have something entitative about itself—in the way in which manifestation in all its forms is a dimension of being—the present celebration would fail to distinguish itself appropriately from the event that occurred only once. The necessary range of differences would not be available to allow the sacramental reenactment of the original action.

Thus, it is in the area of presentation that the new element of the liturgical celebration takes place; it is there that we can find the differences within which the identity of the redemptive action of Christ can be sacramentally disclosed. James T. O'Connor observes that the Council of Trent left many issues concerning the Eucharist open for further theological discussion, and among them "it left unexplained the *novum* (the new element) present in each Mass."[9] It is not that more is offered in the Mass than in the original sacrifice or that something else is offered, but the mode of presentation is changed, along with the new datives for this presentation, who are then drawn into the offering. The sacramental sacrifice both is and is not "new," in the way—analogously—that a picture both is and is not other to what it depicts, and a quotation both is and is not a new statement.[10]

---

9. O'Connor, *The Hidden Manna*, 235. Journet often appeals to the theme of presence to speak of the Mass as the same sacrifice as that of Christ; see *La Messe*, 11, 68–71, 99.

10. One might say that the difference between the sacrifice of Calvary and the Eucharist lies in the bloody and unbloody manner of offering, but for that difference to take place, there already has to be a distinction drawn between the natural and the sacramental enactment. The Eucharist could not be an unbloody sacrifice if it were not already established as a sign and not a natural sacrifice. The difference in the form of presentation is presupposed by the difference in the manner of offering; being a sacramental sign comes first.

The Mass is different from such worldly analogues, however, because at its core it is a presentation not just before us but before the eternal Father. The Eucharist is a reenactment in time of the action of the incarnate Son before the Father; what is it to quote, image, recall, and proclaim this act before God the Father? The original sacrifice is not "past" for the eternal Father in the way it is past for us; hence quotation and representation before the Father are not like quotations and representations exercised simply among men. The Eucharist transcends time for us because it presents itself before the transcendence of God. In these and many other respects, the way in which the Eucharist is a sign is an issue for the theology of disclosure.

5

༄༅

DEEPER THEOLOGICAL
CONTEXTS FOR THE
EUCHARIST

UNTIL NOW we have been speaking directly about the Eucharist. It is also necessary for us to place this sacrament against the background of other, more general Christian beliefs. In this chapter (a) we will discuss the Incarnation as a setting for the Eucharist, and (b) we will examine the Christian understanding of Creation as a still more basic horizon. To amplify our treatment of Creation, (c) we will enter into a discussion concerning necessity and contingency. Then, (d) we will examine a Scholastic expression of the Christian understanding of Creation, and finally (e) we will comment on how the theology of disclosure can help us in the exploration of these themes.

A

Like all the sacraments, the Eucharist cannot be understood except in the context set by the Incarnation. Each sacrament involves some bodily activity: pouring water, anointing with oil, taking and consuming bread and wine, imposing hands, speaking. The material dimension of the sacraments reflects the bodily presence of God in Christ. Furthermore, the sacraments express the manner in which God was presented in Christ. Jesus did not serve merely as an occasion for conversion to God: it is not the case that those who met and reacted to him were just turned toward God by him, as they might have been by a prophet. Rather, they found God in and through Christ: "No one comes to the Father except through me" (John 14:6), and "Whoever has seen me has seen the Father" (John 14:9). Jesus does not *lead* us along the way to the Father; he *is* the way (John 14:6).[1] Likewise, it is in and through the sacraments that the recipient enters the life of grace, is forgiven, and receives the fruits of Redemption; the sacraments do not simply occasion the conversion of the person to God in faith. As van de Pol has written, "Just as the Incarnation is the visible manifestation of God, whom no man has ever seen, so also in the holy sacraments Christ has rendered visible the invisible working of the divine Spirit. It is because of this that the normal way of return to God leads through visible realities to those which are invisible."[2]

Louis Bouyer, in *The Eternal Son*, speaks of Christ's humanity as more than the humanity of a single individual. Bouyer claims that Jesus, because of his divine personality, was able to enter into contact with the whole human race: "Christ is one among us, certainly, but not in opposition to all of us, not in a contradistinction that would make him other to each of us, but in an assumption that can encompass all of us. Far from excluding anything that belongs to any of us, he bears us all, and all the possibilities of our humanity, in a fullness of realization."[3] In the Incarnation, the divine life became embodied in Christ, not as a single episode but as the beginning of the spread of this life in the entire human race. St. Leo the Great expresses a similar thought: "Human nature has been received by the Son of God

1. See von Balthasar, "Mysterium Paschale," 288.
2. Van de Pol, *The Christian Dilemma*, 71–72.
3. Bouyer, *The Eternal Son*, 396; translation modified.

in such a union that one and the same Christ is not only in that man who is the firstborn of all creation, but also in all his saints."[4] In rather striking terms, C. S. Lewis speaks of the Incarnation as installing a "good infection" that now germinates among us and enables us to live the new life of adopted children of God. The human race, the biological species that was elevated by nature to the power of reason, is now redeemed and established as the place in which God's own life becomes imaged and lived in charity. Lewis says, "The whole offer which Christianity makes is this: that we can, if we let God have his way, come to share in the life of Christ. If we do, we shall then be sharing a life which was begotten, not made, which always has existed and always will exist."[5]

Bouyer stresses the corporate character of Christ's humanity in order to avoid the theological error that would isolate the Incarnation and Redemption and see the actions of Christ as exercised in a solitary relation to the Father, with the rest of humanity rendered "miserably superfluous."[6] The new life brought in the Incarnation and Redemption is to be distributed throughout God's creation, until all the elect come to share in the Son's filial relationship with the Father. Bouyer says, "Christ becomes unthinkable if he is separated from the humanity in which and from which he is continually being born, and from the history that attains its fullness in him."[7] When St. Paul says that through his sufferings he is "filling up what is lacking in the afflictions of Christ" (Colossians 1:24), he does not imply that the passion of the Lord was somehow inadequate, but that it was meant to be dispersed among all the faithful, who would be enabled to join their sufferings to those of Christ. The action of Christ toward the Father is an action that is to permeate the human race and make it the instrument of God's glory within

4. St. Leo the Great, "Sermon XII on the Passion," in Migne, *Patrologia Latina*, 54:356. See also Pope John Paul II, "Lord and Giver of Life (*Dominum et Vivificantem*)," 96: "The 'first-born of all creation,' becoming incarnate in the individual humanity of Christ, unites himself in some way with the entire reality of man."

5. Lewis, *Mere Christianity*, 137.   6. Bouyer, *The Eternal Son*, 388.

7. Ibid., 405; translation modified.

the created world. As Hans Urs von Balthasar says, the work of Jesus was "exclusive" in that he alone could accomplish what he was sent to do, but it was "inclusive" in that it allows all of us entry into the life it brought.[8]

Certainly the Eucharist has a place both in expressing this distribution of the divine life and in bringing it about among us: in the eucharistic passage of chapter 6 of St. John's Gospel, Jesus says, "Whoever eats my flesh and drinks my blood has eternal life, and I will raise him up on the last day" (John 6:54). The "scattering" of the Eucharist to all parts of the earth, together with the sowing of the Word of God, lets the new life spread to all places and times. The choice of bread and wine as the embodiment of the memorial of our Redemption furnishes an image of the Incarnation: as the Son took on human flesh and assumed it into the life of God, so the common material elements of bread and wine become transformed into signs and vehicles of that same life. And the fact that bread and wine are food confirms the sacrament's involvement in the distribution of life. It is in being fed that our life is sustained. The Eucharist is the most material of all the sacraments; it establishes a sacramentality in eating. The bread and wine given to us to be consumed are palpable images of the life that is conveyed to us in and through the Church.

B

The way in which sacraments are signs must also be seen against the background of the Christian understanding of the world as created and God as Creator.

In Christian belief, God is understood as having created freely, and not out of any need. God exists in such perfection and sufficiency that he did not have to create anything in order to perfect himself. Indeed, he did not need to create in order to bring about any greater goodness in being. His own existence is

8. Von Balthasar, *Theodramatik*, 3:327.

so complete that the further existence of created beings does not add to the perfection and goodness of being, even though it does add to the number of beings that are. God has indeed created, he has brought about the being of things other than himself, but he need not have done so. The world, according to Christian and biblical belief, might not have been.[9]

We must not underestimate the originality of this Christian understanding of God and the world. It is not an understanding found in all religions, nor is it found in all monotheisms. In the natural understanding of the world and the divine, in pagan religious thought, god or the gods are taken to be part of a more encompassing whole. The divine is the best, the most permanent and necessary, and the most powerful, but it is not and it could not be all that there is. The divine and the nondivine are necessary complements to each other. In the pagan understanding, it would be not false but it would be meaningless to say, "God is all that there is"; such a statement would contradict the sense of the divine found in the natural religious understanding.

But according to Christian belief, God might have been all that there is. In fact he is not all that there is; he has created a world other to himself; therefore in Christian belief it would be false to say, "God is all that there is." However, in contrast with paganism, it would not be meaningless to say so. The sense of the word "God" becomes transposed in biblical belief, so that the statement "God is all that there is" changes from being meaningless to being meaningful, even though false. The word "God" is not used univocally between paganism and biblical faith.

We note in passing that in a pantheistic religious understanding, and perhaps in a Hindu and Buddhist understanding of the whole, the statement "The divine is all that there is" not only would be meaningful but would also be true. Everything that is not divine would in some radical sense not be, or at least

9. On the Christian understanding of the distinction between the world and God, see Sokolowski, *The God of Faith and Reason*, 1–52; also, "Creation and Christian Understanding."

ought not to be. As Bouyer says about the Neoplatonic divinity, "The return to the god of the Neoplatonists signifies that any distinct existence is an error and that it must ultimately be an-nihilated."[10] The difference between Christianity and pantheism lies not only in their respective interpretations of the divine but also in their interpretations of the beings other than God. In contrast with pantheism, Christian belief acknowledges the sub-stantial being of things, as well as the truth and goodness grounded in their act of being. Indeed, for Christian belief worldly things are even more intensely real than they are taken to be in paganism, because they participate through Creation in the independent existence of the God who could be even with-out the world.

God might not have created; he did not need to create. God and the world do not, for the Christian, form a necessary whole. Only if this understanding of the world and God lies behind the doctrine of Creation can Creation be understood as being truly free, achieved through generosity and abundance. Any other understanding of the relation between the world and God would make Creation necessary in some sense, at least as a means of in-creasing the goodness of the whole. It would imply that God needed to be perfected, that he created in order to overcome a deficiency. Creation would not be totally generous; it would be at least partly motivated by need, and God would not be the model of sheer generosity that biblical revelation declares him to be.

The world around us is therefore interpreted differently in pa-ganism and in Christianity. We all start with the same surround-ing world, but for the pagan or for the secular thinker this world is simply there and it remains simply there. It may have changed its form and content in various ways, it may have evolved in the course of its being, but it simply exists as the final context for ourselves and for everything in it, including the ultimate, gov-erning powers, or perhaps the single governing power, that could be called divine. In this pagan understanding the divine is

10. Bouyer, *Le mystère paschal*, 134 n. 25.

beyond the vicissitudes and limitations we must all endure, but in all its power and in its tranquility it remains only the best part of the encompassing whole.

For the Christian, the world takes on a new sort of contingency. Not only might it change in many ways; more radically, it might not have been at all. This possibility is presented to our thinking through biblical revelation. If the world might not have been, then it exists through something like a choice, and the one who chose it to be cannot be reduced to anything, no matter how exalted or powerful, within the world. Furthermore, Christian belief also maintains that if the world had not been, God would not be lessened in any way. Thus Christian faith does not reveal a new god but a new sense of the divine, one only analogous to the sense found in natural religion.

The strategic role of Creation in the encounter between Christianity and paganism is brought out in two events described in the Acts of the Apostles, the visit of Paul and Barnabas to Lystra, and the speech of Paul at the Areopagus. At Lystra, Paul cured a man who was crippled. The people interpreted the cure according to their own religious understanding: they believed that Paul and Barnabas were gods in human form, and they called Barnabas Zeus and Paul Hermes (because he did all the talking). The priest of the city brought oxen and garlands to offer sacrifice to them (Acts 14:11–13). Paul and Barnabas were outraged at this, and the first thing Paul said was, "We are of the same nature as you, human beings. We proclaim to you the good news that you should turn from these idols to the living God, 'who made heaven and earth and sea and all that is in them'" (Acts 14:15). Even with these words, however, Paul and Barnabas could scarcely prevent the people from sacrificing to them. The point we take from this colorful incident is that the first thing to be conveyed to the Gentiles—and this was the first recorded speech of Paul to the pagans—is the understanding of God as Creator. This understanding must be accepted before anything else can be taught.

Nothing can be said about Redemption until we know what kind of God it is who redeems us. Paul uses the same starting point in his speech in the Areopagus. He says he will tell the Athenians about the Unknown God, and the first attribute he describes is that he is "The God who made the world and all that is in it, the Lord of heaven and earth," and that he "does not dwell in sanctuaries made by human hands, nor is he served by human hands because he needs anything" (Acts 17:24–25). Once again, the issue of Creation and the sovereign perfection of God provides the bridge between paganism and Christianity.

We must also add that the radical biblical sense of God comes through hearing and not through direct experience. The gods of, say, thunder and lightning, birth and death, or harvest and nourishment are perceived as the powers immanent in such things, but the God who could be even if there were no world cannot be differentiated from the world by any human perception. We have to be told about him and he must be revealed to us. As Rahner says, "Supernatural reality can display itself only through the medium of the human word, as long as it cannot present itself in its own proper reality. . . in the immediate vision of God."[11] For this reason, the statement "God could be all that there is" is not a report arising from our own experience. It is not the case that we first experience what is meant in this statement by the term "God," and that we then express the feature we have discovered; rather, the full statement comes first, and we are told that we must understand the subject of the sentence in such a way that the statement can be accepted as true. The words and the statement come before understanding; hearing precedes faith (Romans 10:17).

Finally, the introduction of the biblical sense of the Creator is not merely the introduction of a single idea. The understanding is revealed as part of a network of ideas, and as involved in a

11. Karl Rahner, "The Word and the Eucharist," 267.

way of life to which we are called and which we must practice. The revelation of this sense of God took place through the centuries of events and activities in the Old Covenant, and it was brought to perfection in the New Covenant, in the Incarnation and in the death and Resurrection of Christ. The understanding calls for a distinctive response from those who receive it; the virtues of faith, hope, and charity are the dispositions corresponding specifically to the transcendent God of the Bible. The pagan gods, because they are part of the whole, do not require the same response as the biblical God does; as Alain Besançon says, the gods of paganism were not sufficiently distinguished from the world to call for an act of faith.[12] And as we shall see at the close of this chapter and in the next, it is only the transcendent biblical God who could have redeemed us in Christ and who could act toward us in a sacramental way. Both Redemption and the sacraments disclose the nature of the God who could be, in undiminished perfection, even if the created world did not exist.

C

In the Christian understanding, while the world might not have been, God could not not be. As Anselm says about God, "He cannot be thought not to be."[13] God is so understood that it would be impossible for him not to be. Whereas the world exists contingently, God exists necessarily. However, the necessity involved in God's being and the contingency involved in the possible nonbeing of the world are not the same as the necessities and contingencies found within the world.

We must tread carefully as we begin to use the terms "necessity" and "contingency." This pair of terms is used in one way

12. Besançon, *The Rise of the Gulag*, 10: "Gnosticism did not thrive in a pagan environment, where the divine had not yet been gathered into one Godhead, transcendent and separate from the world, and where, as a result, religious adherence was not sealed by an act of faith."

13. St. Anselm, *Proslogion*, chapter 3.

within natural religion and philosophy, and in another way within biblical revelation. The terms become transposed in biblical belief. Their meanings shift. Let us try to mark off the meanings of the terms and the nature of the transposition that occurs when the terms are placed within a biblical context.[14]

For our natural thinking, the whole within which we and all other things are found is divided into necessary beings and contingent beings. The necessary things include, for example, beings that are changeless, motions that never vary, the eternal laws of nature, the changeless essences of things. The contingent things are the beings and the events that do exist but that might have occurred in different ways, or that might not have occurred at all. Whether I am here or there or elsewhere at this moment is contingent, but for me as a man to be a rational animal is necessary.[15] Let us express this in a simple diagram (Diagram 1). For natural thinking, the whole is distinguished into the necessary and the contingent.

DIAGRAM I

| The Necessary |
| The Contingent |

Now the necessity by which the biblical God exists is not the same as the necessity within the world. Likewise, the contingency by which the world as a whole exists is not the same as the contingency that marks things and events within the world. To bring out these differences we can supplement our first diagram with Diagram 2, which expresses the biblical understanding of the relationship between creation and the Creator.

14. The material in this section owes much to Prufer, "Juxtapositions: Aristotle, Aquinas, Strauss." My diagrams are developed from a diagram in Prufer's essay.

15. Our distinction between the necessary and the contingent is not as fine-grained as that of Aristotle. He distinguishes three modes of being: the necessary, that which happens for the most part, and the accidental. See *Metaphysics* VI 2.

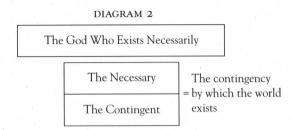

DIAGRAM 2

The God Who Exists Necessarily	
The Necessary	The contingency
The Contingent	= by which the world exists

The major change is that the biblical God could exist without the world; Diagram 3 could represent all there is.

DIAGRAM 3

The God Who Exists Necessarily

But in natural religion and philosophy, it would not be possible for the domain of the necessary to be the whole. It would not be possible for Diagram 4 to represent the whole.

DIAGRAM 4

The Necessary

That is, the worldly necessary could not be all that there is. The worldly necessary can exist only in conjunction with the worldly contingent. The situation illustrated in Diagram 1 is meaningful and possible; the one in Diagram 4 is not.

Furthermore, in natural religion and philosophy, the divine is taken to be part of the domain of the necessary. If we were to try to incorporate the divine into Diagram 1, we would have something like Diagram 5. The divine in this natural understanding could not exist apart from the whole. The divine is the preeminent part of the whole, the best part of the necessary, but it could not be without the rest of the whole, without lesser necessities and without contingencies.

DIAGRAM 5

The Divine	
The Necessary	
The Contingent	

These metaphysical diagrams are meant to help us register the distinctions they illustrate. If we were to state the distinctions simply in words, and were to distinguish two forms of necessity and two forms of contingency (perhaps by using superscripts or supplementary adjectives), our argument would seem to get lost in arcane verbiage. The point of the distinctions would be hard to see and to keep in mind. The use of diagrams makes things and distinctions more vivid and helps fix the meaning of the terms as they are shifted between the natural and the biblical contexts. The spatial configurations help keep the concepts clear.

Let us elaborate these distinctions. We should not minimize the importance of the worldly distinction between the necessary and the contingent, the distinction illustrated in Diagrams 1 and 5. Reaching insight into the necessary is what human reason strives to do, and this desire is not just a matter of academic curiosity: it is a matter of getting to know how things have to be, of realizing their natures and boundaries. Such insight comes not just from reading books, but also from prudence and experience, from getting to know how things really are. Statesmen, parents, automobile mechanics, computer experts, builders, physicians all want to disclose the necessities of things and to get beyond the contingencies of perception and happenstance. They want to know how things have to be, not just how things happen to be. Experts want to have such insight in the fields in which they work, but everyone wants to have it in regard to being human and living a life, in dealing with choices, friendship, the pleasant and painful, the future and the past, one's family and society. No one escapes the need to know some necessities, and no one wants to be lost in contingencies. It is obvious that we want to discover the necessary in theoretical matters, but it is also true that we want to reach an appropriate necessity in practical matters as well. A virtuous character, in fact, establishes stability in our lives and conduct and makes it possible for us to be more vividly aware of what is the just thing to do in situations calling for action. A virtuous character gives us a sense of *decet* and *non decet*, of the moral necessity in the situations before us. A virtuous character is an embodiment of practical reason, a participation of appetite and passion in reason. Thus in both the theoretical and practical domains, reason and the necessary are correlated one with the other.

But the correlation of reason and necessity does not mean that we should want to escape contingency. The contingent— the happenstance and the coincidental, that which could be other than it is, that which happens usually but not always— does exist. We would be denying half of the world if we tried to flee to the necessary and live our lives only there. We would be like the "Friends of the Forms" in Plato's *Sophist* (248A), lost in sheer necessity. The necessary is necessary only as played off against and played with the contingent. There is gist, but not sheer gist; the best for us is to find the gist of things. Chance and the contingent provide opportunity and variety for the human estate. (We should observe that the task of philosophy is not to escape to the necessary and to sheer form, but to contemplate the interplay between the necessary and the contingent and to validate each of these modes of being.)

So, the necessary requires the contingent. However, it remains true that the necessary is the best. The contingent becomes good for us when it is blended with and integrated into the necessary: an actor may have the luck to get a good part just at the crucial moment in his career, but unless he were a good actor already, and unless there were the dramatic world with its necessities and definitions, the contingency of the opportunity would make no sense at all. It is easy for us to sink into the contingent, to be carried this way and that by it; this is the condition of the prisoners in Plato's cave and the kind of mind attracted to the lowest part of the Divided Line. The human challenge is to let the necessary disclose itself and differentiate itself from the contingent. The more mind we have, whether in theory or in practice, the more we can allow this disclosure to take place; to have less mind is to be more at the mercy of the contingent and to attain the necessary, if at all, only indistinctly, only by luck, and never really *as* necessary.

It is important, in our theological reflection, to have a sense of the ultimacy of the world for the natural human situation. It is also important to have a sense of the weight of the distinction between the necessary and the contingent, and to appreciate the nobility and goodness of the necessary. Only when we appreciate the density of the whole can we appreciate the transposition undergone by the terms "necessary" and "contingent" in biblical belief.

In biblical belief, the whole, which is so dense and final outside biblical revelation, is now seen as existing "contingently" and God is seen as existing "necessarily." But when we make this transposition, we must avoid thinking that the domain of the necessary in the world is now somehow dissolved, that everything worldly is diluted into the worldly contingent. That is, we must avoid the understanding that could be expressed in Diagram 6.

DIAGRAM 6

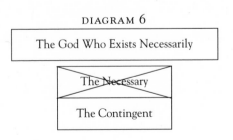

To turn everything in the world into the contingent in this way would be to equate the contingency that marks the world as a whole with the contingency that is found as part of the world. The consequence of such a confusion, of course, would be another confusion regarding necessity; the necessity by which God exists would be equated with the necessity that is part of the world, and the divine choice to create would be assimilated to events that take place within the contingent domain of the world. God's choice would then appear as a "merely contingent" event and would take on the quality of being arbitrary. Cajetan criticizes Scotus for making this mistake. He says, "How uncultivated and upstart (quam rudis et novus) is Scotus's way of speaking . . . when he calls the divine will 'the first contingent cause.' It is nefarious (fas quippe non est) to speak of contingency in the divine will."[16] All such confusions follow if the shifting senses of necessity and contingency are not clearly recognized.

We must also observe that the metaphysical categories found in Aristotle and other pagan philosophers, and the patterns of thought found in natural religion, must be transposed into analogies when taken into Christian discourse and Christian metaphysics. It is not just that we have to add new categories or new names; the old names have to be newly understood. "Necessity" and "contingency," "divine" and "worldly," take on a transposed sense. And the issue that helps us determine the new, analogous senses is the issue of how the world and God are to be understood: although the world does obviously exist, it might not have existed, with no lessening of the perfection of being, since God would still be in undiminished goodness and greatness.

D

The ontological theology of the Scholastics was well aware of the shifts in meaning we have just discussed and it expressed

---

16. Cajetan, Commentary on St. Thomas Aquinas, *Summa theologiae*, I 19 3. This citation and translation are taken from Prufer, "Juxtapositions: Aristotle, Aquinas, Strauss," 38.

them very well. For Aquinas, God is sheer *esse* subsisting in itself; God does not need the world as a further perfection because
all the perfections of creatures are formally and eminently contained in him. God is not part of the world, nor is he one of the
entities taking part in what Aquinas calls *ens commune*, being in
general. God is the cause of the totality of the world and the
cause of *ens commune* and therefore he exists outside them. God
as *esse subsistens* is only analogous to the entities that are.

Aquinas also recognizes the difference between divine necessity and the necessities found in creatures. In the *Quaestiones
disputatae de malo*, he says that the divine will is "beyond (*supra*)
the order of the necessary and the contingent, as it is beyond all
created *esse*."[17] In his commentary on Aristotle's *Metaphysics*, he
says, "Just as being itself is subject to divine providence, so are
all the features (*accidentia*) of being as being, among which are
the necessary and the contingent. It pertains to divine providence not only to make this particular being (*hoc ens*), but also
to grant it contingency or necessity."[18] Both necessary and contingent beings are found within the things created by God. God
stands outside the necessity and the contingency immanent in
created things: "Whatever exists necessarily or contingently depends on a higher cause, which is the cause of being as being;
and from [this cause] is derived the order of necessity and contingency in things."[19] Thus, St. Thomas clearly distinguishes
between the necessity by which God exists and the necessity
that is part of the world. The latter, together with the contingency that is part of the world, is created by God.

Furthermore, as the texts we have just cited imply, the contingency found within the created world is different from the
freedom by which God creates, and the contingency within the
created world is also different from the contingency that marks
the created world as a whole. This is a point that deserves fur-

17. St. Thomas Aquinas, *Quaestiones disputatae de malo*, 16 7 ad 15.
18. St. Thomas Aquinas, *In duodecim libros metaphysicorum Aristotelis expositio*, VI
3 §1220.
19. Ibid., §1222.

ther reflection. We may be quite willing to admit that the divine necessity is different from the necessities we find in creation, but we are less used to saying that the contingency that
marks the created world as a whole is different from the contingencies that occur within the world. These are two different
kinds of contingency. In both cases, contingency means that the
beings that exist could have been otherwise; but the way in
which they could have been otherwise is different. Within the
world, contingency is explained by the indeterminacy of the
causes on which the contingent beings depend. Some of these
contingent beings depend on the free choices of rational agents,
but not all do; many depend simply on chance, on the way
things happen to turn out, on the coincidental confluence of
causes. But the created world as a whole does not have a wider
context of created causes that intervene in its contingency. The
created world as a whole depends only on the freedom, wisdom,
and holiness of God and on nothing else. This sort of dependence is a distinct and unique kind of contingency. The sense in
which the world as whole "could be otherwise," that is, the
sense according to which the world might not have been, is not
the same contingency according to which you could be seated
somewhere else at this moment or according to which it might
have rained in Washington on 31 July 1990.

Our remarks on necessity and contingency in the last two
paragraphs are a technical formulation of the biblical understanding of the relationship between the world and God. Stated
less technically, the biblical understanding holds that the world
(everything other than God) exists through a free divine
choice; the world might not have existed. God himself exists
necessarily and in such plenitude that he did not need to create
in order to perfect himself in any way. His choice to create was
made out of generosity and abundance. St. Thomas expresses
this truth when he explains what it means to say that God
rested after the six days of Creation: "God did not rest in
created things themselves as though in an end, but [rested] from
created things and remained in himself, in whom his blessed-

ness consists (since he is not blessed because he made things, but because, having sufficiency in himself, he does not need the things that have been made)."[20]

E

The remarks St. Thomas makes concerning necessity and contingency are moves within what we have called an "ontological" theology, a form of thinking that examines the mode of being of God and the world. The theology of disclosure can add a new dimension to such a Scholastic analysis; it can offer a study of how the biblical understanding of God and the world differentiates itself from the natural understanding found apart from revelation. The theology of disclosure can help us examine how the "transcendent" necessity and contingency came to light for us and how they differentiate themselves from the "immanent" necessity and contingency that belong to part of our normal worldly encounters.

In our natural and original experience, the world is first presented and taken as the encompassing whole, as the ultimate context, enclosing both necessities and contingencies. Everything, both the divine and the nondivine, is subject to the rhythms and destiny of the whole. But through biblical revelation, through the events and teachings presented in both the Jewish and Christian Scriptures, the new understanding of God was gradually brought forward, and we were taught that the divine is to be found neither in the stars nor in the Canaanite idols, but in the God who could be all that he is in goodness and perfection even if the world did not exist. A new distinction between the divine and the nondivine was introduced, one that deepens and transforms the distinction between the gods

20. *Quaestiones disputatae de potentia* IV 2 ad 5. I am grateful to Susan Selner for bringing this text to my attention. See also the Preface to the Canon of the Mass, Weekdays IV: "You have no need of our praise, yet our desire to thank you is itself your gift. Our prayer of thanksgiving adds nothing to your greatness, but makes us grow in your grace."

and the profane that was known to paganism. The theology of disclosure describes the emergence of this sense of God not simply as a historical fact—although the historical circumstances surrounding it are of great importance—but in the structure of its appearance. The theology of disclosure does not do what positive theology does. It describes the uniqueness of this sense of God and the impact it has on our own self-understanding. It also explains the difficulty we have in sustaining this revealed sense of the divine, showing that we tend always to pull back to a natural comprehension of the world as the final context of being and truth.

The theology of disclosure does not assert all these things as mere historical facts, but it also does not assert them as mere facts of human psychology. This manner of differentiating itself from the natural religious phenomenon is proper to the biblical sense of the divine as such. God is hidden not just because of human psychological limitations, but because he is not one of the things in the world. The way God is manifested to us reflects the way he is. The theology of disclosure avoids both historicism and psychologism, just as phenomenology works its way between both the history of ideas and psychology.

One of the further things a theology of disclosure does is to bring out the relationship between the Christian understanding of God and the world and the doctrine of the Incarnation.

In the mystery of the Incarnation, Jesus is understood to be fully and integrally human, and fully and integrally divine. He is one person in two natures. As St. Athanasius and other Church Fathers have said, Christ could not have redeemed us if he were not both human and divine.[21] In Christ, the God who created the world, and who could exist in undiminished goodness and greatness even without the world, himself became part of what he created, and he did so without becoming lessened in his divinity.

21. See St. Athanasius, "On the Incarnation of the Word," §§8–9, 44.

This understanding of the Incarnation is related to the Christian understanding of Creation in the following way. If the Incarnation is to be possible, the divine nature must be taken as not a worldly nature, as not one of the kinds of beings that are encompassed by the whole. If the divine nature were to be conceived as it is in natural religion, as the best kind of thing in the world but still a part of the world, the Incarnation would become an incoherence. It would be a union of two worldly natures, each of which is defined by not being the other. A union of two such worldly natures would force us to say that one of the two is diminished by the other, or that they only seem to be brought together in one being, or that together they make up a new, unnatural kind of being. Most Christological heresies veer toward some form of these misunderstandings, and in doing so they show how human reason wants to pull the revealed mystery down to its own worldly horizon and its own level of comprehension. Thus, as a matter of disclosure, the full sense of the divine is revealed in the doctrine of the Incarnation, as a kind of theological presupposition for the Incarnation. As St. Athanasius writes, "While yet men were not able to recognize [the Word of God] as ordering and guiding the whole, he takes to himself as an instrument a part of the whole, his human body, and unites himself with that, in order that since men could not recognize him in the whole, they should not fail to know him in the part."[22]

The Incarnation perfects the understanding of divine transcendence that was revealed in the Old Testament. In the Old Covenant it would not have seemed possible for God to become incarnate in his own creation. Such an embodiment would have seemed to compromise the sovereignty of God over the world and his difference from it. Thus the New Testament not only adds belief in the Holy Trinity to the faith of the Old Testament;

22. Ibid., §43. On man as part of creation and as the appropriate place for the Incarnation of the Word, see §§41–43.

it also deepens the understanding of God's nature and transcendence, precisely by revealing that his becoming part of creation does not lessen the difference between him and the world. God is revealed to be so transcendent that he can enter into his creation without suffering limitation in his divinity. His divinity is such that he can become man without ceasing to be God. If, as we have said earlier, there is a transposition between the sense of divinity in nonbiblical religion and the sense of divinity in Christian belief, there is also an intensification between the Jewish and the New Testament understandings of God. There is a difference even though there is not an otherness, as there is between the gods of paganism and the God of Christian faith. The God who is called "Father" by Christ is the same God who spoke to Moses and spoke through the prophets, but he is more deeply revealed to us when he is so addressed by Jesus. The God who is called "Father" by Jesus is not the same god that is worshipped by the pagans: he is the unknown God; he is God in a sense different from the way the pagan god is divine.

The Incarnation therefore sheds light on the understanding Christians have of God as Creator. And once again, the relationship between the Incarnation and Creation, the relationship between the ways each of these comes to light, is not a matter merely of history or psychology; there is necessity in these structures of manifestation, and the necessity is based on the nature of the things that come to light; it is a necessity that can be the theme of theological reflection.

We have explored the relationship between the mystery of the Incarnation and the biblical understanding of Creation. The theme of the Eucharist has been left in the background since the beginning of this chapter. We will return to it gradually in the next chapter, as we explore more deeply how the mystery of our Redemption is related to the Christian understanding of the distinction between God and the world; we will also study how the Eucharist is related to this distinction.

6

⚜

REDEMPTION AS AN ACT OF
GOD AND MAN

IN ORDER to bring out theologically how the Eucharist is related to the new understanding of God revealed in the Bible, it is
necessary to examine more fully the action by which we were redeemed. Accordingly, (a) we will discuss the death of Christ as an
action accomplished by him and (b) we will examine how this
action is sacramentally embodied in the Eucharist. Further, (c) we
will discuss this action as something performed by God the Father
and as completing the divine works accomplished in the Old Testament. This will lead us (d) to examine in what sense our Redemption was achieved by Christ and in what sense it was done
by the triune God. Finally, (e) we will describe the act of our Redemption as an action into which we are drawn and in which we
can participate. All these themes place both our Redemption and
the Eucharist against the background of the Christian understanding of the relationship between the world and God.

A

The death of Jesus was an event in the world, but it was not
only a worldly episode. It was not like the death of Socrates or

the death of Caesar. If it were an ordinary event in the world, there would be no question of its being reenacted as the same event in each eucharistic sacrifice; it could only be commemorated as past and as not occurring now. But the death of Jesus was not simply worldly; it was an event that took place specifically in the context set by the distinction between God and the world. What took place in his death is defined by that context.

The death of Jesus was an action performed by Christ. Christ was not simply passive and overcome by others; he did something when he died. To an onlooker it would have appeared that in his bitter passion and death Jesus was deprived of any possibility of action; all the initiative seemed to be in the hands of his enemies and executioners. But the whole sense of the Gospel narratives of the passion is that Christ was accomplishing something through his suffering and death. He knew these events would come, he anticipated them as his "hour," he accepted them as the will of his Father, and even during the trial, torture, and death he is presented by the Scriptures not as one who is simply crushed, but as one who exercises a kind of command over what is going on. The Gospel of John especially depicts the majesty and initiative of Christ in his sufferings, and St. Matthew's description of the moment of Jesus' death—"Jesus cried out again in a loud voice, and gave up his spirit" (27:50)— has been said to express "both Jesus' control over his destiny and his obedient giving up of his life to God."[1]

But other courageous men have also made their deaths a kind of action before others and for others. The death of Jesus accomplished more than this, and it was an action in a different way from theirs.

An action is a performance done toward and before others that establishes or changes a relationship. If I generously help you in your distress, I am established as your benefactor and you are established as my beneficiary; if I defraud you, I am established as the one who injured you and you are established as the

---

1. *The New Testament of the New American Bible*, ad loc.

one victimized by me. The relationship in each case is instituted by the public action, which involves a material dimension—handing over, taking, speaking—that both embodies and expresses the action.[2] An action is performed in the web of human relationships, toward and before others, and it modifies or confirms that web. An action is always a transaction or an exchange, in the moral sense of these terms.

The death of Jesus, in its substance, was not simply a human exchange. It was done for and before other men, but primarily it was done toward and before the Father. Jesus accomplished his death not primarily toward his executioners and his disciples and the onlookers, but toward God, accepting his death as the will of the Father. It was an action, a transaction performed toward God, and as such it established or modified a relationship. It confirmed the relationship between the Son and the Father, and it affected the relationship of man to God. Since Christ was man as well as God, his death brought the offer of reconciliation, forgiveness, and salvation to all men. When Christ said that his body would be given up and his blood shed "for you," he meant that it would be done for us not just before other men but before the Father. As St. Paul says, "Christ loved us and handed himself over for us as a sacrificial offering to God" (Ephesians 5:2).

Why and how did his death accomplish our salvation? Certainly it was not the case that a vindictive divinity had to be appeased by a blood sacrifice, but somehow it does seem that an action that fell short of death could not have put things right between us and God. Death, human death, seems to be the place where our fall from God is most vividly indicated, and death served as the embodiment, the bodily expression of the action Christ performed toward God. Jesus did not just die; he was active in his death. He took death, his death, and gave it to the source of life and being, and in doing this, in the living choice expressed in his dying, he overcame death.

2. See Sokolowski, Moral Action, 48–54.

But the struggle that Jesus was engaged in on Calvary was not simply the conflict between human life and death, even as carried out in the presence of God. Jesus overcame not only the natural force that brings death to all men, but more specifically the sin that is joined with human death and is its cause, as *human* death, in a deeper way than are the destructive but innocent powers of nature that simply bring an end to life. Jesus conquered death because he conquered sin.

He conquered sin by somehow taking it upon himself. As St. Paul says, "For our sake [God] made him to be sin who did not know sin, so that we might become the righteousness of God in him" (II Corinthians 5:21).[3] This aspect of the passion of Christ must have been far more terrible than the physical and emotional suffering he endured; God's wrath against sin fell on Christ, who became sin for us. It must have been this aspect of his passion, far more than the "worldly" suffering, whether physical or psychological, that Jesus prayed might be kept away from him: "My Father, if it is possible, let this cup pass from me; yet, not as I will, but as you will" (Matthew 26:39). Christ prayed that he not have to drink the "cup" of God's wrath against sin.[4]

His prayer in Gethsemane is addressed to his Father. During his life, Jesus used the word "Father" to address and to name the one who sent him, the one to whom he was related as no one else is. When as a boy he was lost and then found by his parents in the temple in Jerusalem, where they had gone to celebrate the Passover, his response to them was "Why were you looking for me? Did you not know that I must be about my Father's work?" (Luke 2:49). In Gethsemane, at the time of his final Passover, the word "Father" acquires an especially sharp poignancy. In St. Matthew's account (26:39, 26:42) Jesus twice uses the phrase "My Father," intensified by the personal pronoun, and in the corresponding passage in St. Mark (14:36) the Aramaic word *Abba* is used: "Abba, Father, all things are possible to you. Take this cup away from me, but not what I will but what

3. See also Galatians 3:13 and I Peter 2:24.
4. See von Balthasar, *Theodramatik*, 3:315.

you will." (Only in Romans 8:14 and Galatians 4:6 is the Aramaic term *Abba* used elsewhere in the New Testament.)

When we recall the strength Christ showed under all circumstances and in the face of all troubles, we must conclude that
these prayers to the Father reveal an agony more profound than
anything that could have been caused by the fear of suffering
and death. The same distress is expressed in the Lord's cry of
abandonment just before his death, as recorded by Matthew and
Mark: "My God, my God, why have you forsaken me?" (Matthew 27:46, Mark 16:34).[5] Again, remembering the unity that
Christ always claimed between himself and the Father, we can
only wonder what sort of dereliction must have forced these
words from him. We might be able to comprehend the physical
and emotional suffering of Jesus, since we all must die, and some
people may well have endured more painful deaths than Jesus
did, but no one of us could comprehend what it was for him to
become sin for our sake and to accept God's judgment of sin
as he did. No one could be abandoned by God as Christ was: as
"made sin for us," Christ was abandoned precisely because, as
Son, he was one with the Father in holiness, which abhors sin.
In this respect his suffering and death were unique, not because
he died only once, as we all are destined to do, but because the
final judgment of sin, through his abandonment and death,
could occur only once: "He entered once for all into the sanctuary, not with the blood of goats and calves, but with his own
blood, thus obtaining eternal Redemption" (Hebrews 9:12).[6]
The priests of the Old Law offered many sacrifices, "but this one
offered one sacrifice for sins" (Hebrews 10:12).

We must also note the prominence of Jesus' cry of dereliction.
It is recorded only in the Gospels of Matthew and Mark, but in
these two Gospels the words of abandonment, taken from the beginning of Psalm 22, are the only words said by Christ from the
cross. He is not presented as saying anything else. The Gospels

5. See von Balthasar, "Mysterium Paschale," 212.
6. On the once-and-for-all and eternal aspect of Christ's death, see von Balthasar, *Theodramatik*, 3:465.

are written with economy of expression; if these words are all
that Christ is recorded as saying, they must be meant to define
forcefully what his condition was during the crucifixion.

Christ was sent to redeem us because we were in need of Redemption. The world created by God had suffered an estrangement from him, an estrangement somehow chosen by what he
had created. This estrangement, this sin, was not a mere irritant
or blemish. At its core it is malevolence, the direct movement
toward what is evil and rejection of what is good: at its core it
actively detests goodness at its source; it detests God and hence
becomes detestable itself. It is the only thing in creation that is
irreconcilable with God. Most of the malevolence that we as
human beings encounter is mixed with weakness, confusion,
error, and ignorance, and therefore its full nature and its aversion from God are obscured to us. Most of the sin we encounter
is blended with mitigation and excuses, so that what it is is not
clearly disclosed to us ("It's not that he wanted this terrible
thing; he only wanted something else, something quite reason-
able, and this is how it turned out"). Sometimes the malevolence does appear more vividly and we get a sudden view of its
real face, but such occasions are relatively rare, and we might
wonder whether that particularly horrifying vision really took
place or was something we imagined. But the redemptive death
of Jesus showed us what sin is. The action that saved us from sin
showed what we were saved from. It cleared away the mitiga-
tions and obscurities and lifted the cover for a moment, showing
what sin is in itself and by itself, showing what it is that "nourishes" the more feeble and confused instances of malevolence
that run through the ordinary states of our lives. Henceforth all
those other instances, all those more or less excusable, under-
standable, and mixed cases, become more ominous: if they are
"kept alive"—or rather if they are nursed into death—by this
core of malevolence, then they are less harmless and less toler-
able than they might have appeared. The sins that form part of
the everyday scene, the sins to which we can so easily get accus-
tomed, share in the detestation of God that sin itself is.

The estrangement of the world from God had somehow been chosen. It was not placed there by God himself, who looked at everything he had made and saw that it was good. God could not but hate this estrangement, this sin, because it is hateful in itself: "A God who loved simply, and did not hate evil, . . . would be a contradiction."[7] We ourselves were caught up in sin and found ourselves sharing in it. It brought us death, not simply in the sense that our biological life would come to an end, but in the sense that we find ourselves inclined to take part, and that we actually do take part, in the aversion from life that makes up its core. Instead of leaving us to die in sin, God sent his Son to take it upon himself and to drink the cup of his justice. It is not that Jesus somehow pacified God's anger; rather, he overcame through his action that which provokes the anger. His charity conquered the malevolence in which we are caught. "The wrath of God toward the denial of divine love encounters a divine love, that of the Son, that exposes itself to this wrath and disarms it and, literally, renders it objectless."[8] Jesus took upon himself the greatest alienation, the greatest distance there could be between God and his creatures, and extinguished it through his obedience. This was his action, this was his conquest, and it was revealed and confirmed by his Resurrection from the dead.

B

It was this action of overcoming sin that Jesus anticipated and identified at the Last Supper and embodied in the bread and wine of the Eucharist. He did not simply foresee his own dissolution before the stroke of his enemies and the force of mortality; he anticipated the action he would perform in this very dissolution. His body was to be given and his blood poured out "for you," for us.

---

7. Ibid., 315; see also von Balthasar, "Mysterium Paschale," 209–10.
8. Von Balthasar, Theodramatik, 3:326.

It is also this action of Jesus that is reenacted in the liturgy of the Eucharist. There could not be a sacramental reenactment of the simple death of a good and courageous man, because as a worldly event it is confined to the moment in which it occurs. It can be remembered or depicted but not reenacted. But as a transaction toward the God who is not part of the world, as an action that changes the relationship between the world and God, the sacrificial death of Jesus contains an aspect that escapes the restrictions of history. His death was a different kind of action; it is only by analogy that we call it an action. Because it was so distinctively done toward the God who is not part of the world, this redemptive exchange can be reenacted. Indeed, its sense is more fully manifested as it is reenacted, as the event itself becomes complemented by its many representations in the Eucharist. Bouyer claims that the death of Jesus was itself interpreted as a sacrifice in the light of the eucharistic sacrifice that reenacted it: "Historical evidence leads us rather to the supposition that the terminology of sacrifice came to be applied to the cross by the Church because the cross was felt to be at the heart of the sacrifice offered by the Church in the eucharistic celebration."[9]

The Last Supper, which anticipated the death of Jesus; the eucharistic sacrifice, which reenacts it; the biblical narratives, which describe it; and even the prophecies and events of the Old Testament, which prefigured it, as well as the terrible vision itself on Calvary, are the various disclosures or appearances, the views within which the saving action performed by Christ toward the Father is made manifest and glorified. All these appearances are important; all are essential. It is not for us to argue which of these God might have dispensed with. They all are part of the manifestation of the sacrifice of the cross, and all must be theologically recognized.

There are some theologies of the Eucharist that place the identity between the sacrifice of the cross and that of the altar

9. Bouyer, *Liturgical Piety*, 76; see p. 131.

in the will of Christ.[10] They claim that the essence of a sacrifice is the complete giving of one's self to God. They admit that an external rite may be required to express this internal donation, but the rite, they say, is only a sign of the internal disposition. The will of total consecration was present in Christ throughout his life and is present now in his glory, but his will was especially expressed in accepting death on the cross, and it can also be expressed in the Eucharist. Critics of these theologies state that the bodily aspect of sacrifice is not a mere sign of the true sacrifice but an intrinsic part of it.

Our interpretation of the sacrifice as an action must be distinguished from the concept of sacrifice as a continuous will. An action is different from a will. An action is not continuous; it happens once. An act of generosity or an insult occurs at a given moment and determines a relationship from that moment on. Furthermore, a human action not only is expressed in a material sign but is also embodied in it. If the generosity or the insult did not involve a handing over or a spate of spoken words, it would not have taken place as that particular action at that particular time. Something very much like the action, another generosity or another insult, might have been embodied in another material, but in fact this action took place in this material at that moment and it is to be bound to that embodiment from then on. The material is part of the individuality of the action. The act of Redemption, therefore, embodied and expressed in the crucifixion of Christ, was a single action and not a continuous will. The "Lamb that was slain" described in the Apocalypse

10. This emphasis on the "oblation" as the center of the sacrifice is not one of the major theological theories concerning the Eucharist, but it is useful for us as a foil against which to develop our emphasis on the bodily action as the center of the sacrifice. For a summary of the oblation theory and the criticisms of it, see Ott, *Fundamentals of Catholic Dogma*, 411. See also Vonier, *A Key to the Doctrine of the Eucharist*, 164: "There is a clear danger besetting us in our own days, that of over-spiritualizing the Incarnation and its circumstances, of attaching value only to such things in Christ as may be called his spiritual acts. The sacrifice of the cross is not primarily definable in terms of spirit, but in terms of the body; it is not the heroic fortitude of Christ on the cross which constitutes the sacrifice, but the material fact—we need not hesitate to use the word—of the pouring out of the blood."

(Revelation 5:6–14) does not represent a new heavenly sacrifice nor the continuous obedience of the Redeemer, but "the eternal manifestation (*Ewigkeitsaspekt*) of the historical bloody sacrifice on the cross."[11]

When the sacrifice of the cross is reenacted on the altar, it becomes embodied in the bread and wine taken up and consumed, and not in the shedding of blood. Does this not make it into another action, just as an act of feeding the hungry is a different act of generosity than an act of visiting the sick? It does not become another action, because the bread and wine are meant to be not a simple embodiment but a representative one. It is not the bread and wine as such that are offered but what they represent. They are involved in a sacramental and not a natural sacrifice.[12] They signify the embodiment of the action at Calvary, but still as representative they are another embodiment at another moment. A new difference is established within which the same action of Calvary can be reidentified sacramentally. And the reason the bread and wine, as taken up and consumed, can become substantially the same as the action of Calvary is found in the nature of what occurred there: the sacrificial death of Jesus was an action performed by Jesus toward the God who is not part of the world. It was therefore an action that is not simply part of the history of the world, even though it does belong to that history. As it can be eternally manifested in heaven, so can it be repeatedly reenacted in time, in the eucharistic quotation and representation that the Church accomplishes before the Father.

C

We have spoken of the sacrifice of the cross as an action performed by Christ toward the Father and for us. It can also be described as an action accomplished by the Father. It can be seen as

11. Von Balthasar, "Mysterium Paschale," 152.
12. See above, Chapter 4.

similar to the great deeds performed by God for his people in the Old Testament, and the Eucharist can be seen as the memorial of what God has done for us on Calvary. Instead of emphasizing the action of Christ, we can emphasize the action of God the Father. The Father did not merely receive the action of Jesus; the sacrifice of the cross was willed by him and it was accepted and achieved as such by Jesus. The initiative behind our Redemption was not only that of the Son; rather, "God so loved the world that he gave his only Son, so that everyone who believes in him may not perish but may have eternal life" (John 3:16). The sacrificial death of Jesus was equally the gift of the Father.

The action of God in redeeming us completed the saving actions God performed for his people and the words he spoke to them in the Old Covenant. As Louis Bouyer has written, there was little distinction in the Old Testament between the words of God and the acts of God. God's word is itself effective; his word "is not a discourse but an action."[13] Even in Creation, it is the word of God that brings things into being. What God *does* is like a speech because it reveals who and what he is, and what he *says* is like an action because it accomplishes what he asserts: God's word "produces what it proclaims by its own power. God is 'true' not only in the sense that he never lies, but in the sense that what he says is the source of all reality. It is enough that he says it for it to be done."[14] Bouyer says that "the great distinction between God's word and man's word is that when God says something he also does it; he does it by the very fact that he says it. In him, saying and doing are one and the same thing."[15] This union of word and deed does not mean that the word and its intelligibility are absorbed into an action that is arbitrary and blind. Rather, the deed preserves the sense of being a word, of being something that can be understood and known, something that reveals not only the way things are but also who it is that speaks the word and accomplishes the deed. The "intellectual

13. Bouyer, *Eucharist*, 32.   14. Ibid., 33.
15. Bouyer, *Liturgical Piety*, 105.

content"[16] of the words and actions of God concerns first and foremost God himself and the actions he performs, but it also concerns the manner in which things are related to God.

In the Old Testament, the great works of God are his Creation of the world, his election of Abraham, the deliverance of his people from slavery, his guidance of them through the desert and into the land he promised them, and his actions throughout their subsequent history, including what he did for them in and through their exile. God frees and preserves his people, moreover, not simply to make them independent of the power of others, but to provide a place and a community in which his glory can be manifested and his praises sung, by his people and before all men.

All God's actions were epitomized in the deliverance from Egypt, which the Jews commemorated in the Passover service. The sacrificial death of Jesus was taken as the new Passover, the new deliverance from bondage of the new people chosen by God. This Redemption also was accomplished not merely that the people who were chosen would enjoy the benefits of freedom, but "that, rescued from the hand of enemies, we might worship him without fear in holiness and righteousness before him all our days" (Luke 2:73–75). It was done for the glory of God. This Redemption was the great deed accomplished by God in the New Covenant, and it was accomplished through the final Word he spoke to the human race, his Son, through whom he made all things. Just as the Jewish Passover commemorated and reenacted the great work of God in delivering his people, so the Christian Eucharist commemorates and reenacts God's action of redeeming us from sin.

In his treatment of the Passover liturgy, Bouyer also describes the Jewish blessings or *berakoth*, which celebrated and proclaimed the works of God and formed part of the religious ritual of both the Passover and other Jewish meals. These blessings were a human response to God's words and deeds. St. Paul says

16. Bouyer, *Eucharist*, 34.

that in the Christian Eucharist we are to "proclaim" the death of the Lord (I Corinthians 11:26). Bouyer takes this proclamation in the sense of the Jewish *berakah*; it was not primarily an announcement to other men, but a prayer before God: "Every time Christians celebrate [the Eucharist], as St. Paul says, they 'announce' or 'proclaim' this death, not first to the world, but to God, and the 'recalling' of Christ's death is for God the pledge of his fidelity in saving them."[17] In this spirit, we can also recall that the narration of the institution of the Eucharist is recited in the Mass not as a story told to the congregation but as part of the prayer addressed to the Father.

When understood against the background of Jewish liturgy, the Christian Eucharist can more easily be seen as a commemoration which is also a true reenactment of the saving work of God. The question of how the Eucharist can itself be a sacrifice and yet be the same sacrifice as that of the cross becomes less perplexing when seen against the Old Testament understanding of God. The God worshipped by the Jews was always the same God, whose actions expressed his fidelity to his people. In a sense, since it was always he who was acting, it was always the same thing that was being done, both in the deliverance from slavery and at all the commemorations of that work. The Christian Eucharist requires a more intense unity of action than does the Passover, because of the uniqueness of the sacrifice performed by Christ as man, but the Jewish sense of God working in history provides a better context for the understanding of the Eucharist and the cross than does the modern notion of historical events, each fixed exclusively in its own moment in time and thus separated from all the others.

Indeed, Bouyer claims that the Reformation controversy between Catholics and Protestants, concerning whether the Mass is an actual sacrifice or the commemoration of a past sacrifice, is not a genuine problem arising from the Eucharist itself, but a dilemma arising from ill-formulated theologies. He claims

17. Ibid., 105.

that the controversy arose when words like "sacrifice" and "memorial" were given meanings that did not belong to them in the ancient eucharistic prayers: "Eucharistic theologies so constructed create and multiply false problems. They cannot resolve them (which is not surprising, since they are badly posited), nor can they ignore them, since these theologies themselves are what created them in the first place."[18] As an example of such a false problem, Bouyer mentions the question "How can a unique action from the past become present again every day?"[19] The first step in dissolving such a problem, he says, is to turn to the sources of our eucharistic belief and to try to recapture the understanding found in them. His description of the Jewish understanding of God's work as being the same throughout history, and his description of the early Christian eucharistic prayers as continuing this understanding, are steps in his attempt to formulate Christian eucharistic belief in a more appropriate way.

The ancient Jewish understanding of God's work does shed light on the way the sacrifice of the altar and that of the cross can be distinct and yet the same, and it is true that some of the polemical formulations of this relationship should be abandoned. However, raising the question of the relationship between the altar and the cross need not be an exercise without theological meaning.[20] Our understanding of time is not simply the same as that of the Jews in antiquity; we do think of events as defined by their historical location. It is therefore necessary for us to examine not only why the Christian Eucharist seems to transcend history, but also why the Jews thought that the action of God did so as well. This transcendence could only occur if God himself is to be understood in a special way, as not being reducible to part of the world and its history, whether cyclic or evolutionary. The ancient Jews may have thought the way they

---

18. Ibid., 7.   19. Ibid., 8.

20. The issue of how the Eucharist overcomes time and how the Mass can be the same sacrifice as that of Calvary continues to return as a problem. See, for example, Journet, La Messe, 81–82, 93; Stevenson, Eucharist and Offering, 202–203; and O'Connor, The Hidden Manna, 243.

did because they still had not grown beyond a rather primitive understanding of time. The Jews did not distinguish clearly between "then" and "now," and they also did not distinguish sharply between name and object, and word and deed. But we have become vividly aware of the separations that time and history bring, and we have also become vividly aware of many other distinctions. We realize, for example, that a word can become a purely formal marker deprived of any specific sense and reference, and hence can be radically distinguished from the thing that it names.[21] And while we acknowledge a performative aspect in every speech, we distinguish that aspect from the constative: we distinguish between the dimensions of doing and saying. It therefore becomes theologically necessary for us to clarify what sense of divinity lies behind both the Passover mystery of Jews and the eucharistic mystery of Christians. If we merely refer to the mode of thinking present in the Old Testament, we run the risk of trying to resolve a problem by merely historical means. We might be left stranded with the observation that the people of the Old Testament had one "conceptual framework" while we happen to have another.

Both the Passover mystery and the mystery of the Eucharist could be accomplished only by the God who is not part of the

21. One of the best treatments of the phenomenon of words taken as formal markers, and of the importance of this phenomenon for computer science and artificial intelligence, can be found in Arsac, La science informatique, 34–47. In another place, Arsac observes that the inability of the Islamic tradition to take words in such a purely formal manner may bring about a cultural and religious crisis for it: "I do not know how the Islamic civilization will take the shock of science in general and of informatics in particular. . . . For them, there is an identity of name and person, and when that happens one does not have the freedom to consider words independently of their signification" Jacques Arsac. Un Informaticien, 78. He goes on to say that being able to take words in a purely formal way, apart from their meaning, is what made modern science possible (and hence, he says, such science is essentially nominalistic). Computer science is only the completion of a movement that began with the nominalists in the late Middle Ages. Arsac criticizes the term "computer science" and prefers the name "informatique," because the former names the science through the instrument used in it; speaking of "computer science" is like calling astronomy "telescope science." On a contribution made by Husserl to the philosophy of computer science and artificial intelligence, see Holenstein, "Eine Maschine im Geist. Husserlsche Begründung und Begrenzung künstlicher Intelligenz," 84–93.

world, the God who could exist in undiminished goodness and greatness even if the world did not exist. Thus, the Eucharist is a perpetual reminder of the transcendence of God; the Eucharist could not be what the Church takes it to be unless God were able to receive again the one sacrifice of his Son each time the Eucharist is celebrated. Only through God so understood can all of history be sanctified. Only before him could the sacrificial offering of Jesus be accepted as the work of both God and man, the work of the incarnate Son of God, and only before him could the same sacrifice be reenacted on the altar.[22]

D

The sacrificial death of Jesus was an action performed by Jesus toward the Father, but it can also be understood, as we have said, as an action performed by the Father himself. It was God's final action, the one that concluded the divine actions accomplished in the Old Covenant.

In what sense can our Redemption have been accomplished by the Father? The acts described in the Old Testament clearly were performed by God. They were received and responded to by Israel. But in the New Testament the decisive action seems to have been carried out not by the Father but by the Son. No one in the Old Testament acted in the way Jesus did in the New. Jesus acts in obedience to the Father's will, but it still seems to be Christ and not the Father who accomplishes our Redemption.

This issue brings out some of the trinitarian aspects of Redemption. The last of the great Christological Councils, the Sixth Council of Constantinople (680–681 A.D.), stated that there were two wills in Christ, a human and a divine will. The

---

22. Theologians often appeal to God's creative power to explain the possibility of transubstantiation, but it is also true that the eucharistic presence proclaims and reveals the eternity, transcendence, and creative power of God. The former issue would be a typical concern for an ontological theology, the latter a concern for the theology of disclosure.

Council condemned the heresy of monothelitism, which held that there was only one will, the divine, in Jesus. If there are two wills in Christ, and if, as the theological tradition asserts, the will is correlated with the nature and not the person, then it follows that there is only one will in God, one will for the Holy Trinity.

The mission that Jesus accepted as the will of the Father flowed from a decision of the Holy Trinity, a determination made by the triune God to send the Son "in the likeness of sinful flesh" (Romans 8:3) for our Redemption.[23] It was a decision according to which the Father sends the Son in the power of the Holy Spirit, but it was a decision made by the triune God. St. Thomas addresses this issue by making a helpful distinction.[24] He says that insofar as we speak of one of the divine persons as being sent to accomplish a certain *work*, to bring about a certain effect (in this case, the Incarnation and Redemption), we can say that the entire Trinity is the one who sends, but insofar as we focus on the divine *person* who is being sent, we must say that he is sent by the person or persons from whom he proceeds within the Trinity. Thus the eternal Son is sent by the Trinity to achieve our *Redemption*, but as the eternal *Son* he is sent by the Father. Likewise, the *sanctification* achieved by the Holy Spirit is accomplished through the decision of the Holy Trinity, but the *Spirit* is sent by the Father and the Son.

The decision to bring about the Incarnation and Redemption was made by the triune God. Jesus as the eternal Son takes part in that timeless choice. His mission stems from the will of the Holy Trinity, but it is called the will of the Father because the Trinity itself comes ultimately from the Father, and because the Son in particular comes directly from him in the divine filiation, and because his mission in the world reflects his eternal procession from the Father. As von Balthasar says, "Jesus as man does not obey himself as God, he also does not obey the Trinity, but as Son he obeys the Father in the Holy Spirit."[25] Still, his

23. Von Balthasar, *Theodramatik*, 2/2:172.
24. St. Thomas Aquinas, *Summa theologiae* I 43 8 c.
25. Von Balthasar, *Theodramatik*, 2/2:208.

work of Redemption is chosen not by the Father alone; it is chosen by the Holy Trinity, by the triune God.

The fact that our Redemption was the work of the entire Trinity is shown by the role played in it by the Holy Spirit. Jesus was guided throughout his public life by the Spirit and what he said and did was accomplished in the Spirit. (He transmitted the Holy Spirit to his disciples only after he was glorified and his mission completed.) The part played by the Spirit in the work of Jesus is brought out in one of the prayers recited by the priest just before communion at Mass; the priest says that the death of Jesus brought life to the world "by the will of the Father and the work of the Holy Spirit (*cooperante Spiritu Sancto*)." The Spirit did not enter into the work of our sanctification only after the death of Christ, but participated in it from the beginning, even at the Annunciation (Luke 1:35). Thus the action that Jesus accomplished was the outcome of the decision of the Holy Trinity. The plan of Redemption was formulated by the triune God; it was "the mystery hidden from ages and from generations past" (Colossians 1:26).

Within the life of the Holy Trinity, the generation of the Son by the Father and the spiration of the Holy Spirit by the Father and the Son are accomplished not by choice or by will but by divine necessity (which is beyond the necessity, contingency, and freedom that occur within the world). The procession of the Son does not occur because the Father sees that it would be good for it occur; the procession could not be chosen not to occur. The redemptive mission of the Son beyond the Holy Trinity, however, is accomplished by a choice, but by a choice carried out by the three persons as God, not by the Father alone nor by the three persons acting together in distinct but united choices. Therefore Jesus, as the eternal Son, takes part in the decision leading to our Redemption, but since everything in the Holy Trinity comes from the Father, he was able even as Son to speak of it as the will of the Father, as what the Father willed.

However, as man Jesus did not share in the divine choice of Redemption, so what God willed still had to be accepted by him. In Jesus there had to be human acceptance as well as divine decision. And although Jesus as man was intent on doing the Father's work from the moment he took responsibility for his actions, still as man he had to reaffirm and confirm his human decision in the ever new circumstances that life brought to him; this confirmation occurred most vividly at the eve of his passion, as his "hour" drew near. This is how human dedications are made. We have to keep acting to maintain a decision. A decision may be made once at a given time and may even become habitual in us, but it still needs to be reaffirmed by what we do in new situations. Christ as man had to continue to act. The divine choice, in contrast, does not need to wait on new circumstances to confirm itself. It is made once, in a way that does not involve before and after. This eternal decision was there already in Christ as God, but it had to be appropriated by him as man: there are two wills in the incarnate Word.

Jesus appropriated this decision not only throughout his life, and not only as his "hour" drew near, but also at the final point of his obedience, when he said, "It is finished" (John 19:30). He did not say, "I have done it," as though it were a conquest achieved through his own effort; he said, "It is finished," as an expression of having done what was to be done in and through and by him.

However, the divine decision did not have to be appropriated by Jesus as something decided externally for him by someone else, since he was the same agent, the same person who shared in making it as the eternal Son. His human choice was added to the divine decision as to something he himself had already made. Just as a new human choice can confirm another choice that the same agent made earlier, and so blend with that earlier choice and make it manifest in a new situation, so Christ's human acceptance of his mission and his hour was the new confirmation of the divine choice of our Redemption.

Moreover, the obedient action of Jesus was not a simple act of consent to the decision of the Holy Trinity, not a mere statement of agreement. Jesus took on the condition of sin; without sinning, Christ became what we become through malevolence and detestation of God, and he did so in obedience to his mission, in obedience to the decision made by God. Christ did this most fully in the *action* of his suffering and death, not in the consent that preceded the action. There is a tendency for us to see the substance of actions in the decisions or acts of will that take place before the actions are performed; we tend to think that what really counts in an action is a choice that temporally precedes the performance. But such choices are merely the anticipation of the actions themselves. The climax, the full actuality of a personal exchange, occurs when the deed is done, not when we resolve to do it.[26]

Christ's love for the Father was most fully embodied and expressed in his dereliction and death; even his acceptance of this suffering at Gethsemane was only an anticipation, not the full action of his obedience. Furthermore, his sacrificial death was also the embodiment of the decision of the triune God to redeem us. The *plan* of our Redemption was "the mystery hidden from ages and generations past," but the *act* of our Redemption took place only when Jesus suffered and died. The one death embodied and expressed not only the obedient action of Jesus as man but also the divine action of the triune God.

We may be inclined to think that the center of the mystery of our Redemption was an act of God's will, a decision made by the triune God from all eternity, and that the actual suffering and death of Jesus were merely the outcome of this decision. But in fact the opposite is true. The substance of our Redemption occurred on Calvary. When we speak of God's will, we refer to what is willed by God; we refer to the thing that God has decided to do. It is not the decision that should be stressed, but the thing decided upon, the thing that is done "decidedly." Even in human affairs the "decision" merely anticipates the performance. All the weight is in the action itself, not in the in-

---

26. On the need to see true human action in its external performance and not in an internal shadow or anticipation of action, see Sokolowski, *Moral Action,* 52–53, 57, 208–11.

tention to act; the performance does not merely echo a decision. The decision receives its full meaning and reality only when the performance takes place. In the decision made by God, there is no before or after, no temporal span between making the resolution and carrying it out, so the divine decision is even more thoroughly united with the action that is performed. The sacrificial death on Calvary was therefore the gift of the Father as well as the accomplishment of Christ.

It seems that the Incarnation allowed a kind of response by God to God himself to take place, a response that could not have occurred in any other way. The processions of the Son and of the Holy Spirit allow there to be reciprocities among the divine persons, but this kind of eternal reciprocity, this circumincession or perichoresis, is carried out through divine necessity. There are no choices within the Holy Trinity, no determination of something that could have been otherwise. The choice of the mission of the Son, however, did not occur through divine necessity; it did not have to happen. It was a determination that need not have occurred. When it did occur as an action, it opened the possibility of a response, of a reaction by another will: the obedient choice of the man Jesus. In becoming obedient to death, even to death on the cross, Jesus allowed an exchange to take place between God's choice and a created counterchoice.

And the eternal Son was the person who made this human choice. It was not just a creature that did so, even though he did it as a creature. In this regard, the central action of the New Testament is different from the actions of the Old Covenant, because the responses to God's actions in the Old Testament were made by his people, but in Christ the one who responds as man is God himself. The splendor of our Redemption lies not simply in our liberation from sin, but primarily in the admirable exchange of choices between the creature and God. The Son as eternal could not have done this, because his will as eternal is not different from that of the Father. The response of the incarnate Son, as man, was, furthermore, not merely an adequate re-

sponse; because it was done by the Son, it was a full and appropriate response to the decision of the Father: it "came up to"
what God had decided. Jesus was the Son in whom the Father
was well pleased.

We have been using words like "decision" and "choice" in
describing the exchange between God and Christ, but we
should not let the common meaning of these terms trivialize
the action we are talking about. We are not speaking about
things like the decision to buy a car or the choice of a piece of
clothing. In our context, more appropriate analogues would be
things like the decision to marry a certain person, the decision
to adopt this child, or the choice to enter a particular religious
community. Such serious decisions and choices clearly involve
decisions and choices made in response, and they also involve
further decisions and choices made to confirm them, but as important as they are, even they would give us only a glimpse of
the exchange that occurs between God and the man Jesus.

E

Christ's obedient acceptance of his mission becomes the
paradigm for our own acceptance of the salvation brought to
us by God. God the Father did not only send us his Son but
also "chose us in him, before the foundation of the world, to
be holy and without blemish before him" (Ephesians 1:2). We
become adopted in the sense that we can choose and decide in
imitation of Christ. The obstacle of sin is removed and we are
called to enter the exchange of choices that took place
between God and Christ: the exchange was accomplished not
merely to be admired but also to be shared. We are made able
to participate in Christ's perfect conformity to the will of
the Father: "God, who is rich in mercy, because of the great
love he had for us, even when we were dead in our transgres-
sions, brought us to life with Christ" (Ephesians 2:4–5). The
life to which we have been brought is the ability to choose
and to act in the way Christ did in accepting and fulfilling his

mission. In Christ, we can take our lives as the will of the Father and act in accord with the mission that has been allotted to each of us.

The central action in which Christ conformed his will to that of the Father was his redemptive death. The Eucharist reenacts this action for us at all times and places. It represents not simply the dying of Jesus, but the action he performed in his dying and the Redemption God achieved in it. The Eucharist calls us to enter into that action ourselves. In our Eucharist we announce the death of Jesus not merely to ourselves and to others, but to the Father; we proclaim it before God, in whom there is no before or after, and before whom the perfect sacrifice of the Son is always present. Our Eucharist brings us into this presence before God. It both calls and enables us and all the faithful "to offer your bodies as a living sacrifice, holy and pleasing to God, your spiritual worship" (Romans 12:1). How we participate in the sacrifice of our redemption can be illuminated theologically by some thoughts of Louis Bouyer and Alexander Schmemann. Bouyer, in his book, *Rite and Man*, clarifies the nature of sacrifice.[27] A sacrifice is usually understood as the dedication of something to God, the setting apart for God of something that does not belong to God, something profane. In this understanding, the Latin term *sacrum facere*, from which the word "sacrifice" is derived, would mean to make something to become holy, to make something that is profane to become sacred. But Bouyer challenges this understanding and says that *sacrum facere* originally means to perform a holy action, to "do" the "sacred thing"; it does not mean to render something holy. A sacrifice is not a dedication of something profane to God but an entry into and a participation in what God already possesses.[28] We are elevated into a sacrifice; we

27. Bouyer, *Rite and Man*, 78–94.

28. Bouyer says the rites, rather than making something sacred, "merely preserve what has been sacred from the beginning" (*Rite and Man*, 81). A sacrifice "cannot be made to consist in an offering to God of something which up till then has not been his" (p. 82). A fortiori, Bouyer continues, sacrifice does not primarily consist in a slaying or a destruction or an immolation. It is, rather, the performance of a sacred act, and basically a sacred meal, the "richest hierophany" in which man recognizes

do not make something into a sacrifice. However, man is unworthy of such participation in the sacred activity, both because of his limitations and because of his sins and failures; consequently, there needs to be an element of purification and expiation in sacrifice. Sacrifice is not first and foremost a sin offering, but it does involve as an immediate, if derivative, feature a remedy for sin.[29] Thus, according to Bouyer, the usual order of emphasis in the notion of sacrifice needs to be reversed: it is not the case that expiation is primary and that praise and thanksgiving follow, but that the entry into the divine glory is primary, and expiation and purification serve as the condition or consequence.

These thoughts of Bouyer can be applied even to the sacrifice of Jesus. The deepest core of Christ's action in his passion and death was his act of obedience to the Father, which reflected his eternal procession as the Logos from the Father. This reflection of the divine glory comes first; this obedience was the summit of the divine action. But because Christ approached the Father from a world of sin, and indeed in the form of a sinner, the aspect of expiation necessarily accompanied the sacred action. The death of Jesus was a sacrifice of redemption, but only because it was an act of perfect love of the incarnate Son toward the Father. It is not the case that the death of Jesus was an act of perfect love because it freed mankind from sin; if that were so, the act of obedient love would have depended on the existence of sin. And our sacramental participation in Christ's action brings about the forgiveness of sins, but only because we are brought by Christ into the life of the children of God, where

his "total dependence, both for his creation and his continued existence, upon a God who is at the same time apprehended as the one who possesses the fullness of life" (p. 84; see also p. 90).

29. Bouyer, *Rite and Man*, 87: "The essence of a sacrificial act is not this expiation for, or purification from, sins. This factor is only the necessary prelude to going into the sanctuary." On p. 86 he writes, "Neither Scripture nor the manifold varieties of natural religion make any essential connection between sin and sacrifice." See also p. 88: "The expiatory ritual ceaselessly reminds man that he is of himself basically unworthy of that contact with the divine which is effected in sacrifice."

we can praise his glory and give thanks for his deeds. Grace and the glory of God are primary; forgiveness is derivative.

Alexander Schmemann, in *The Eucharist*, also speaks of a reversal of emphasis, one different from that proposed by Bouyer. Schmemann reverses the familiar order of emphasis between the Last Supper and the death of Jesus. Usually it is said—as in the course of this book—that the central action was the death of Christ on the cross; the Last Supper is taken as anticipating that action. But, according to Schmemann, the Supper was the center, and the death of Jesus followed from it. Schmemann says that at the Last Supper, Jesus manifested the kingdom of God as he established the Church, but he revealed this kingdom in a world of sin: "In the night of the fallen world, enslaved to sin and death, the Last Supper manifested the otherworldly, divine light of the kingdom of God."[30] Schmemann beautifully develops the manifestation of the kingdom at the Last Supper; in a deeply Johannine spirit he draws out the meaning of the night outside, the treachery of Judas, the brilliance and love of the new community being established around Jesus. He also observes that because of sin, this revelation of the kingdom led to the death of Christ; Jesus "condemned himself to the cross with the Last Supper, with the manifestation of the kingdom of love."[31] The presence of the kingdom is first; the redemptive death follows.

Schmemann then says that the Eucharist recalls primarily the manifestation that took place at the Last Supper: "The whole meaning, the entire endless joy of this commemoration, is precisely that it remembers the Last Supper, not as a 'means' but as a manifestation, and even more than a manifestation, as the presence and gift of the very goal: the kingdom for which God created the world."[32] Schmemann develops these thoughts to counter what he calls a "reduction" found in many theologies of the Eucharist, "the identification of the commemoration of the

---

30. Schmemann, *The Eucharist*, 200. On the Last Supper as the beginning of the life of the Church, see p. 201.

31. Ibid., 206.   32. Ibid., 203.

Last Supper with the commemoration of Christ's death on the cross, and hence the interpretation of the Eucharist as the sacrament above all of the sacrifice on Golgotha."[33] The "reduction" that Schmemann argues against is the interpretation proposed by Vonier (and very many others, of course), and represented also in this present book. Indeed, Schmemann explicitly criticizes Vonier.[34] He admits that there is a close link between the Supper and the redemptive death of Christ, but he reverses the usual order of emphasis and finds the eucharistic center in the Supper and not in the cross.

While appreciating the theological richness of Schmemann's analysis, we wish to differ from him and defend Vonier's position by proposing the following considerations. We must distinguish between manifestation and action. It is true that the kingdom of God's love was achieved and manifested at the Supper, but the action of Jesus after the Supper, his redemptive death, was not just a further manifestation and consequence nor was it simply a victory over sin; as we have shown earlier in this chapter, it was a deed, an act of obedience. It was not just a conquest over the prince of darkness, not just the triumph over sin and death, but the highest act of filial obedience. At the close of chapter 14 of St. John's Gospel, Jesus says, "He [the ruler of the world] has no power over me, but the world must know that I love the Father and that I do just as the Father has commanded me" (John 14:30–31). This action is more than a manifestation to the world; it is the doing of what the Father has commanded, the fulfillment of the mission of Christ. This incarnate action mirrors the eternal procession of the Son. This action was not yet achieved (except as a preenactment, described in the synoptic Gospels) at the Last Supper. The incarnate and divine *doxa* of the Last Supper needs to be completed by the incarnate and divine *praxis* of the cross. Schmemann's emphasis is on manifestation, but the emphasis of Vonier and the others is on action. The issue is one of disclosure and appearance and mirroring and

33. Ibid., 202.
34. See, for example, ibid., 28, 32–33, 216.

representation, but also one of the irreducibility of praxis. God is not only at the heart of disclosure, but also at the heart of action. Vonier, in seeing the Last Supper as reflecting sacramentally the sacrificial action of Golgotha, would certainly not want to make the Last Supper merely instrumental, merely a "means," as Schmemann puts it. He too would see it as a manifestation, a sacramental manifestation, but he would also claim that something more than a victory was achieved in the death of Christ. The victory over sin was only the external aspect of the obedience of the Son. Likewise, our eucharistic participation in the Last Supper makes us share also in the redemptive and obedient action of the Son of God.

7

꧁꧂

EUCHARISTIC TENSES AND CITATIONS

IN THIS CHAPTER, (a) we will discuss how the words and actions of Christ at the Last Supper are quoted in the Eucharist, and (b) we will make some general remarks concerning the character of this quotation. Then, after having discussed the way the Eucharist takes us back to an earlier moment in time, (c) we will mention the importance of the present moment of the liturgical action. In a final section (d) we will discuss devotion to the Blessed Sacrament as it is related to temporality.

A

We have discussed the role of the words "my" and "you," as first- and second-person pronouns, in the eucharistic narrative of institution. These two words signal a change of perspective from that of the Christian congregation here and now, which is expressed by the pronouns "we" and "us," to the perspective of Jesus and his disciples at the Last Supper. But there is a third word which is similarly important, the demonstrative pronoun "this." It is used in the phrases "Take *this* . . . and eat it: *this* is my body," and "Take *this* . . . and drink from it: *this* is the cup of my blood." These three words, "my," "you," and "this," deserve further examination.

To bring out the force of these words, let us consider what would happen if the eucharistic narrative were expressed without them. Suppose that during the liturgical prayer and ceremony, the celebrant were to speak in simple narrative without quotation. Suppose he were to say, "The Lord Jesus took bread and gave you thanks and praise. He broke the bread, gave it to his disciples, and said that they should all take and eat it, for it was his body, which would be given up for them." Suppose an analogous statement were to be used for the cup of wine, concluding with the words "And he said that they should do what he did in memory of him." The element of direct quotation would be removed from such a restatement of the narrative of institution.

Such a formulation might be acceptable as a description of what happened at the Last Supper, but it would be inappropriate in the liturgy.[1] If we reflect on this formulation, and if we can come to see why it is inappropriate, we will be helped to appreciate better the liturgical words we do use; we will be helped to see what these words achieve and why they are fitting. We will discover how important "mere" grammar can be.

First, in the formulation we have imagined, the word "it" is used instead of "this." It refers to the bread that Christ took into his hands and only to that bread, not to what is present on the altar. Consequently, even if the celebrant were to carry out the gestures expressed in the words, the words he used would not refer to the bread he himself takes up; they would refer to the

1. Our analysis is based on the eucharistic prayer as it occurs in practically all the liturgies in the history of the Church. There have been some interesting variations. The East Syrian Anaphora of the Apostles Addai and Mari, for example, seems not to contain any words of institution; that is, the narration of the Last Supper and the quoted words of Christ seem to be absent from the rite. See Hänggi and Pahl, eds., *Prex Eucharistica*, 375–80, and Jasper and Cuming, *Prayers of the Eucharist*, 39–41. Bouyer, following the opinion of Dom Bernard Botte, O.S.B., claims that the absence does not indicate an early practice of omitting the narrative and words of institution; he claims they were omitted in the text because everyone knew them and they did not need to be written down. See Bouyer, *Eucharist*, 146–52. The Didache

bread that was taken up by Christ, which would be explicitly distinguished from the bread taken up at the altar. The two actions—the action of the priest and the action of Christ that the priest describes—would be carried out, so to speak, in parallel. The priest's action would imitate that of Christ, but it could not be considered to be the same action; it would remain the priest's own gesture. A separation would be introduced between the action of Christ and the action of the priest.

Second, the use of the words "his body" in place of "my body" would forestall any identification between the voice of the liturgical celebrant and the voice of Christ; the priest would refer to Christ there and then, at the Last Supper, but he would not let Christ speak here and now. The voice of the celebrant would not be lent to Christ; the priest would speak entirely in his own voice (or, perhaps more precisely, in the voice of the Church). Once again, a separation would be introduced between the saying that occurred at the Last Supper and the saying that occurs now.

Third, the radical distinction between the liturgy and the Last Supper brought about by the new pronouns would be reinforced, in the formula we have imagined, by the continuous use of the past tense and the preservation of the context set by the past tense. The speaker would say that Jesus "took" and "gave," and he would continue in this past tense and would declare that Jesus said "that they should take and eat" and "that his body would be given up." That past context would remain wholly past and would not be allowed to merge with the present context of the liturgy. What happened at the Last Supper would not be permitted to happen again.

---

is also considered by some to be an example of a eucharistic prayer without an institutional narrative. See Crockett, *Eucharist: Symbol of Transformation*, 40–48. For a recent summary of the arguments against taking the Didache and the Anaphora of Addai and Mari as eucharistic prayers without an institutional narrative, see O'Connor, *The Hidden Manna*, 7–9. Even if such instances did exist, they do not represent the normal and complete form of the eucharistic prayer.

Another interesting variation is found in some Eastern anaphoras in which the prayer leading up to the words of institution is directed not to God the Father but to Christ. See Hänggi and Pahl, *Prex Eucharistica*, 183, 328–29, 365, 413.

All this is *not* what occurs in the Eucharist, but it is what would happen if the grammatical changes we imagined were to be introduced. Thinking about this proposal, and seeing why it would be theologically inopportune, helps us to realize the liturgical power of the formulas actually used in the Eucharist. The words we do use allow a dovetailing of perspectives and contexts, not a mere reference from within one context to another. In our present liturgical context, the context of the Last Supper is activated, and this in turn activates and preenacts the context of Calvary. The voice of the priest can be identified with the voice of Christ, and the bread and wine taken up by the priest can become identified in their substance with the bread and wine taken up by Jesus. All this becomes set by the distinctive quotation carried out by the priest when he recites the words of institution. These dimensions of presence, this arrangement of presentations and identifications, is constituted through the words used in the eucharistic narrative.

It is also important to note that the gestures carried out in the Eucharist by the priest are quotational gestures.[2] When the priest takes the bread and the cup of wine, he does not just do what he is doing here and now. His actions, as the accompanying words indicate, are meant to "be" the actions of Christ. As the encyclical *Mediator Dei* states it in the passage cited earlier, the priest gives Christ not only his voice but also his hand.[3] The gestures are important in the display that occurs in the Eucharist, in the reenactment of the Last Supper and the sacrifice of the cross. Christ told his disciples not only to say

2. For an example of what is meant by a quotational gesture, imagine someone saying the following: "John said, 'I don't care what happens next,' and when he said these words, he did this: [the speaker shrugs his shoulders and makes a sour face]." The speaker in this case does not become an actor; his citation of John's gesture is a quotation, not a dramatic reenactment. It is also not a simple imitation. A dramatic reenactment would not be part of a narration but would be a play from beginning to end. A mere imitation would present something like what John usually does ("Look: this is how he walks"), but a quotation re-presents the gesture he performed at that particular moment.

3. See above, Chapter 2, n. 5.

what he said but to "do this," and the priest "does" what Christ did.[4]

To specify more exactly how the actions of the priest are the same as the quoted actions of Christ, we must discuss a new, rather complicated issue concerning the mode of presentation that occurs in the Eucharist. We have said that the priest quotes the words of Jesus and that his actions quote the actions of Christ. But it would be wrong to conclude that the priest is involved in a dramatic reenactment of the Lord's conduct at the first Eucharist. The Mass is not a depiction of the Last Supper. We have said earlier, in Chapter 2, that the Mass is not a ritualized Passion Play, that it reenacts the death and Resurrection of Christ sacramentally and not mimetically. But it is also true that the Mass is not a play, a dramatic reenactment, of the Last Supper, with the celebrant taking the role of Christ and the congregation the role of the apostles.[5] It is true that the priest lends his voice and his hand to Christ, but he does not do so in the manner of an actor. Quotation, even bodily quotation, is not the same as dramatic representation. There is a presentational difference between quotation and dramatic depiction, and the difference comes to the fore in the Eucharist.

The current form of the liturgy makes us somewhat inclined to think of the Eucharist as a depiction of the Last Supper, a small drama representing it. The priest stands facing the people, who are assembled around the altar as the apostles must have

4. The gestures, which vary in detail, are very ancient. They are absent, however, in the Byzantine liturgy. On this topic see Jungmann, *The Eucharistic Prayer*, 15: "Only in the Byzantine liturgy does the priest omit any gestures of this kind, although this is an innovation as the result of controversy. The gestures in question were only abandoned when the Byzantine theologians adopted the theory that it was not the words of consecration but the epiclesis which completed the consecration" (translation modified). See also Jungmann, *The Mass of the Roman Rite*, 2:202–203. On p. 202 Jungmann says the ritual actions are done "in dramatic fashion," but the category of quotation could be used instead of drama.

5. I owe to John Tomarchio the point that the Eucharist should not be taken as a dramatic reenactment of the Last Supper, as well as the observation about the rubrics that I make in the two paragraphs following this one.

been assembled around the table before Christ in the upper room. The bread and wine are taken up and later distributed. The ritual seems very much like a dramatic representation of what occurred at the first Eucharist, with the priest in the role of Christ and the people in that of the apostles. The impression of being a dramatic reenactment is strengthened by a practice that has become very common in the new liturgy. Very often the priest, at the consecration, will look at the congregation when he says, "Take this, all of you, and eat it," or, with the wine, "Take this, all of you, and drink from it." It might seem, therefore, that his words are being directly addressed to the people participating in the Mass. The priest and the congregation seem to be depicting the Last Supper.

However, the rubrics do not indicate that the celebrant should look at the congregation when he says these words. The rubrics state that he should bow slightly (*parum se inclinat*) before saying the words. When he says the words he is to look at the host (or the chalice) and repeat what Christ said to his apostles at the Last Supper. When he bows in this way, it becomes clear that the priest is not depicting but quoting, since it is unlikely that Christ bowed in this manner when he addressed his disciples. Indeed, the "slight bow" that the rubrics call for can be considered a kind of gestural quotation mark. What is being said during the bow is said quotationally. The quotation is broken off when the priest closes the bow and elevates the bread or the chalice, showing them to the congregation, and then genuflects in adoration. The elevation and genuflection, bodily gestures, are actions done by the priest himself. He is no longer quoting when he performs them. They are a return to the present and no longer a quotation drawing on another context. They are directed toward the Christ who is present here and now. The acclamation made by the people is also directed toward Christ the Redeemer present here and now; Christ is addressed by words such as "Dying you destroyed our death, rising you restored our life, Lord Jesus, come in glory." The context of the Last Supper gives way to the present context and the sacramental presence of the Redeemer.[6]

There is a complicated sequence of shifts in voice and gesture during the central part of the eucharistic prayer. The first setting is that of the prayer addressed by the priest, in the name of the Church, toward God the Father. This prayer encloses a narrative, the narrative of institution, which is also directed toward the Father. The narrative encloses quotations, not only in words but also in gestures, of the act of institution and the prefigurement of the death and Resurrection of the Lord. The quotations are followed by a reverencing, in gestures alone, of the consecrated bread and wine; this silent action is then followed by a verbal acclamation directed toward the Redeemer. Finally, the original setting, that of the prayer to the Father, is restored.

It has been said that the priest's genuflection after the words of consecration and his elevation of the host and chalice are inappropriate gestures because they interrupt the focus of the eucharistic prayer, which is directed toward the Father. Because they are Christocentric they are said to break the unity of form and meaning in the eucharistic Canon. This observation has been made, for example, by Enrico Mazza in his work on the eucharistic prayers in the Roman rite.[7] Mazza does not mention the acclamation, but presumably he would consider it to be an interruption as well, since it is also directed toward Christ. However, since the words and actions of the Last Supper are themselves directed toward the sacrifice on Calvary, and since

6. Every liturgical form will have some inconveniences that it must guard against. The current liturgical form has many advantages, but, as we have noted in the text, it does have the tendency to make the institutional narration look like a drama, and it also inclines some celebrants to look toward the congregation (who are not the addressees) while reciting the prayers directed to God. There were inconveniences in the older rite; as early as the fourth century and through the Middle Ages, there was a tendency to see the Mass as a drama, with various parts of the Mass being said to represent various events in the life of Christ; there also were allegorical interpretations of various gestures and parts. See Mitchell, *Cult and Controversy*, 55–61, 196–97; Crockett, *Eucharist: Symbol of Transformation*, 107, 123; Jungmann, *The Mass of the Roman Rite*, 1:107–21.

7. Mazza, *The Eucharistic Prayers of the Roman Rite*, 8–10.

the Eucharist reenacts that sacrifice, it does not seem inappropriate to signal this ultimate focus of the ritual by words and gestures that are directed toward it. It does not seem out of place to acclaim the presence and the saving action of the Redeemer, both in words and in gestures. This response of the participants to the presence of Christ is especially fitting for us who live in the aftermath of what the Last Supper prefigured, who have the memory of the Redemption. If the reverence and acclamation were removed, the ultimate focus of the Eucharist on the act of Redemption would be weakened liturgically.

The kind of quotation that occurs in the Eucharist is not the same as that found in ordinary discourse. In the Eucharist, the one who is quoted, Christ, acts through the quotation in a way in which the person quoted in ordinary quotation does not. When the words and gestures of Christ are quoted sacramentally, what Christ did is done again in a sacramental manner. Such an identification of action and achievement does not take place when, in normal discourse and conduct, we cite the words and gestures of another person. In ordinary quotation, what the quoted person did remains fixed in the time and place in which it was done. Sacramental quotation is not the same as regular quotation.[8]

Sacramental quotation is different because it is carried out before the eternal Father, in a prayer addressed to him. The eucharistic citations are not primarily addressed to the congregation but to the Father, before whom the original sacrifice of the cross is eternally present. The image and the citation can blend with

8. Mazza seems not to differentiate sufficiently between sacramental quotation and normal quotation and repetition. He compares sacramental identity with the identity of a parable (say, that of the Prodigal Son). He says that the parable once stated by Christ can now be restated by others in a new situation and with other words, but "in fact, it is really not 'another' parable." He observes that "if this is true of the word of God, there should be no problem in saying that the bread and wine on our altar are the very bread and wine of the Lord's final meal" (ibid., 353). But the kind of sameness at work in words and in meanings is quite different from that occurring in the sacrament. A verbal meaning can be quoted or repeated as one and the same in any form of natural human discourse; it enjoys an "ideal" type of being. Sacramental reenactment goes beyond this.

the original before the Father in a way that they cannot in our merely human representations. Because the Eucharist reenacts the decisive action between the incarnate Son and the Father, the sacrifice of the Mass can also be for us the same as that of Calvary. The identity that is manifested to us is dependent on the identity achieved before the Father.

It might be well, as a final point, to correct a possible misunderstanding. From what we have said about quotation, it might appear that the primary initiative in sacramental action lies in the present moment, with the Church and the local community and the celebrant of the Mass; when the Church and the priest determine to celebrate the Eucharist, the sacramental action occurs. But to see things in this perspective would be to put the emphasis in the wrong place. It is rather the case that the initiative lies with God and Christ: God has acted in Christ, and now he extends this action by elevating the words and actions of the Church and its priest and people into a reenaction of what he did. The Mass is celebrated in obedience to Christ's command, a command that is repeated, almost as a kind of warrant, in the liturgical words of institution. Christ elevates the voice and gestures of the celebrant and allows them to reembody his own words and gestures, thus allowing his redemptive action to be embodied sacramentally in the Eucharist. The priest *lends* his voice and hand to Christ; he does not order or conjure. To ascribe the initiative to the present Church, community, and minister would be to misunderstand who is acting and the kind of action being performed in the Eucharist.

And yet, even though the deepest initiative comes from God, it is also true that those who celebrate the Eucharist do act when they celebrate it. They are not only recipients but also offerers. The Church and its members act in the sacrament; as Vonier says, "Suppose the eucharistic sacrifice to be what some are inclined to make it, an entirely divine act, done by Christ, of which the Church is merely the witness, in which she has no part as sacrificant, as a sacramental power, there could be really no eucharistic Liturgy, in the true sense of the word."[9] If we were simply passive, "we should be merely a circle of worshippers, whilst the Liturgy is essentially an act, a doing of a mystery."[10] The Eucharist reflects the economy of Christian salvation, in which God redeems us but also calls us to act in accepting his grace. It is an economy that reflects the being of Christ, in whom both man and God acted to perform one and the same deed.

B

We have said, in Chapter 2, that the Eucharist reenacts the death and Resurrection of Christ indirectly, by reactivating the context of the Last Supper, in which Christ anticipated and pre-enacted his redemptive action. We have also stated, in the present chapter, that the Eucharist reactivates the Last Supper not by theatrically depicting it, but by quoting the words and the gestures of Christ, by letting Christ act here and now to achieve what he achieved at the Last Supper.

Quotation is, in fact, a more suitable vehicle than dramatic depiction for allowing the Eucharist to reenact the redemptive action of Jesus. Pictures, including dramatic representations, serve to draw the depicted into our present context, whereas quotations move us from our present situation to another context, to the context in which the person quoted was speaking.[11] A dramatic reenactment of the Last Supper would seem to make the Last Supper present here and now, while a quotation of the words and gestures of Christ more clearly takes us back to

9. Vonier, A Key to the Doctrine of the Eucharist, 245; see also p. 227.

10. Ibid., 245. Léon-Dufour, Sharing the Eucharistic Bread, 66, compares the apostles at the Last Supper with the apostles and the Church after the Resurrection. He says that at the Last Supper the apostles were merely recipients, merely passive. In the Gospel accounts they do not say or do anything as regards the institution. At that point they do not offer; Christ alone acts. But after the death and Resurrection of Christ, and after the coming of the Holy Spirit, they and their successors and the whole Church do act in the celebration of the rite.

11. See Sokolowski, "Picturing," in Pictures, Quotations, and Distinctions, 5–10.

the time and place of the Last Supper. We are displaced by quotation into the context of the Last Supper: "It is not the original event that is made present anew, but those celebrating the
rite are made present to the event."[12]

Furthermore, to consider the Eucharist as a depiction of the
Last Supper would obscure its reenactment of the death and Resurrection of Christ. The vividness of the dramatic presentation of
the Last Supper would tend to "crowd out," so to speak, the sacramental presentation of the act of our Redemption. The Eucharist
would tend to become understood primarily as a commemoration
of the Last Supper; it would tend to be taken primarily as a meal
and not a reenactment of the redemptive sacrifice.

To take the Mass as a dramatic representation of the Last
Supper would also make us overlook the fact that the institutional narrative in the Eucharist is set within a prayer addressed to God the Father. The quotation of the words and gestures of Christ is made with the Father as the one being addressed, not the congregation. If the Mass were to be taken to
depict the Last Supper, the emphasis would be placed on the effect the representation has on the congregation; the center of
gravity would be moved from addressing the Father to presenting a play to the congregation or to involving the congregation
in the play. Once again, the Eucharist would tend to become
interpreted simply as a meal and not a sacrifice to the Father. If
we are to respect the sacramental integrity of the Eucharist,
therefore, we must be clearly aware of the form of presentation
or making present at work in it.

The presentational form at work between the Eucharist and
the Last Supper is that of quotation. Quotation is more spiritual
than depiction (which involves a bodily imitation). It is also
more transparent. It is, so to speak, "lighter." It fits better into a
narration than a depiction would.[13] By referring to the Last Sup-

12. Giraudo, "The Eucharist as Re-Presentation," 156.
13. The form of presentation of the sacrament, because it involves quotation and
because it is so complex, makes the sacrifice of the Mass more spiritual, more "rea-
sonable" than either a depiction or a natural sacrifice.

per through quotation and not depiction, the Eucharist makes it easier for us to go through the Last Supper to the death and Resurrection of Christ. The Eucharist mentions the Last Supper and alludes to it and quotes from it and in one sense it repeats what happened at it, but the terminus of the Eucharist is the redemptive action of Christ. The Mass reactivates the context of the Last Supper only to reenact the saving action of Christ on Calvary. The Eucharist sacramentally reenacts the death of Jesus, not the Last Supper; yet it does so through the Last Supper, and it would be misleading to leave this dimension out of our theological consideration.

C

Quotations draw our attention to the content of what is quoted.[14] When we quote someone, we and our listeners focus on the content of the quotation. We think back to what was said at another time and place and we think about the other speaker's saying it. The same displacement occurs in the Eucharist. The quotation of Christ's words presents what he said at the Last Supper and presents him as saying it. The quotation of his gestures presents what he did at the Last Supper and presents him as doing it. Since these cited words and actions of the Last Supper themselves looked forward to the act of our Redemption, we are led to the Lord's sacrifice on the cross and his Resurrection; this is our ultimate focus when we celebrate the Eucharist. We hear and look through the various modes of presentation and come into contact sacramentally with the sacrifice of Calvary and the exchange that occurred there between Christ and the Father.

However, as our attention is drawn to the past event that was once preenacted and is now reenacted, we must not overlook theologically the present situation in which our quotation takes place. In being drawn to what is quoted and to the person being quoted, we must not overlook, theologically and religiously, the

14. See Sokolowski, "Quotation," in *Pictures, Quotations, and Distinctions,* 27–33.

present activity of quoting, the present activity of offering anew the one perfect sacrifice to God.

A similar reminder is necessary when we think about quotation in ordinary speech. There also we are drawn toward the quoted, but we tend to overlook the importance and prominence of our own activity of quoting. Without the present activity, the quoted would lose the life it newly gains in our speech. The activity of quoting has features of its own, even though it seems so transparent in relation to what it brings back to presence. When we quote, we as speakers are displaced into the speakers we cite, and our minds are displaced into what was thought and stated by someone else somewhere and sometime else, but *we now* are the ones who are so displaced. Our own speech acquires a hidden prominence, even as it subordinates itself to the speaker and the speech that it brings back to life.

One feature of the eucharistic liturgy that brings our present action to the fore is the epiclesis before the consecration, the calling down of the Holy Spirit on the gifts we are about to present to the Father. The epiclesis occurs just before we begin to narrate the institution of the Eucharist and quote the words of Christ. It is spoken explicitly by us here and now; it speaks of *our* offering and *our* celebration of this mystery. It refers to *these* gifts of bread and wine that we have set apart in the offertory. It asks God to make them holy through the power of the Holy Spirit so that they may become the body and blood of the Lord; the demonstrative "these" that we use here and now to indicate our bread and wine will blend with the demonstrative "this" used by Christ when the institutional narrative is recited and we displace ourselves into the perspective adopted by Jesus at the Last Supper. But the epiclesis occurs before this displacement and this change of voice—from prayer and narrative to quotation—take place: it highlights our present activity and the perspective from which we begin when we move on to quote the words of Christ. It highlights the perspective to which we return during the elevation and reverencing of the consecrated bread and wine, and which we adopt after the consecration, as we continue with the memorial prayer and offering, the prayer for the Church, the prayer for the dead, and the prayer for ourselves in union with the saints. It is this perspective from which we recite the doxology that closes the eucharistic Canon, and in which we go on to sacramental communion with Christ the risen Savior.

We should therefore not permit the actual eucharistic celebration here and now to become theologically invisible. It is true that our celebration takes us back through the Last Supper to the event on Calvary, but the event on Calvary itself was meant to be distributed throughout the world. Its reenactment now is part of what it was intended to be when it occurred. Its eucharistic re-presentation is part of its being. The Eucharist does not live simply from the past; it draws from whatever present it may inhabit wherever it takes place, and it lends a present voice and hand to Christ. Its ancient form of words is always newly spoken by us and by Christ to the Father.

D

The devotions to the Blessed Sacrament that developed during and since the Middle Ages are another way in which the present is graced by the Eucharist. Worship of the Blessed Sacrament in adoration, exposition, visits, holy hours, benediction, and processions engages a kind of temporality different from that of the celebration of Mass. The Mass involves the blending of two actions into one (the sacramental celebration and the redemptive sacrifice of Christ), while prayer before the Blessed Sacrament involves a continuous form of presence. The Mass is an action, a single, punctuated performance, even though it takes time to be completed. As an action, the Mass is like the saying of a sentence or the performance of a moral transaction or the presentation of a gift. As an action it blends with the action of the sacrifice of Christ on the cross; the "two" actions are sacramentally one action, one deed. In contrast, the manner in which the Blessed Sacrament presents itself to us is one of continuity in both presence and response.

It is true that eucharistic devotions are derivative from the Mass; they developed during the Middle Ages, rather late in the Church's history, and even now the directives the Church gives for them clearly make them subordinate to the eucharistic celebration.[15] The Blessed Sacrament always points back to the Mass and always retains the sense of food that the bread and wine of the liturgy possess; the sacrament is there ultimately to be consumed and to nourish us. Still, it has developed its own spirituality as a variation on that of the Mass itself. A study of eucharistic presence that omitted any discussion of devotion to the Blessed Sacrament would be incomplete.

Two of the major theological issues concerning the Eucharist are that of the Real Presence of Christ in the sacrament and that of the identity of the sacrifice at the altar and at Calvary. The two issues are obviously related, but it does seem that an ontological theology is more immediately focused on the former, and a theology concerned with manifestation on the latter. In the thought of St. Thomas Aquinas, for example, the focus is on the Real Presence, and the identity of the sacrifice is understood derivatively; Thomas says, "The Eucharist is the perfect sacrament of our Lord's passion, because it contains Christ himself who endured it; *tamquam continens Christum passum*."[16] The sacrifice is the same because of the identity of Christ. In contrast, in some of the more recent theologies of the Eucharist, such as those of Vonier, Journet, and Casel, the emphasis is on the iden-

15. A history and an evaluation of the cult of the Eucharist outside Mass are presented in Mitchell, *Cult and Controversy*. For a discussion of the rites promulgated by the Church in 1973 for such worship, see pp. 337–54. Mitchell's book is very informative and clear, but I find that his philosophical claims about the control language has over reality are too strong (for example, see pp. 73, 118–19). Furthermore, it seems to me that his treatment of ambiguity in sacramental presence (pp. 389–403), helpful as it is, does not take into account the special kinds of presence and absence that arise as possibilities in the light of the Christian distinction between the world and God.

16. St. Thomas Aquinas, *Summa theologiae* III 73 6 ad 2.

tity of the sacrifice and the Real Presence is seen in reference to that identity: for the sacrifice to be the same, Christ must be truly present. These theologies have been developed since the early years of this century, and perhaps they reflect a concern with manifestation that had lapsed into the background when Scholastic theology took the place of Patristic thought.[17]

Devotion to the Blessed Sacrament is more closely allied to the theme of the Real Presence. It responds to the continuous presence of Christ in the sacrament. It is interesting that such devotion involves the consecrated bread but not the wine. This is not just for practical reasons. The bread has a kind of priority and prominence in the symbolism of the Eucharist. Léon-Dufour points out that in the institutional narratives, the bread and the wine are not treated simply in parallel; rather, the two statements of Christ, the one concerning the bread and the other the wine, "represent a progression."[18] We might say that the bread and the wine are not two equal things placed in a simple sequence, but that they are rather like an ordered pair, with one being primary and the other accompanying it, something like the ordered pairs of father and son, mother and daughter, tree and shade, or light and shadow. The bread symbolizes the body or the full person of Christ; the cup of wine symbolizes his blood as separated from the body and poured out in a violent death.[19]

17. O'Connor, in *The Hidden Manna*, 243, asks, "How . . . can a past historical act (as distinguished from the person who performed the act and the consequences of the act) be present to us now?" He raises this question as an objection to the position of Journet and others who follow the thought of Casel. In his interpretation, it would seem that the Real Presence (the presence of "the person who performed the act") is what explains the identity of the sacrifice. O'Neill, in *Meeting Christ in the Sacraments*, 192, 196–203, expresses a position similar to that of O'Connor, along with a criticism of Casel. But it seems to me that a theological discussion of appearances and time can allow us to speak more directly about the sameness of the sacrifice itself; I hope that the reflections that we have developed in this book may be of some help in responding to the question O'Connor raises.

18. Léon-Dufour, *Sharing the Eucharistic Bread*, 198; see also pp. 63–64.

19. Of course, the body of the Lord is also present in the consecrated wine by virtue of what St. Thomas calls "concomitance," but the symbolism of the wine is still somewhat different from that of the bread. St. Thomas also makes the interesting point that in the words of institution, Christ adds the reference to the "cup" to

The double consecration, the use of bread and wine, symbolizes Christ in his sacrificial death, with the separation of blood from the body. Hence the reenactment of the sacrificial death of Christ requires the action of consecrating both bread and wine. But in eucharistic devotion, the body of Christ, which represents his whole person, not the body as separated from the blood, is presented to the believer.

Devotion to the Blessed Sacrament is a confirmation of the Real Presence of Christ in the Eucharist. During the growth of such devotion, the Church was also developing its teaching on transubstantiation, asserting not just that Christ is present in the bread and wine, but that in the Eucharist they cease to be bread and wine in their substance and become the body and blood of the Lord.[20] As St. Thomas observes, Christ did not say, "*This bread* is my body," which would allow us to think that the bread remained bread while serving to make Christ present to us; rather, he said, "*This* is my body," which indicates that it— "this"—is not bread any longer.[21] However, although the devotion to the sacrament was influenced by the doctrinal development,[22] it was not merely the outcome of theological controversy, no more than devotion to Mary the Mother of God was merely the outcome of Christological controversies. The devotion and the controversies are two aspects of a common development, the deepening of the Church's eucharistic faith.

Another theological distinction related to the Blessed Sacrament is that between the matter of the sacraments and the use of the matter. All the sacraments involve an element called the

what he says about the blood because, whereas bread is normally understood as something to be consumed, blood is not, so it was necessary to indicate by its being contained in a cup that it was to serve as food for the believer. See *Summa theologiae* III 78 3 ad 1.

20. Just as the issue of the Real Presence must be distinguished from that of the identity of the sacrifice, so must the issue of transubstantiation be distinguished from that of the Real Presence. See O'Connor, *The Hidden Manna*, 219–20.

21. See St. Thomas Aquinas, *Summa theologiae* III 78 2, objection 3 and ad 3. A similar point is made in *Summa theologiae* III 75 3 c.

22. See, for example, King, *Eucharistic Reservation in the Western Church*, 53.

matter (as opposed to the "form" or verbal part of the rite), such as the water used in baptism, the oils used in anointing the sick, and the bread and wine used in the Eucharist. But there is a difference between the Eucharist and the other sacraments in regard to the role of the matter. St. Thomas says that "all the other sacraments are brought to completion only when the consecrated matter is being used."[23] Even though the matter for these sacraments may have been blessed or dedicated, the actuality of the sacrament is not achieved until the matter—the oil or the water—has been used. But in the case of the Eucharist, "this sacrament is fully established when the matter is consecrated." The matter of the Eucharist is not just a vehicle for sanctification; it is not just instrumental in making Christ present to the believer or recipient; it is changed in itself into the person of Christ.[24] The change of the matter is what establishes the possibility of eucharistic devotion, since Christ is present not only during the Mass or at communion but permanently in the consecrated bread and wine.

Devotion to the Blessed Sacrament is one of the great legacies of the Middle Ages, and through the centuries it has fostered the sanctity that the Eucharist was instituted to nourish in the Church.[25] It reflects the mystery of the Incarnation. The eucharistic celebration does so as well, but with a concentration on the redemptive action of Christ in his death and Resurrection; devotion to the sacrament brings out more fully the fact that the Logos dwelt among us and conversed with us. He did not appear for a single action only, even though that action marked the hour toward which his life was directed. His continuous presence during his life called for a response. It still does so in the sacra-

23. St. Thomas Aquinas, *Summa theologiae* III 78 1 c.
24. Thus, Aquinas states in *Summa theologiae* III 84 3 c: "In the sacrament of the Eucharist, which consists in the actual consecration of the matter, the truth of this consecration is expressed when the words *This is my body* are said."
25. For a defense of the importance of the eucharistic theology and the eucharistic devotion of the Middle Ages, see O'Connor, *The Hidden Manna*, 186–206; also Clark, *Eucharistic Sacrifice and the Reformation*.

mental presence. Eucharistic conversation is understood only by the believer; it is a version of the intimacy of the disciple with Christ that is expressed in the Gospel of St. John. In eucharistic worship the believer responds to Christ and the Father who love him and make their dwelling with him (John 14:23).

8

⚜

THE TIME OF THE EUCHARIST

THE CELEBRATION of the Eucharist engages the temporal dimensions of present, past, and future in various ways. It also activates various temporal contexts and relates them to one another.[1] We will now explore the temporality of the Eucharist. We begin by considering the Jewish Passover, which provided the setting for the first Eucharist.

1. When the Passover was celebrated by the Jews on the fourteenth day of the month of Nisan, the first month of the year, it recalled God's deliverance of his people from slavery in Egypt. It recalled this event by following the ritual injunctions that were set down by Moses for the first Passover, which took place on the eve of the Exodus and prepared the Jews for the action God was about to perform.[2] On that first Passover, each family was to slaughter a lamb, mark with its blood the door-posts and lintel of their dwelling, roast the animal, and eat it along with unleavened bread and bitter herbs; the family was to

1. Léon-Dufour discusses the many dimensions of what he calls the "temporal axis" in the Eucharist and the Last Supper. See *Sharing the Eucharistic Bread*, 55, 60–72, 105–13, 234.

2. The description of the first Passover is contained in chapter 12 of Exodus, which presents both the ritual of the Passover lamb and that of the unleavened bread.

consume it "with your loins girded, your sandals on your feet, and your staff in your hand; and you shall eat it in haste" (Exodus 12:11). They were to eat the meal as people who are ready to depart. The blood sprinkled on the doorposts and lintel protected the people within from the tenth plague, the death of "all the firstborn in the land of Egypt, both man and beast" (Exodus 12:12).

The subsequent Jewish Passovers thus looked back to the deliverance from Egypt, but they also looked back to the first Passover, which anticipated that deliverance. When Moses gave the instructions for the first Passover, he himself looked forward to its future repetition by the Jews: "You shall observe this rite as an ordinance for you and for your sons forever. And when you come to the land which the Lord will give you, as he has promised, you shall keep this service" (Exodus 12:25). In speaking of these future celebrations, Moses also told the people that they should in the future remember the event he was preparing them for: "And when your children say to you, 'What do you mean by this service?' you shall say, 'It is the sacrifice of the Lord's passover, for he passed over the houses of the people of Israel in Egypt, when he slew the Egyptians but spared our houses'" (Exodus 12:26–27). Moses anticipated not only a future celebration but also a future remembering or memorial of what God did for his people at the time when he, Moses, gave the people these instructions.

2. Within the context set by the Passover, another context was set by Christ at the Last Supper. Jesus also engaged the temporal form of present, past, and future. He celebrated the first Eucharist against the background of the Jewish Passover and its recollection of the past, and he anticipated the death he was about to undergo in the immediate future. He also anticipated, in the more distant future, the repetition by his disciples of the action he was performing, just as Moses anticipated the future celebrations of the Passover. Jesus anticipated this future when he told his disciples to do as he did. Finally, and still more re-

motely, he anticipated the eschaton, the final state of God's kingdom, when he said, "I tell you, from now on I shall not drink this fruit of the vine until the day when I drink it with you new in the kingdom of my Father" (Matthew 26:29).[3]

3. Within the first context set by the Passover, and within the second context set by the Last Supper, our celebration of the Eucharist establishes its own form of present, past, and future. Ours is chronologically later than the other two, but it takes its place within them and blends with them temporally in several ways. It repeats the actions of Jesus and revives the context of the Last Supper, but it also revives the more ancient context of the Passover. When it reenacts the death and Resurrection of Jesus, it also reenacts the action God performed in the Exodus. The Last Supper invoked the Passover, so when we invoke the Last Supper we also invoke the Passover that preceded and was drawn into it. Our Eucharist thus has a double revival of the past, with one of its reenacted pasts, the Last Supper, enclosed within the context set by the other, the Passover. The past of our Eucharist is the present of the Last Supper and the sacrifice of Calvary; in a deeper dimension, the past of our Eucharist is the present of the Passover and the Exodus.

But at the Last Supper, Jesus also anticipated the repetition, by his disciples, of what he was doing; he told his disciples to do as he did in memory of him. Thus our present Eucharist coincides with the future that was anticipated by Christ.

The remote future to which our Eucharist looks is the final coming of Jesus and the restoration of all things in God's kingdom. This distant future, along with the past and present dimensions of the Eucharist, are well expressed in one of the acclamations used after the words of consecration: "Christ *has* died, Christ *is* risen, Christ *will* come again." The same eschaton

3. In the parallel passage in Luke 22:17–20, Jesus makes the statement about the kingdom of God not in regard to the cup he calls the cup of his blood, but in regard to another cup from which the apostles drank at the Last Supper, one that is shared by all even before the bread is taken up.

was also anticipated by Jesus at the Last Supper, so in this respect his future and ours coincide.

More proximately, we in the Eucharist anticipate our own death as to be joined to the death of Jesus. Our death becomes part of the divine mystery, part of the great saving action of God, because it can be identified with the sacrificial death of Christ. Even if our death is not to be especially heroic or memorable in the eyes of the world, it can become sanctified through the death of Jesus, through the action that he performed before the Father when he let himself be put to death. The celebrations of the Eucharist at which we assist are like so many rehearsals of the one transition, the one exodus that is reserved for each of us, the one offering in which we no longer sacramentally but bodily participate in the death of the Lord. As Jesus acted toward the Father in his death, so we are enabled to make our death an act before God, an act in which life is changed, not taken away. It is an act in which we respond to rather than initiate what is to happen, but through the death of Jesus we come to know that this apparent dissolution is really a word spoken to us by God, and spoken to each of us only once. Our death, which is the horizon marking off the edge of our life, becomes a particular image of the final restoration of all things in Christ, an image of the death of things that is now to be understood as a transition into the kingdom of God. The Eucharist thus presents a double future to each of us as we participate in it: it presents our own entrance into the death and Resurrection of Jesus, and it presents the more remote setting in which everything will be restored in the kingdom of God.

These enchainments of past and future are all woven into the Eucharist we celebrate in the present. The celebration of the Eucharist is surrounded by temporal ripples through which past and future things are refracted. The Eucharist does not give us merely images or signs of what is past and future; it presents these things as past and as future to us now.

The Eucharist involves memory and anticipation, but it does not involve them as mere psychological states; rather, it reenacts and preenacts things God has done and will do. In this respect, the Eucharist resembles our ordinary memories and anticipations. When we remember and anticipate natural things in our natural representations, we are not locked into our psychological states: if I anticipate meeting someone, I anticipate the meeting itself, not an idea of the meeting; if I remember parting from someone, I remember the separation itself, not an image of it. In the case of the Eucharist, the public action of the liturgy does not just put us in mind of past and future events; it reenacts an event—the sacrificial death and Resurrection of Christ—that truly happens again in a sacramental way, and it gives us a foretaste and promise of the Paschal feast of heaven.

The implicatures of present, past, and future that occur in the Eucharist resemble the blends of time that occur in all our natural activity and being. We are and we act always "now," but our now is always the recapitulation of a past and the anticipation of a future. In our conscious life we are aware of this constant emergence of the present out of the past and its steady transformation into the future; we are aware of it because we constantly displace ourselves into the past and into the future through remembrance and anticipation.[4] Although we are aware of this emergence and this transformation, the emergence and transformation go on quite independently of our awareness. The transitions of time go on whether we pay attention to them or not; everything in the world is subject to the succession of time. Even as we live a biological life and take part in the processes of matter, we recapitulate the past and are determined into the future. The time of the world, the temporal succession of the world, provides a kind of raw material for the Eucharist. The Eucharist draws on time and could not be without it. It draws on the world's temporal existence as it reenacts one of the

4. See Sokolowski, "Timing," in *Pictures, Quotations, and Distinctions*, 124–27.

events that once took place in the world, as it reenacts the death of Jesus on Calvary.

But the Eucharist repeats that event not merely as one of the things that happened in the development of nature and the movement of history. It reenacts it as occurring before God and reenacts it in a prayer that addresses God. In this presence before God, the emergence of the present and the determination of the future now show up as not being the final context for what occurs. The succession of things and events, which in the natural order is the ultimate setting for whatever is, now becomes an image.[5] Time becomes a moving image of eternity. Succession, which seemed to lie under everything that happens and seemed to be the "last thing" there is, now seems itself to rest against a life or an event that has no before or after, the eternal life of God, and this life is directly involved and invoked in the Eucharist.

In celebrating the Eucharist, we do not "feel" the life of which succession is the image, since whatever we can feel must move along in time. If we were to "feel" this life, it would not be imaged any longer; it would be given to vision, not to faith. But because succession is now understood as an image, what it images is somehow presented to us: not merely in words, but in the image we have of it specifically in succession.

The very temporality and public movement of the eucharistic celebration are perhaps a more effective presentation of eternity than might be a religious moment "out of time," precisely because the time and motion of the Eucharist can serve as a privileged image of eternal life. The Eucharist takes time when it is celebrated, but it also overcomes time as it reenacts an event that took place at another time. In doing this, the Eucharist calls time into question. It claims to go beyond time and thereby indicates that time and its succession are not ultimate. It makes time to be an image; it makes succession to be a representation. Thus the Eucharist, in its reenactment of the past

5. On what I call succession, see ibid., 132–37.

and anticipation of the future, also enacts for us the context that encloses past, future, and present: it enacts the eternal life of the God who could be all that he is, in undiminished goodness and greatness, even if the world and its time were not. The Eucharist engages, and perpetually reminds us of, the Christian distinction between the world and God.

Because the Eucharist engages the relationship between the world and God, it reaches beyond the context set by the Passover, which we took initially as the first setting in our chronological study of eucharistic contexts. In our exposition in this chapter, we first examined the Passover, then the Last Supper, and finally the present eucharistic celebration; our discussion reached back to the Passover as the widest horizon for the Eucharist. But now we find that the Eucharist extends back into Creation itself, into the biblical understanding of the relationship between the world and God. In reaching back to Creation, the Eucharist finds itself in the same context as that of the eschaton, the moment in which all things will be restored in Christ. The widest horizon is the place for both the beginning and the end. What the Eucharist anticipates as the eschaton is found to be in the same place as what it attains when it reaches back to Creation, the context in which all things begin and end in God.

This final setting, in which worldly time becomes profiled against eternal life, in which worldly time itself becomes relativized against eternity, permeates the Eucharist and gives it its sense. Only the God who lives in eternal plenitude and independence could become part of his creation; only he could save us in the way we have been redeemed; only he could achieve in the Eucharist the sacramental reenactment of our Redemption. Our celebration of the Eucharist, our sacramental way of looking back on the one sacrifice of Christ and being present to it, becomes a temporal icon of how we will look "back" on that same sacrifice from the eschaton, from the eternal present of our life with God.

If God were not as Christians understand him to be, the Eucharist would be either a mere symbol or a kind of idol. A worldly divinity that intervened in human affairs would have to become subject to the inevitabilities of time: either it would only seem to enter into history, and hence only be symbolized by a commemoration of that "event," or it would be captured by its own worldly involvement and hence idolized in it. Only the God who is so independent of the world as the biblical God is revealed to be could become incarnate and sacramentally present in the Eucharist. Only before this God could sacramental time become an image of eternity. The Eucharist is a constant reminder of the transcendence of God.

9

꧁꧂

THE PLACE OF CHOICE IN
THE WORLD

THE EUCHARISTIC prayer is a prayer of praise and thanksgiving. If we are to thank God and praise him for his deeds, we must understand his actions to have been chosen by him. Some reflection on the place of choice in the being of things is appropriate for our study of eucharistic thanksgiving. In developing this theme, as well as those found in the next four chapters, we will be moving away somewhat from our study of the Eucharist. We will develop issues that belong rather to the second concern of this book, the theology of disclosure. In Chapters 9 and 10 we will discuss how the world appears to Christian belief; we will show how the world as taken by the Christian differs from the world as taken by the unbeliever. In Chapter 11 we will examine how Christian understanding is based on and yet differs from the Jewish, and in Chapter 12 we will show how the Christian understanding differs from the pagan. In all these differentiations, the central topic will be the Christian understanding of the difference between the world and God, hence the Christian understanding of the divine. We will then be led to a fuller discussion, in Chapter 13, of the nature of the theology of disclosure. As we explore these themes, however, the Eucharist is never really lost from view, since as a central article of Christian faith it both presupposes and reminds us of the way we are to understand God, the world, and ourselves.

Since Christians understand the Creator to be distinct from the created, they also understand the world in a way different from the way it is naturally understood. In the Christian view, the world is taken not as simply there, not as an unquestionable background for the being of particular things, but as existing through something like a choice. In this understanding, it makes sense to be grateful that the world exists. In the natural understanding, we may marvel at the world and its articulation, but there would be no sense in thanking someone for its being there. For the natural understanding, the world simply is, ineluctably, and we could not authentically imagine its not being, since it could not have come out of nothing.

What we might call the ontological place of choice changes in this Christian understanding. For pagan philosophy, choice is a restricted phenomenon. It is a human activity, a human perfection, but it arises from the limitations of the human estate. We have to make choices because we are not perfect and must try to make ourselves and our situations better. The domain of choice is surrounded by the necessities, regularities, and contingencies of the cosmos, which are simply there as a background for the human condition, and which are devoid of choice. The fact that other beings do not choose does not necessarily make them less perfect than the things that must make choices: in their highest excellence, the things that surround man are more admirable and more noble than human things.

Aristotle, for example, says, "It would be strange if someone were to think that the art of politics or practical wisdom is the best [knowledge], if man is not the best of the things in the cosmos."[1] He goes on to say, "If [the argument be] that man is better than the other animals, this makes no difference; for there are

---

1. Aristotle, *Nicomachean Ethics* VI, 7, 1141a20–22.

other things much more divine in their nature even than man, such as, most conspicuously, the things of which the cosmos is framed."[2] Aristotle thinks that the principles of nature and the highest beings, which do not need to make choices, are more excellent in their being than man. Even St. Athanasius thought that some parts of the cosmos were higher than man; regarding the Incarnation, he raises the question "Why did [the Word of God] not appear by means of other and nobler parts of creation, and use some nobler instrument, as the sun, or moon, or stars, or fire, or air, instead of man merely?"[3] His answer is that the Word came not just to appear but to heal, and in creation only man "had gone astray." St. Athanasius thus acknowledges that there are beings greater than man in the visible cosmos, but the Word did not choose them as the place in which he would appear.

In a more modern register, someone who believes in evolution and in an evolving universe would also find human choice to be rather diminutive. Nature and evolution themselves would be seen as the causes of human existence, and they would also be seen as the more remote causes of human choice; nature and evolution would therefore at their best be higher than the human beings that they bring about. The self-correcting mechanisms of evolution would seem to be more effective and successful, and hence more excellent, than human deliberation and choice, which operates on so small a scale and really affects only the human estate. Choices are very important for us who have to make them, but if we look at things from a large-scale perspective, and if we consider the size and age of the universe, it does not seem that our choices affect things very much. And once again, there would be no reason for us to thank nature and evolution for our existence. Nature and evolution, as presently conceived, seem to operate through a combination of blind necessity and blind chance, and neither of these powers could have chosen us to be.

2. Aristotle, *Nicomachean Ethics* VI, 7, 1141a33–b2.
3. St. Athanasius, "On the Incarnation of the Word," §43.

Thus in a naturalistic understanding, whether ancient or modern, choice arises because one kind of entity, man, is able to look a few steps into the future, discover various possible ways of behaving, and select one action or another. This entity needs to choose; it needs to be resourceful in order to preserve itself, satisfy its desires, and make itself better. In being capable of choice, this entity is more perfect than the other animals, who must find ways to adapt to their environment but who do not have the range of possibilities that choice opens up, but this entity's need to choose also reflects its limitations; it is neither happy nor satisfied just as it is; it needs to make choices in order to try to be happy and to become more fully what it is; it has to bob and weave in response to the pressures of nature and the opportunities opened up to it. Its choices, moreover, do not only enable it to cope with its environment; they also shape its own way of being (its character) and make it into a morally good or bad, strong or weak agent. But it needs to make choices before it becomes either good or bad, excellent or depraved; it is neither good nor bad by nature. The higher beings do not need to choose in order to perfect themselves. Aristotle's celestial beings, and the laws of nature and mechanisms of evolution, are simply as perfect as they can be. In a naturalistic understanding of things, choice shows up as a symptom of limitation, and it shows up within a context of natural necessities and contingencies that do not involve choice.

In the Christian understanding, choice acquires a different ontological place. Instead of being a subordinate phenomenon nested within the world, it becomes that within which the world itself is nested. It is placed at the origin of the world in Creation and remains at the heart of the world in divine preservation and providence. The necessities and contingencies of the world—whether the heavenly bodies or the laws of nature or the force of evolution or the way things happen to work out—now appear as derived necessities and contingencies, necessities and contingencies that are but that might not have been, and the events that occur in nature and even in history are seen to be the work of the divine will. Gratitude for the being of the world and prayer for divine intervention become not only possible but appropriate.

Clearly, the kind of choice that is believed to underlie the existence of the world is not the same as the choices exercised within the world itself. The divine choice to create is called a choice only by analogy. When human beings make choices, they determine themselves to one action and leave many possibilities undone; human choice stems from limitation, from the need to be made better, and it also brings about restriction. The restriction concerns not only the things that are left unrealized but also the perfections of the agent that will never come to be. If we enact ourselves to be in *this* way, we forego the self-enactment that would make us be in *that* way. But in the divine choice to create, God could not be restricted by his choice to be only this or that sort of Creator, the Creator of this world only and not the Creator of another. God is not confined by his choice to being only this way or that, because his choice is not the sort of thing that confines him at all; more radically, he is not the kind of being that could be confined at all. For God to choose one thing does not deprive him of the perfections he might have had if he had created something else. God does not suffer lost opportunities. He is neither restricted nor perfected by what he does when he creates.

Furthermore, while human choices can be made only when a situation calling for action has presented itself, the divine choice is sovereign over all situations and does not have to wait for the right time to come. We depend on the moment to act, but God is not subject to time in this way. St. Ignatius of Antioch brings out this distinction, regarding both time and action, when he writes to Polycarp, "Be even more diligent than you already are. Weigh every opportunity (*tous kairous*) carefully. And wait for him who does not need any opportunity (*ton hyper kairon*), being beyond time and invisible, who became visible for us."[4]

4. St. Ignatius of Antioch, "Letter to Polycarp," in Migne, *Patrologia Graeca*, 5:721–22.

Because the divine choice to create is so different from human choices, we might be inclined to say that the former only faintly resemble the latter, that God's choices are only a dim shadow of human choice. To think this way, however, would be to take human choice as the paradigm of freedom and to claim that divine choice is not a full and clear instance of freedom. But theologically it would be more appropriate to reason in the opposite direction and to say that human choice is the derived thing and divine freedom the paradigm. The inherently restricted and restrictive character of human freedom need not belong to freedom as such, but only to its exercise in the conditions that mark the human estate. In the light of revelation, we come to see that choice could in principle be purely positive. How a purely positive choice could be exercised remains mysterious to us, but in the light of revelation, human choice now provides us a glimpse of how it could happen. Instead of being the only kind of choice there can be, human choice becomes an image of a kind of choice that escapes the limitations of human freedom. Moreover, human choice serves more perfectly as such an image when it is purified by grace and exercised in charity. The life of Jesus and the lives of the saints show what kind of human choices reflect most accurately the choice of the Creator.

In theological writings, the divine act of Creation is usually expressed in the categories of making or producing. Even in the creeds, God is called maker of heaven and earth, of all that there is, whether seen or unseen. Creation is like fabrication in that both yield something that endures as a "product," but the product in each case is different. Human making brings about products that remain when the activity of making is finished and the human maker departs—tables, cars, buildings—but Creation brings about a world that needs God's continuous preservation to remain in being. Human fabrications do not need the continuous support of their fabricator to remain in being; once made, they endure apart from him.

One of the reasons why human products become independent of their makers is found in the material out of which they are made. Human making always involves some pregiven raw material on which it must work: wood, metal, clay, or even words and grammar, in the case of both written and spoken texts. This raw material, which has its own independent existence, remains as a support for the transformations it receives from the human maker, so that when the maker finishes his activity, the thing he made can go on in being. The need for raw material in human making brings about a theological problem when the category of making is used to express Creation. There seems to be a need for some sort of matter into which God brings order and form, and if such matter is accepted, then the world seems to have some sort of independence of God. God would be not the Creator but a demiurge. To correct this tendency, which arises because human production is used as the model for Creation, Christian belief has to assert that God creates the world out of nothing, out of no preexistent material.

It would be helpful, when speaking of Creation, to supplement the use of the category of making with the category of action. Whereas making (*poiēsis*) establishes a product that becomes independent of its maker, acting or doing (*praxis*) is simply a transaction between agents which is nothing more than the transaction itself, and which establishes or modifies a relationship between the agents. An act of thanking someone, an act of insulting someone, an act of benevolence, an act of betrayal, all are examples of actions. There is no product made in an action as such, but the agents and the relationships between them are changed by what is done.[5] One agent remains henceforth as the one who was betrayed and the other remains as the betrayer; one remains as the beneficiary, the other as the benefactor. Actions do not require raw material in the same way that making does,

5. For a good contemporary expression of the nature of human action, see Arendt, *The Human Condition*, 175–247. See also Oakeshott, *On Human Conduct*, 31–107, and Sokolowski, *Moral Action*, 54–63.

but they do need something material in which to be embodied and expressed. There have to be words or gestures, there has to be something handed over or taken away, if there is to be an action among human agents.

If Creation were to be interpreted as an action, then the being of the world would be seen not as an ineluctable background for everything that happens, but as the embodiment and expression of the Creator's choice to create. Whereas we have to carry out our exchanges by taking up things that are already there and expressing ourselves in them—in words, objects, bodily motions—God both acts and establishes the embodiment of his action. Indeed, his making of the embodiment of his action is equivalent to his action. What is distinguished in our conduct is united in his.

One way of understanding Creation as an action is to call it a gift, as Kenneth Schmitz has.[6] To understand Creation as gift is in keeping with the biblical and the liturgical interpretations of Creation as one of God's saving deeds. It is not the case that God first simply created the world as a kind of stage and only subsequently began to act within it. Such an understanding would take Creation to be only a making and not an acting; it would take God's actions to be only what he does when he intervenes in history. But such a disjunction between making and acting would not conform to the way the liturgy understands Creation. In the biblical passages read during the Easter vigil service, for example, we recall the various interventions God made for his people in the Old Testament: we read about the call of Abraham, the Exodus, the promise of an eternal Covenant, the gift of the Law, the restoration from exile; all of these actions lead up to the divine action achieved in the death and Resurrection of Jesus. But the first of the Easter readings is the narrative of Creation taken from the Book of Genesis; Creation is certainly taken in this liturgical context as the first of the divine interventions. It is the first of the actions of God, not

6. Schmitz, *The Gift: Creation.*

just the fabrication of the stage on which his actions are to be performed. As Herbert Haag writes, "Creation itself was for the Israelite a saving action of his God."[7]

It is one thing for us to understand the world as created by God, to see it not as just being there always but as existing through a divine choice; it is another thing to make the inference and realize that we too exist through divine election. In our natural understanding, we take ourselves to be the outcome of natural forces and contingencies, and more proximately we see ourselves as the children of our parents. All of us know that we so easily might never have come into being and that someone else might have been there instead; our existence depends radically on chance. But in our natural understanding, none of us thinks that the forces of nature, or even our parents, in their hopes and plans, wanted and chose *us* to be. Even our parents have to accept *us* when we appear on the scene; we in our individuality were not selected or made by them. But if we owe our existence to God's choice, then *we* in our individuality were chosen by him to be. Our being is the outcome of an action of the Creator. We do not appear before him with our own warrant, as we do before our parents and before the laws of nature, and as we would before Aristotle's god or the god of process theology. In the biblical understanding, we are there because God wants us to be. In this light, we take ourselves in our continued existence as created and sustained by divine choice, and the whole sense of our life takes on a different tone. This self-understanding, which we have through our biblical faith, is correlated with our belief that the domain of choice and of the personal is not just one component of the being of the world, but is the ultimate setting within which there is a world at all.

7. Haag, *Vom alten zum neuen Pascha*, 18.

10

❦

THE CHRISTIAN UNDERSTANDING
OF THE PERSON

OUR TREATMENT of choice in the last chapter leads us to an investigation of persons as the agents who choose. We must also examine the meaning of the term "personal" as it is used in reference to God and his actions. In this chapter, (a) we will examine the philosophical teaching that the possession of reason is the root of personal being, and (b) we will see how the biblical understanding of Creation recognizes a personal source for the existence of the world. Then (c) we will examine a definition of the person proposed by Hans Urs von Balthasar, and finally (d) we will contrast the biblical understanding of the world as created by a personal God with other understandings of the world that have been presented in Western thought, both ancient and modern.

A

Traditionally, the person has been defined as an individual substance of a rational nature. This definition was formulated by Boethius and was generally accepted by the Scholastics. "Person" signifies an individual; strictly speaking, from the philosophical point of view, the term should not be used as a common noun. In this respect it is something like a demonstrative pronoun.[1] It cannot be used to name a nature or a kind of thing, as the terms "man," "animal," and "plant" can. The term "person" is used simply to denote individuals who possess reason: a person is an individual substance of a rational nature. It is rationality, and the freedom that stems from rationality, that marks a being as a person.

Being a person is different from being an individual in a species. As Yves Simon writes, an individual is a part of its species and is subordinated to the species to which it belongs.[2] Individuals as such are not ends in themselves. Individuals are expended in preserving the species, in allowing the form of the species to pass through them to others. Plants and animals are there to be instances of their species and parts of it, and much of what they do is directed toward promoting their species. Human beings also are individuals in the species "man," and in some respects they too are there to instantiate and propagate their species. But they also transcend their species and are each, individually, ends in themselves. They transcend their species especially through their rationality and the freedom founded upon it: as persons, as rational and free, human beings are no longer mere parts but wholes and ends in themselves. As Simon says, "Considered as a complete substance which owes to its rationality a unique way of being a whole and of facing the rest of the universe, [a human subject] is more properly designated as a person."[3] Through their reason, human beings are able to have a sense of the whole; they can have an opinion about the whole, orient themselves in regard to it, and determine them-

1. Heidegger's use of the term *Dasein* to name human being (and as a kind of substitution for "person") brings out the demonstrative character to which we refer.
2. Simon, *A General Theory of Authority*, 67.
3. Ibid., 67; see pp. 67–79. Jacques Maritain, in *The Person and the Common Good*, also describes how a human being is part of a larger whole (of a political society, of the species, of the cosmos) and yet as a person transcends any whole. Maritain works out at length the logic of parts and wholes for individuals and persons.

selves in respect to it. This possibility frees them from being simply instruments in a larger process and makes them each to be a whole of a distinct kind.

So far we have been discussing the person as it is defined by Boethius. Our method has been that of the Scholastics: we have examined the ontology of the person. Let us now shift to the approach followed by phenomenology and the theology of disclosure. We will describe how the personal presents itself to us and how it differentiates itself from the impersonal. Let us imagine two different scenarios as a basis for our analysis.

Suppose I am on an expedition in the far north. I am attacked by a polar bear. The bear injures my arm, but my colleagues drive the animal away and I escape with no further harm. Now imagine a second situation. We are again on an expedition. Tensions build up among the members of the group. At one point, perhaps out of revenge or jealousy, one of my colleagues attacks me and injures my arm. The others put a stop to the fight. We return from the expedition and go our separate ways. Let us say that the damage to my arm, the cuts and bruises, is practically the same as that inflicted by the bear in our first imagined case. I may have suffered the same material injury in both instances, but obviously there is a difference in the kind of thing that happened to me. I carry resentment to-

---

He makes use of a passage from Aquinas, "The sense of being a part is at odds with the sense of being a person (*ratio partis contrarietur rationi personae*)" (*In III Sententiarum*, 5. 1. 2, c). See also *In III Sententiarum*, 5. 3. 2, ad 2: "It belongs to the sense of person to be whole and complete." It is interesting to note that in the Incarnation God became part of his creation when the Logos was hypostatically united to a human nature, but because this human nature, through its rationality, could somehow be all things, in the Incarnation God became united with his creation as such, not with "merely" a part of it.

As regards persons and the logic of parts and wholes, the way of being of angels provides an interesting contrast with the being of man. St. Thomas understands each angel to be a species, hence individual angels are not subordinated in any way to a species extending beyond them. Human rationality, in contrast, distributes and regenerates itself through many individuals. It is, consequently, more feeble and more fragile in any particular individual, but it also becomes capable of certain virtues that angels neither need nor enjoy.

ward the man for what he did, but I have no resentment toward the animal for what it did.[4] The man's act was a personal action while the bear's was not.

The difference lies in the fact that an exercise of reason, an "exhibition of intelligence," was present in the man's action but not in the bear's.[5] The man understood me as one who was to be injured, and his action occurred through this assessment and because of it. Because he understood *me* as to be injured—whatever his motivations might have been—he acted in a way that was injurious to me. It was not just a will that moved him to attack me, but an understanding that provided the context for the will. The bear, on the other hand, acted entirely out of inclination. It wanted food or it feared danger and it attacked; there was "nothing personal" in what it did. The bear acted simply according to the way it was born to be, not according to the way it had come to be and to think because of earlier choices, actions, and thoughts. The bear did not see *me* as to be injured; it just wanted something or was trying to avert something. The difference between the two acts lies in the rationality that Boethius says is the distinguishing characteristic of persons: in the conduct of the man and the behavior of the bear we directly experience the presence or the absence of rationality. I experience the man's behavior as exhibiting intelligence, and I experience the bear's behavior as not manifesting intelligence. The intelligence in question, furthermore, is not the discovery of means toward an end, nor the abstraction of a universal out of particulars, nor the discovery of the cause of a fact, but the assessment and identification of me as to be injured, as one who, for whatever reason, ought to be injured. The exercise of intelligence is a rational identification. I am a personal target for the man but I am simply an object for the bear.[6]

4. See Strawson, "Freedom and Resentment."

5. The term "exhibition of intelligence" is used by Michael Oakeshott in his analysis of responsible action. See *On Human Conduct*, 39.

6. For further remarks on the role of rational identification in moral conduct, see Sokolowski, *Moral Action*, 54–76, 156–62.

We have used the example of a harmful action, but the same difference between the personal and the impersonal can be found in beneficial performances. I am grateful to someone who, out of kindness, gives me a valuable object, because the "handing over" takes place through and with the assessment of the person who gives me the item; he understands me as one to whom this thing should be given and I receive the object as coming to me through that understanding. But I am not grateful to the chicken that lays the eggs that I eat for breakfast, because the chicken acts merely out of inclination and not through a benevolent understanding. The chicken does not give me the egg. Likewise, I am not grateful to the market where I buy the egg, because it too does not identify me as one to whom the egg should be given. Thus, whether harmful or benevolent, personal actions are achieved through moral understanding.

Because understanding is at the root of personal action, it makes sense for us to talk to human agents in order to try to change the understanding they have of their situations and of the persons involved in them; we sometimes try to persuade people to appraise their situations differently and therefore to act in different ways. We do not argue with animals because they are not rational and cannot respond to argument. Still less do we argue with plants or with simply material forces. We also carry no resentment toward them. I am not resentful toward the tree whose roots damage my waterpipe, or toward the tide that ebbs and leaves me stranded, because such processes are not the outcomes of assessments. The things acting in such ways are not persons.

B

We might, however, see even such natural processes as the growth of trees or the movement of tides as the expression of a divine will or providence. We might also take accidents or coincidences as the expression of the will of a higher power. Besides being recognized as simply natural processes, both the regularities and the accidents in our world might be seen as somehow embodying a personal decision. If we were to accept such things and events in this way, we would see them as the outcome of an assessment, as an exhibition of an understanding. They would not be taken as the expression of a sheer will, but of a choice made within an understanding. Providence does not involve merely a will but also a comprehension from which a choice emerges, a comprehension that takes us to be the targets of a particular exchange. When we accept things as the will of God, we take them as ordered by divine wisdom as well as governed by the divine will. Put another way, we begin to look through them—they no longer are simply and ultimately "there" as brute facts—toward a person expressing himself in them. A dimension opens up beyond them. We do not rest merely with something, as we might have, but arrive at someone, and correlatively we take ourselves as the ones toward whom that someone acts.

We can even see the actions performed by other people toward us as being chosen by providence. This person's generosity toward me or that person's injury inflicted on me can be seen as what the divine will, in its wisdom, sees as what I am to undergo here and now. There can be a dovetailing of two personal actions: that of the human agent and that of divine providence. The human and the divine choices function, of course, in different ways; the divine will is not to be understood as like a hidden human transaction added to the one I consciously experience. The manner in which the two choices come together needs to be explored, and such exploration will help us appreciate the difference between human and divine personality and choice.

The biblical understanding takes not only particular events but the very existence of the world to be chosen through an assessment. The Bible presents the world as an expression of divine wisdom and particular events as chosen by divine providence. In this respect the biblical understanding is very different from the philosophical understanding of Aristotle, who thought of the world as eternal and ineluctable, and who thought that the divine did not intervene in worldly affairs; indeed, for him the divine did not even think about things lesser than itself, because such knowledge would be unworthy of the highest mind.

The Bible does not just encourage us to see things and events as the work of God's providence; it also gives us the example of the most intense and complete recognition of the divine will that was ever achieved by a human being. It gives us this example in its description of the life, work, and words of Jesus of Nazareth. As Hans Urs von Balthasar has shown, Christ understood himself simply and totally as sent by the Father, and he appreciated everything that happened to him, especially what he called his "hour," as involved in the work the Father sent him to accomplish.[7] More profoundly than anyone else, Jesus took the world as the expression of a divine understanding and will, and he took himself as sent by that understanding and will. He did not consider himself as simply the outcome of natural forces and contingencies; he considered himself as having been sent by the Father. As his words recorded in the Gospels testify, Christ did not have merely a vague appreciation of something personal behind the rhythms and events of the world; that "something personal" was *everything* to him. He saw himself as immediately and uniquely sent by the Father and he saw himself as the one through whom the kingdom of God was to come.[8] He was not only to bear witness to that coming; the kingdom was to occur in and through him.

The mission of Jesus was radically different from that of any of the prophets. Each of the prophets was chosen and commissioned at some point in his life. Isaiah was chosen when he saw a vision in the temple; he proclaimed his own uncleanness and was purified by one of the angels in the vision, after which he said, "I heard the voice of the Lord saying, 'Whom shall I send, and who will go for us?' Then I said, 'Here am I! Send me'" (Isaiah 6:8). When Jeremiah was called, he blurted out that he was too young and could not speak well: "Ah, Lord God! Behold, I do not know how to speak, for I am only a youth" (Jere-

7. Von Balthasar, *Theodramatik*, 2/2:140–44.
8. Ibid., 152.

miah 1:6), but the Lord sent him anyway. Amos was chosen from the life of "a herdsman and a dresser of sycamore trees" (Amos 7:14), and Jonah tried to run away from his election and mission, but fulfilled it nevertheless in a rather roundabout way (Jonah 1–3). Even John the Baptist, the prophet who stood at the threshold of the New Testament, was chosen at a certain moment during his lifetime, though he had not yet left his mother's womb (Luke 1:41–44).[9] But Jesus was not elected in this way; he was sent from the beginning. He was sent but never chosen. God did not call him at any point in his life. From the moment he began to be, he was sent by the Father. The first words of Jesus recorded in the Scriptures, spoken when his parents found him in the temple, were "Why were you looking for me? Did you not know that I must be in my Father's house?" (Luke 2:49). No one had to tell Christ who he was and at no point did he have to be called. He knew who he was, because he knew who sent him, from the time he became aware of himself at all. The shape of what he was to do may have become more definite as he grew in wisdom and age and favor (Luke 2:52) and as circumstances developed in the course of his public life, but the knowledge of having been sent did not have to come to him from anyone or anything outside himself.

The mission of Jesus was to do the will of the Father. His fulfillment of the Father's will was not simply one among many other things that he did in his life. Rather, Christ lived just to do that will; he was defined entirely by his mission. Moreover, Jesus did not have a merely contemplative attitude toward his mission; he did not merely *know* that he was sent by the Father. The response he had toward his mission was one of obedience; his obedience was a response to the personal agency he recognized as the origin of his own being and as the providence behind the events that occurred to him. Christ did not just speak about the personal dimension he recognized behind the events

9. Ibid., 241–43. Von Balthasar observes that Samson is said to have been chosen before his birth (Judges 13:7) and that he provides a kind of model for John the Baptist.

in the world, nor did he only speak toward that personal presence in prayer; he also acted in an obedient response to it.

The appropriate response to a mission is not contemplation but obedience. Obedience is one of what Peter Strawson has called the "reactive attitudes," the responses we make toward personal agency that is directed toward us.[10] Gratitude is one of these responses, the kind appropriate to benevolence, and resentment is another, the kind appropriate to malice. Obedience is different from gratitude and resentment because it essentially requires conduct and not just thought, emotion, and disposition; obedience involves the attempt to accomplish what was set down for us to do.

We can be obedient to different kinds of injunctions. I can obey a *command*, which is an order explicitly directed by someone toward me as an individual here and now. I can obey a *law*, which is an order formulated in a general way toward anyone who falls into the circumstances spelled out by the rule. The obedience of Jesus to the will of the Father was not the acquiescence to a command or to a law imposed on him by the Father; it was deeper than that and it dealt with something not as external as a command or a law. Christ was obedient to his *mission*, the mission that determined his being.[11]

The mission of Jesus is a worldly reflection of the procession of the eternal Son from the Father in the internal life of the Holy Trinity.[12] In God, the Father gives his entire substance, his divinity, to the Son, who, as Word, expresses fully the divine nature of the Father. The complete obedience of the incarnate Son is a reflection of the complete reception of the divine nature by the eternal Son. It is also a joyful response in the world infected by sin to the generosity of the Father. The redemptive mission of the Son in the world is therefore not something merely added to

10. Strawson, "Freedom and Resentment," 6.

11. Von Balthasar, *Theodramatik*, 2/2:140.

12. In the "immanent" activity within the Holy Trinity, there is *processio ad intra*, and in the "economic" activity of the Holy Trinity, there is *missio ad extra*, but in both cases there is an *esse ad*, a "being related to another." The relations in the economic activity reflect those of the immanent.

the being of the incarnate Son; it determines who and what he is and it reflects what he always was. And his obedience to his mission is an acceptance not of a command or a law but of a way of being.

Thus, when the Bible exhorts us to take the world not as simply there, not as subject merely to its own natural elements, powers, and necessities, but as existing through divine wisdom and freedom, as profiled against something personal, it does not try to persuade us merely with metaphysical arguments about being, the finite, and the infinite. At its apex in the New Testament, the Bible presents to us the way Jesus understood the world and himself in it, and in this dramatic presentation it discloses a way of thinking, acting, and being into which we can enter.

C

We began this chapter by reflecting on Boethius' definition of the person, and we have given a phenomenological analysis of the disclosure of personal agency. We should also examine a new approach to the understanding of the person, one proposed by Hans Urs von Balthasar.[13] He claims that the formula of Boethius, "individual substance of a rational nature," can serve to define a spiritual or intellectual subject (*Geistsubjekt*) but that it is not adequate as a definition of the person. He admits that a subject is endowed with the rationality, self-awareness, and self-possession that allow it to say "I"; a subject is self-conscious and responsible, and it distinguishes itself from others even as it communicates with them; however, a subject as such does not yet have the uniqueness that we associate with the concept of person, the uniqueness that fully identifies *who* this individual is.

Von Balthasar does not begin with a general philosophical definition of what is meant by person, but takes the Christological and trinitarian sense of the term as primary and paradigmatic. He also recalls that etymologically the word "person"

---

13. See von Balthasar, *Theodramatik*, 2/2:136–259. On the spiritual subject (*Geistsubjekt*) see 186–91, and on Boethius' definition of person see 199–202.

stems from the Latin *persona* and the Greek *prosōpon*, both of
which mean a mask worn by actors and also a character or a dramatic role in a play. Von Balthasar says that the concept of mission or role is intrinsic to the concept of person; it is the feature
that differentiates the person from the spiritual subject. A person
is not just a subject, but a subject commissioned with a particular
role that gives it its identity. Who we are depends on what we
are meant or called or sent to be. How do we acquire our role?
Von Balthasar says that who we are cannot be determined by any
impersonal elements in the world, nor can it be determined by
society or by other people; it can only be determined by God as
the absolute subject. To paraphrase his statement of this claim: a
subject can be said to be a person only when God declares to
that subject who he is before God; God must declare to the subject why he exists, what purpose he is to serve; the subject is a
person only when God grants the subject his mission and so defines who he is.[14] Von Balthasar says that such a declaration occurred "archetypically" in the case of Jesus, who was defined by
God as "my beloved Son."[15] In this declaration the mission of
Christ was revealed and who he is was brought to light: not just
who he was as a man, but who he was from the beginning with
God. The Christological revelation was also a revelation of a
trinitarian relationship. The uniqueness of this subject, his personality, was revealed when his role was revealed.

This understanding of the person of Christ is then applied to
each human being. Von Balthasar says that the uniqueness and
hence the personality of each human being—who each human
being is—derives from the personality of Jesus. The divine "purpose" we are given in life, what, in the mind of God, each
human being is meant to be, is a participation in the mission of
Christ. Jesus was completely identified with his mission and so
was a person in the fullest sense possible; he was *nothing but* his
mission, which reflected his eternal procession from the Father
in the Holy Trinity. Other human beings acquire a mission, and

14. Ibid., 190.
15. Ibid., 190, 201.

hence a personal definition, by their relationship to the mission of Christ. They are not as wholly identified with their mission as Christ was; they are essentially "less personal" than Christ. Indeed, sinners are defined precisely by their rejection, to a greater or lesser degree, of the idea that God has for them. However, even though the mission that identifies other subjects does not saturate them as Christ's mission did him, still their mission is not a mere accident added to them, since it expresses what they were created to be. This personal dimension of all human existence was both achieved and revealed by the incarnate Son of God: "*In Christo* each man has the hope of not remaining a mere individual spiritual subject (*Geistsubjekt*), but of becoming a person through God's action, with a definite task that is also bestowed on him *in Christo*."[16] Each person's task is a gift of being sent, of being given a mission.

This definition of the person would explain why the concept is not found in the ancient philosophers, even though the concept of spiritual or intellectual subject is; those philosophers thought of human beings as capable of living a spiritual and a rational life, but they did not see them as each being "sent" by God or by the gods to perform a certain role in life. The pagan thinkers did not see that a human being was identifiable in that way, and hence the deepest aspect of human individuality remained unknown to them. The concept of person was formulated during the Christological and trinitarian controversies of the fourth and fifth centuries, and von Balthasar's definition places the concept back into the context of these theological discussions. He claims that it was a distortion to try to treat the concept in a purely philosophical manner.[17]

Von Balthasar's understanding of the person does not contradict or render otiose the aspects that are brought out by Boethius' definition and by a phenomenological analysis. The role of reason is still essential to the person. The sense in which a person is identified by having a mission within a particular set

16. Ibid., 202.
17. Ibid., 185.

of circumstances involves the ability of that person to understand the mission, to see it as his own and as the source of his identity, to see it as the divine will, and to respond to it in obedience. All this is done through reason. Being a person involves an aspect of self-definition, even though it is not a matter of simply deciding for ourselves who we will be; it is an understood response to God's creative and redemptive action, but it could not occur without rational self-understanding.

It is the rational part of our nature that allows us to be aware of ourselves as different from others and to take a position toward the whole of things; our rationality allows us to be able to use self-referential terms such as "I" and thus to be able to declare something of our own privacy, uniqueness, and responsibility. Reason allows us to identify ourselves. But when this power of reason is placed within the context of Creation, when "the whole" toward which we orient ourselves is seen to exist through God's free decision; the sense of the "I" that we express through our reason is changed. We now understand ourselves as chosen to be, and if we are chosen to be, then the divine wisdom behind that choice defines who we are in a more profound way than any other interaction or determination that could follow. And although in some sense our Creation comes "before" our Redemption, the truth of our Creation is disclosed only in the redemptive action of God described in the Bible and preserved in the Church, and our Creation itself is shown to have been done in view of our sanctification in Christ. As St. Paul says, God "chose us in [Christ], before the foundation of the world, to be holy and without blemish before him. In love he destined us for adoption to himself through Jesus Christ" (Ephesians 1:4–5).

D

Christ's understanding of himself and his mission has decisively influenced the way human beings can understand themselves and the whole of which they are such a conspicuous part. To appreciate what is distinctive in this Christian understanding, let us examine the major alternatives to it that have existed in the West. There are three nonbiblical or extrabiblical ways in which we can interpret ourselves and the world.

1. The first is the ancient pagan understanding of the world, the gods, and ourselves. It thought that what we call the processes of nature were governed by divine powers and that the gods intervened directly, even casually and frequently, in the world and in human affairs. The ancient myths and legends, the epics and tragedies, depicted not only a divine reason behind the way things are, but also divine choices and actions. The gods were understood to be capable of acting on the worldly stage. The pagan gods were limited in many ways, both in relation to one another and in relation to the world as a whole; they were part of the world and were subject to destiny and necessity, but they were recognized as being far superior to the mortals. Men saw themselves as subject to the divine powers and decisions and obliged to revere the gods. The divine reason and divine choices were far more comprehensive and powerful than the human, and men had to cope with them as best they could. In this understanding, therefore, the whole was thought to contain a reason higher than our own, one that intervened in the affairs of the world.

2. This mythical understanding was radically transformed by philosophy. The form of thinking introduced and developed by the Presocratics, Socrates, Plato, Aristotle, Epicurus, and the Stoics demythologized the pagan religious understanding. It distinguished the natural from the conventional and the legendary. Things were recognized as simply having their own natures; they came to be and acted according to their natures, not according to the way the gods wanted them to act. Philosophy did not acknowledge divine choices in regard to human and worldly affairs, and so did not recognize the possibility of what von Balthasar calls *Theodramatik*; however, it did leave intact the divine reason

as a principle of natural order. Philosophy accepted, behind the forces and elements of nature, a reason higher than our own. The statement of Peter Wust concerning ancient thinkers holds both for philosophers and for theologians: "The assertion sometimes put forward that the man of the classical age is in reality nothing more than the purest form of the rationalist *homo sapiens*, must once for all be emphatically contradicted. We should rather say that the man of antiquity is the *homo naturaliter oboediens*, man naturally submissive to the sacred sanctions of being."[18] However, the divine reason recognized by philosophy does not intervene in the events of the world. It was understood in its perfection as being beyond choice and uncontaminated by contingency.

3. The third understanding we must distinguish is materialistic atheism. This understanding sees the whole as simply material and devoid of any divine principle: the world is just there as matter in motion. Matter may be much more mysterious than Newtonian and Cartesian physics would make it out to be; it may, in its complexity and under the rule of the laws and forces that guide it, yield complex forms of organization and life, but there is no personal choice or will, and also no intelligence, behind it. We are the only examples of rational life that we know. Matter may have developed into other forms of rationality, perhaps very different from our own, in other parts of the universe, but reason is not behind such development. Whatever may have evolved, everything is made up of matter in its transformations and everything is subject to the natural laws that govern the processes and developments of matter. There is no dimension of choice and no dimension of reason behind matter. This materialistic atheism obviously differs from ancient pagan religious belief, but it also differs from ancient philosophy, which acknowledged a divine principle in the world. Such atheism has been conspicuous in the West since Machiavelli and Hobbes; some ancient thinkers, such as Thucydides and Epicurus, may or may not have subscribed to it.[19]

18. Wust, "Crisis in the West," 97.
19. Most of the ancient writers speak about the gods, but some commentators

Over against these three understandings is the understanding
of ourselves and of the whole that is presented in the Bible. But
even here we must distinguish two forms: The first is the understanding found in the Old Testament. Through the patriarchs,
Moses, the Law, and the prophets, the Jews came to understand
the world as created by Yahweh, and themselves as elected from
among the nations to enter into a Covenant with him. Creation
and the Covenant went hand in hand; it was in the context of
the Covenant that the Israelites came to appreciate what kind
of God had entered into the Covenant with them. Israel had a
sense of mission as a nation, and the individual elections and
missions of the prophets took place within the larger mission of
the whole people.

The second is the understanding found in the New Testament, in which everything is compressed into the mission of
one man, Jesus Christ. His mission is unique and he accomplishes it by himself. Even the apostles could not have cooper-
ated with him in his "hour." As Jesus said to Peter, "Where I am
going, you cannot follow me now" (John 13:36). Christ was not
part of a larger mission or part of a more comprehensive relationship to the Father. He is sent as no one has ever been
sent, and he is united with the Father as no one else has ever
been united with God.

The Old Covenant provided the context and the terminology
within which Jesus expressed his understanding of himself and of
the whole. He compressed and intensified the religious understanding of the Old Testament, the understanding of God as
Creator and as the one who chooses and sends his people. But
Jesus also transformed the religious understanding of the pagan
world. This transformation is not immediate; the pagan religious
understanding must first have been "processed," so to speak,
through the understanding of the Old Testament, which remains
always as the setting for the New. But when properly interpreted
the divine interventions described in the pagan legends and

---

claim that in some cases at least they may well not have believed in them, and only
pretended to accept them in order to avoid persecution.

tragedies can now be seen as anticipations, at a greater distance, of the definitive *Theodramatik*, the one final action, that was accomplished in Christ. Furthermore, as von Balthasar has said, the action and understanding of Jesus reveal a divine activity that can withstand the demythologizing that philosophy carried out in regard to the pagan religions.[20] Whereas the pagan myths had to give way before the philosophical critique, the biblical understanding of the divine does not. The biblical God does not need to be transformed by philosophy into the intelligence that encompasses the world but does not intervene in it; the biblical God can be recognized as the one who acts in Christ.[21]

In Christian belief, the saving action of Christ is recognized as the most decisive event in the relationship between human beings and God. But it is also important to consider the impact Jesus had on human understanding and human history from a worldly point of view. We know that individual persons can exercise great influence in the various domains of human accomplishment: Newton in science; Homer, Dante, and Shakespeare in letters; Napoleon in strategy. All those who follow after such figures bear the mark of their work. But Jesus, in his understanding of his mission and his relation to the Father, imprinted on the human race not merely a way of writing poetry or fighting military battles, but a way of understanding the whole and ourselves as conspicuous parts of the whole. Even from the point of view of human history and human self-understanding, some-

20. See von Balthasar, *Theodramatik*, 3:58: "Although there once was a kind of confused *Theodramatik* in the mythical world, now, after having gone through philosophical reflection, it can exist only in Christianity."

21. Within biblical religion, a distinction must be made between the Old and the New Testament. Leo Strauss has frequently observed that revealed religion and philosophy, Jerusalem and Athens, cannot be reconciled and that the tension between the two makes up the motive force for European history; see especially, "What Is Political Philosophy?" Strauss's observation may hold for the Old Testament, but it need not hold for the New; the Incarnation shows that all human powers, including reason, can be reconciled with Christian belief. Scholasticism, the use of reason within revelation, is not an intellectual abnormality but a human and metaphysical possibility in the New Law.

thing decisive was achieved by Christ (by him, and not by
those who remembered him and wrote about him). A turn was
given to the way we understand ourselves within the whole of
things.

Christ did not keep his mission and his relationship to the
Father only to himself. Once he accomplished what he was sent
to do, he allowed his mission to be continued and shared by
those who believe in him and receive the power of his Spirit in
his Church. As he said to St. Peter in the rest of the passage just
cited, "You cannot follow me now, but you will follow later"
(John 13:36). What was not possible before Christ's action is
made possible after it. He told his disciples, "It was not you who
chose me, but I who chose you and appointed you to go and
bear fruit that will remain" (John 15:16). He also said that
"whoever believes in me will do the works that I do, and will do
greater ones than these," and the reason he gives for this is "because I am going to the Father" (John 14:12). The mission and
self-understanding of Christ become shared by others who are
sent by him as he was sent by the Father. The "personal dimension" that Jesus saw in and behind the world becomes available
for those who come after him. They become adopted into his
Sonship and become persons in him.

This sharing in the life and mission of Christ is described in
great detail in the Acts of the Apostles and in the New Testament letters, especially those of St. Paul. Paul came into faith
later than the other apostles and thus entered into it from a distance, as an outsider; for this reason he may have been more
vividly aware of what was new and different in it. He expresses
the new way of living and understanding both in general, doctrinal terms, and in response to particular issues that arose when
people tried to live according to the mind of Christ. Often his
more general theological comments are made on the occasion of
some particular situation. Paul spells out how Christians can take
on something of the self-understanding of Jesus, of the compressed and intensified way in which Jesus saw the world as the

expression of God's choice and the way he saw himself as the recipient of a divine mission.

In the centuries following the age of the apostles, during the Hellenistic period, the Christian understanding had to define itself against the pagan religious and philosophical understanding. Some historians claim that during that time the Christian message was forced to adapt itself to Greek concepts and that it clothed itself in pagan patterns of thought. Von Balthasar, however, says that the opposite occurred: in that intellectual struggle, Hellenistic thought, both religious and philosophical, was decisively overcome by the Church and its theologians, the Fathers of the Church.[22]

In our present situation in the Western world, the chief intellectual alternative to the Christian understanding of the whole is materialistic atheism. Some of the old pagan ways of thinking still survive, but in forms that show the effect of their encounter with Christian faith. The pagan religious belief in the divine and demonic powers of nature shows up in various forms of what is now called superstition, in various cults, and also in some forms of religion that may call themselves Christian but that are more concerned with good luck, worldly success, and bodily health than with Redemption, grace, and the glory of God. The old philosophical understanding, which acknowledged a divine element in the whole but thought it could not intervene in the world, can still be recognized in various forms of deism, in movements like process theology, or in the vague, diffuse religiosity that accepts some sort of divine ordering of the world. But certainly the most prominent and active alternative to Christian understanding in the West is materialistic atheism, which may oscillate between classical and romantic forms, between rationalism and Nietzschean deconstructionism. The two traditions, materialist and Christian, differ on many individual cultural and moral points, but these differences all stem from one basic issue: the question whether the whole is

22. Von Balthasar, *Theodramatik*, 2/1:172.

impersonal, with ourselves as rational and responsible entities that emerge by chance within it, or whether the whole is somehow there as the outcome of a divine choice, with ourselves as both created and redeemed, as called and sent, by the one whose choice it was.

I I

꙳

DISCLOSURE IN THE

SCRIPTURES

THE CHRISTIAN understanding of the world as having
been created by God was not reached through the exercise of
mere natural intelligence. It was disclosed through biblical revelation. Biblical revelation does more than to give us new information: it provides an entirely new perspective on the world, on
the divine, and on ourselves. It engages new forms of intentionality, new modes of presentation, and new distinctions. In this
chapter we will discuss the special form of appearance that occurs in the reading of the Bible.

The Sacred Scriptures draw on the presentational possibilities
given to us by writing. Writing has its own way of manifesting
things, one different from those of the spoken word and direct
perception. Some philosophical observations about the nature of
writing and reading will be of service in our theological reflections on the Scriptures. To begin, therefore, (a) we will examine
the role of writing in the origin and preservation of biblical
faith, and (b) we will discuss several facets of the written word:
the text, the referent, the reader, the act of reading. Then (c)
we will examine how the Old Covenant distinguished itself

from the religion of the Gentiles, and how the New Covenant distinguished itself from the Old. This will lead us (d) to discuss the "more than literal senses" of the Old Testament when read in the light of the New and (e) to speak about how the Church now uses the Old Testament in its prayer. We will close (f) with some remarks about the Gospel of St. John.

A

Our discussion of the Eucharist led us to examine the Jewish Passover. More generally, our discussion of Christian faith leads us to reflect on the Covenant made by God with the Jews; the study of the New Testament is inseparable from the study of the Old.

The names Old and New Testament refer, strictly speaking, to the Old and New Covenants between God and his people, but they have also come to mean the two parts of the Bible, the two collections of books that narrate the events associated with the two Covenants. The fact that these events were written down is not incidental to them. It seems almost impossible to imagine how the Jewish and Christian religions could have existed without the book, without writing. In one respect writing may seem to be only accessory to Jewish and Christian faith, since God's saving deeds took place as actions before being recorded, but these actions were meant not just to occur but to be displayed and proclaimed. They were meant to have their effect not anonymously, but by being known and responded to. The memorial of these actions, their presentation and distribution, could hardly have been effected without the written word. What would these actions have been if they were known only to the few generations of people who could repeat them orally, and what sort of a witness would such an oral tradition provide as the years went on? How could the actions have escaped becoming the matter of mere legend and myth? How could they have been accurately translated into other languages and cultures? Could the nuances of the message be preserved if they had not been written down? The Exodus of the Jews and the

Paschal feast of Good Friday and Easter were meant to be reen-acted through the ages; could this have been done without writing? Was the development of the written word in the centu-ries before Christ, like the spread of the Roman Empire, not part of the providential *praeparatio evangelica*?

Writing seems necessary to preserve the biblical events and message, but it may also have played a role in the establishment of biblical faith. Biblical revelation took place at a particular moment in human life, when the human race was achieving a reflective sense of its own history. The distinction between leg-end and historical truth was beginning to arise, and writing is a necessary condition for the emergence of this distinction. As long as the only record of "what happened" was an oral account, the events recorded were likely to become merely legendary, be-cause the only report people would have of them would be what the narrator told to those who could listen to him speak. Every-thing would be absorbed into the story that is told. But once a written record becomes available, it becomes possible in prin-ciple to appeal to an eyewitness account of the event, or at least to something approaching an eyewitness account. We become able to appeal not only to what a narrator is telling us now, but also to what someone recorded when the event was still fresh. We can compare the two. A distinction arises between what is being stated now and what was stated at a time when people were closer to or in the presence of the event in question. Writing embalms an earlier registration. Thus the very notion of a historical fact depends on the possibility of writing, and so does the sense of documented events preceding and following one another at definite times; writing permits us to order the past in a temporal sequence.[1] Without writing, the past becomes bleached into a kind of omnitemporality, the dreamtime or the time of myth and legend, which is expressed only in the present.

1. We may be able to arrive at particular facts without the benefit of written records, but the very idea or category of historical fact requires the documentation made possible by writing. It allows us to refine the distinction between hearsay and direct acquaintance, which is familiar to us in our unwritten exchanges with others.

Biblical religion, both Jewish and Christian, is concerned with God's interventions in history; it must therefore describe how God dealt with particular people at particular times and places. Biblical faith depends on at least a rudimentary sense of history. It might even have been particularly appropriate for biblical faith to arise when writing was just starting to take hold and when the historical sense was only just differentiating itself from myth and legend, before the time of rigorous critical history and the journalistic report of information. The birth of writing and the transition from myth to history do not keep occurring over and over again in the development of the human race; they marked the change from the tens of thousands of years of unrecorded human life to the few thousand years in which we have been critically aware of what we have done and what has happened to us. This change took place only once and it provided a moment for biblical revelation that cannot be repeated. At that moment, biblical faith was inscribed into the human race. In its uniqueness, this inscription resembles the resolutions of psychological conflicts and separations, identifications and differentiations in the life of an individual human being; such resolutions—Oedipal stages, adolescent separations and attachments, entrance into maturity—also occur only once and only at a particular stage in life, and they make an unrepeatable imprint on the person's being. Thus the written text played a strategic role not only in preserving the events and teachings that are believed in biblical faith, but also in allowing the development of historical awareness as a condition of biblical religion.

B

Once we recognize the fact that the written word is a prerequisite for biblical revelation, however, we must be careful to avoid the danger of making the text the primary focus, of making the text and not the things it discloses the center of our attention. Words, whether spoken or written, present things. We never have "just" words: words are vehicles to articulate and disclose things. Whenever words appear, there arises that shimmering contrast between words and things, between name and named, that allows us to focus either on the thing or on the word.[2] When this distinction arises, however, it becomes possible for us to substantialize the word and forget its subordination to the thing.

Words are sometimes used to articulate things that are directly present to us, but in most instances, and especially in narrative, words are used to present things that are absent. The written word in particular almost always reports about absent things and events. When we focus on what is printed in a book, we nearly always are made to think about something other than the book, something in some other place and time. Furthermore, while spoken words are stated by a speaker who is there before us, written words are usually given to us without the immediate presence of the writer. We have the narrative but not the narrator. Written words thus involve a double absence: the writer is no longer there, and what the words describe is usually absent as well. Because both the writer and the events are absent, the written text takes on a prominence greater than that of the spoken word. Writing therefore intensifies the temptation to make the text stand on its own and become an object in its own right.

A further distinction can be made regarding how the written word is to be read. If the writing is read aloud, then the text becomes more subordinate to what the text is about. The reader and his listeners think through the text to what the words report. But when a text is read silently and privately, when the solitary reader is the entire immediate audience for the text, the text becomes more exclusively the focus of attention. In silent reading the text is still about something other than itself, but it looms larger to the reader than texts do for those who read or hear them in public. Thus the tendency to substantialize the

2. On the relationships among words, meanings, and things, see Sokolowski, *Presence and Absence*, 99–115; also, "Grammar and Thinking," in *Pictures, Quotations, and Distinctions*, 213–25.

word, which is increased when the word is written into text, is increased still more when the text is read in solitude and silence.

We now tend to do our reading silently and privately. Our books are studied and not declaimed. When books were more rare and fewer people were able to read, writings were read aloud and in public. When a book—whether poetry, narrative, or even a philosophical work—is read aloud before others, it is activated in a way that is lost when it is read by one person in silence. Indeed, even in academic life, where so much solitary reading is done, the importance of public reading is recognized: texts come most to life when they are read and discussed in class or in a seminar; even the silent readings carried out in preparation for this quasi public reading find their fulfillment in the oral presentation.

But sacred religious texts especially are meant to be proclaimed in public. The natural place where the Bible is to be read is not at the scholar's desk or the contemplative's prie-dieu, but at the lectern in the synagogue or the church. The Bible, both the Old and the New Testaments, comes to life in its proper form when read in the liturgy. When it is so read, it does not draw attention to itself as a text—as it does for the scholar—but presents to us the things it is about. It points beyond itself to the things it records and manifests. We go through the reading to what is presented in it, to God and his saving actions in the world. Our pressing scholarly and philological concerns have made the text itself more prominent in our reading of the Scriptures, but the biblical text can never become an end in itself. If it were to do so, its sacredness would be lost, since it is made holy by what it carries and presents, not by its own interwoven discourse. Indeed, "textualism" can be considered a deviation analogous to the rationalism, historicism, and psychologism that we discussed in Chapter 1. In each case a form of manifestation—a text, a thought, a situated appearance, a perception—is taken to replace the thing manifested.

That the biblical text refers beyond itself is vividly demonstrated in the New Testament by the fact that there are four

Gospels and not merely one. The four narrate the same thing, the life of Jesus. The fact that there are four shows that the important thing is not the texts themselves but what they are about; each Gospel is relativized by the other three. If there were only one account of the life of Christ, the narrative and the events would be much more closely united and the account would be much more prominent and ultimate.

Thus the text has to be seen as subordinated to the things that it presents, and it must be seen in its relation to the reader and the act of reading. In biblical reading, the reader in question is not an isolated individual but the Church in its members, and the paradigmatic act of reading is the one carried out publicly in the prayer and liturgy of the Church. Thus the saving acts of God are disclosed in the Church through the reading of the biblical text. It is not just words that come to life in such reading, but also the things that the words express, and both of them, words and things, become actively displayed to a dative of manifestation, to the Church and the faithful as readers.[3] This reading, furthermore, is taken to occur before God, so that the proclamation of the divine actions is made not only for the salvation of those individuals who hear the reading, but also as a display before God of his own glory, a display accomplished simply for its own sake.

C

Everything in the New Testament arose against the background of the Old Testament. Even the Christian understanding of God is achieved as an intensification of the understanding that had been revealed during the Old Covenant. When we consider the Christian things under the aspect of their disclosure, it seems that they could not have come to light simply and directly by themselves; it seems that they had to be manifested as a fulfillment of a prior expectation, as a determination within

---

3. On the dative of manifestation, see Sokolowski, *Presence and Absence*, 128, 170–71.

a context that was set in preparation for them. The profiling of Christian things against the background of the Old Covenant seems to be a presentational necessity and not merely a matter of historical accident.

If the Christian understanding presupposed the Jewish, the Jewish understanding required a context in turn: that of the other people, the Gentiles, and their gods. The Jewish religious understanding was centered on Yahweh, who was taken to be different from any of the gods worshipped by other nations. This understanding, however, did not concern only God; it also concerned God as having elected Israel and as having made a Covenant with them, a Covenant that raised them to responsibility and obligation and not just to privilege.[4] The understanding was about God in his actions, about the people toward whom he acts, and about the world as a setting for these actions. In all this the Jews sharply distinguished themselves and their God from other people and their gods; indeed, the myriad distinctions enjoined by the Torah—between different kinds of animals and different kinds of food, different periods of time, different forms of clothing and utensils—may have been not just ceremonial rubrics or practices useful for preserving health and public order; they may have served as a training for the Jews in the very habit of seeing that *this* is not *that*, so that they would be all the more able to realize that "they," the other nations, are not "us," because their "gods" are not Yahweh.

The Jewish understanding of God could not occur except as a modification of another sense of the divine. The Jewish belief in Yahweh could not arise as the first thing men believe about the divine. It had to arise as a correction of something else, a truth grasped by being distinguished from the error of the Gentiles. The Jewish understanding of Yahweh had to arise as an interpretation. It had to presuppose a name for the divine (*'elohim*) that it shared with other people, but that it then interpreted, modified, and claimed to assert in truth. Then, to em-

4. See McKenzie, "Aspects of Old Testament Thought," §81.

phasize the difference between their God and the gods of the Gentiles, the Jews were given a name that was proper to their God, the name of Yahweh. All the ancient Semitic peoples believed in the gods, but "whether or not there are many 'elohim, there is only one Yahweh. No matter what one understands by "elohim,' Yahweh is 'elohim in a way in which no other being is. The question is not whether there is only one 'elohim, but whether there is any 'elohim like Yahweh."[5] Yahweh does not reveal himself just simply and positively to Israel, but in contrast with the other "gods." He reveals himself not just as another one of the gods, but as God and as divine in a new sense.

A distinction is drawn between Yahweh and the gods that is much more than the mere introduction of a new word and a negation, much more than a merely theoretical discrimination. It is a distinction that both emerges from experience and practice and has to be embedded in what the people do; it has to be lived as well as stated. But as important as life and action are to this distinction, it still requires words if it is to be achieved. It has to be communicated. It is not a distinction we pick up simply by looking and touching and tasting, like the distinction between hot and cold or that between apples and stones. Yahweh was not just the power of thunder and lightning or sun and moon: he had to be distinguished from nature and from the forces in nature that were worshipped by other people, and such a distinction could only come about through words and teaching.

Within this Jewish tradition, which had already distinguished itself so sharply from the others, another distinction was drawn when Christ and his Church appeared. The new distinction, between the New Covenant and the Old, was not like that between Israel and the Gentiles. The God of the New Covenant is the same as that of the Old. The Father whom Jesus addresses is not somehow the truth of which Yahweh is only the shadow: the Father by whom and from whom Jesus was sent is Yahweh. And yet a slight new distinction is drawn between the God who

5. Ibid., §17.

could not ever become part of his creation—it would be degrading to him and blasphemous to make him part of what he created—and the God who became incarnate. It is not just that we must now distinguish between the Father and the Son, but that we must now distinguish a deeper sense of the divinity, a deeper sense of the Godhead. It is not another and different God, as Yahweh is other than and different from the 'elohim, from Baal and Moloch and Zeus, but it is the same God newly understood. No new proper name is revealed, but Yahweh is now called Father in a distinctive way; he is called Father instead of being called Yahweh. There is a change in the way the transcendence of God is understood. Not only does God create the world and sustain it, not only does God act toward his people, but he also enters into his creation, without diminishing his divinity. He is so transcendent that even this will not compromise the Godhead. The Old Covenant educated Israel in the transcendence of God by preventing any embodiment of the divinity, even any image of it. This pedagogy was necessary to distinguish Yahweh from the gods of the Gentiles. But in Christ the New Covenant shows that God could become incarnate, that he could humble himself and take on the form of fallen man and become obedient even to death on the cross, and that this humiliation, rather than dishonoring the divine majesty, showed forth its glory in a way that no other act of power could have done.

D

This shift of the meaning of the divine between the Old and the New Covenant establishes a difference which allows the entire Old Testament to be interpreted as anticipating the New. It is not the case that the overall context of the two testaments is the same, with the sense of the divine exactly the same across both, and with differences found only in the new deeds that God performs in the messianic act of salvation. It is not the case that the differences have to be discovered only in the details. Rather, there is a comprehensive change of context, even though it is not the kind of change that took place between the world of the Gentiles and the world of the Jews. The change of context between the Old Covenant and the New affects not only the sense of the divine, but also the sense of the Covenant and the response that the believer makes to God's saving action. The New Covenant is not merely one more stage in the process carried out in the Old. The Christian response in faith, hope, and charity is different from the response appropriate to the Exodus and Sinai and the words of the prophets, even though the Christian faith was prepared and anticipated by the faith of Abraham. This shift of meaning is distinctive and particular, and it must be described on its own terms. It is not like a move from an old religion into a new one, nor is it a readjustment into a sect within a religion that is never abandoned. It is not like other changes in religion or culture. It has its own logic of sameness and difference.

The difference between the Old and the New Covenants does not stem, moreover, simply from interpreters within the Church who compare the two texts and describe a relationship between them. The difference was established by Christ in his words and actions; he is presented in the Gospels as the authoritative and definitive interpreter of the Covenant, and as the one who establishes the new kingdom of God.

If we recognize that the New Testament brought about a fuller revelation and a deeper understanding of God, it becomes easier to discuss the problem of how the Old Testament prefigures the New and is fulfilled in it. If God is understood differently in the New Covenant, then everything he did in the Old takes on a new coloration. If in the New Covenant he did something unlike what he had done before, then what he did before has to be seen in a new light, as leading to what he did later. What he did earlier now appears not to have been simply what it was thought to be when it was originally done. It becomes easier to address the hermeneutic problem of the "more than literal" sense of the Old Testament.[6]

6. See Brown and Schneiders, "Hermeneutics," §§30–77.

One of the ways in which this problem was addressed in the middle of the twentieth century was through the doctrine of the *sensus plenior*. Scholars suggested that the words of Scripture possessed not only a literal meaning but also a fuller sense that went beyond the sense intended by the human author. Although not grasped by the human author, this deeper sense was said to be intended by God as the ultimate author of the Bible. The theory of *sensus plenior* was criticized because it did not seem to give an acceptable explanation of how the divine inspiration and the human author worked together in the composition of the Scriptures; it seemed to imply two authors working almost in parallel, and it made an unsatisfactory use of the Scholastic notion of instrumental causality, with God seeming to use the human author to achieve an effect that would be beyond the author-instrument's ability. Because of such criticisms, the doctrine of *sensus plenior* has not been much invoked in recent decades.[7]

However, if we recognize that the understanding of God presented in the New Testament adjusts the understanding presented in the Old, and that it does so in a rather specifiable way, it becomes possible to say that everything in the Old Testament can be seen in a different light when considered from the New. What was being revealed and what was being done in the Old Covenant was completed in the New in a way that the participants in the Old were not able to discern. It is not the case that there was one meaning in the mind of the human author and another meaning intended by God, but that the one *thing* intended by the human author had dimensions that had not yet come into view, dimensions that could not appear until more had happened. There is only one meaning concerning God and his saving action, but that one meaning was indistinctly grasped until God sent his Son into the world. It is not that God uses the human instrument to convey a sense that is beyond the human author's ability to understand, but rather that the one sense that the human writer conveys is imperfectly known.

7. Ibid., §§49–51.

Another way of formulating this is to say that we should not focus on meanings when we talk about the "more than literal" sense of the Bible, but on the things that the Bible reveals. If we focus on meanings and texts we become inclined to turn away from the things being presented; we begin to look merely at the words, comparing the content of some words with that of others, and concluding that the texts written later seem to contain more than those written earlier. Instead of focusing on words and meanings in this way, we should look at the things being revealed and claim simply that the thing the human author speaks about and discloses in the Old Testament is not yet fully manifested: the God who is acting in the Old Covenant is not as fully disclosed as he will be in the Incarnation, and the saving action he performs has dimensions that will be more fully brought out later on. The emphasis should be not on the meaning of the words, but on the thing presented by the words.[8]

This point can be clarified by an analogy with words used in regard to human affairs. The word "mother" can be said to have one sense for a young girl and to have a fuller sense for an adult who has become a mother. In describing this difference, it is better not to speak of two meanings or two senses. Rather, it is more accurate to say that the *thing* the adolescent is talking about, "being a mother," has aspects that have not yet come into view, and when they do come into view, she will realize that what she was talking about earlier when she used the word "mother" was only partially manifest to her.

It is remarkable how quickly the Church was able to reinterpret the Old Testament. Within a few years after the death and Resurrection of Jesus, the Church reevaluated and reappropriated the entire Jewish tradition. The Church did not have to do this piecemeal, isolating each prophecy and incident and item of the Law, determining which of them anticipated the new kingdom and how they did so. It was not a matter of accumu-

---

8. See Sokolowski, "Exorcising Concepts," in *Pictures, Quotations, and Distinctions,* 173–85.

lating details one by one and constituting the new order gradually. Rather, the change was sudden and comprehensive, because
the center of the Covenant, the understanding of God and his
saving actions, was reinterpreted, first by Christ and then by the
Church. The details then fell in place. The fall of Adam and
Eve, the Messiah, the Son of Man, the Suffering Servant, the
Exodus and the Passover, the manna in the desert, the temple
and the synagogue, the Law itself, all began to look different because the God to whom these things were all related could also
come among his people, make his dwelling with them, and die
for them on the cross.

E

We have seen how the Old Covenant arose by being distinguished from the pagan world, and how the New Covenant
arose in distinction from the Old. These differentiations occurred when the two Covenants were first brought into being.
When we turn our attention to the present day, we must talk
not only about the two Testaments, but also about the contemporary act of recalling them. When we spoke of the celebration of the Eucharist, we reminded ourselves that in our
theological reflection we must not only focus on the redemptive
action that the Eucharist reenacts, but must also consider the
celebration that occurs now: we should not allow the contemporary action to become purely transparent and to lose its proper
presence. Likewise, in the reading of the Scriptures, we must in
our theological reflection think not only about the text of the
Scriptures and the events recorded in them, but also about the
contemporary activity of reading the Bible.

As we have seen, in Christian belief the paradigmatic reader
of the Bible is the Church, and the paradigmatic reading of the
Scriptures is the one that takes place in the liturgy. The center
of the Church's reading of the Scriptures is its reading of the
New Testament, but because the New Testament emerges from
and fulfills the Old, the Church can read the Old Testament in

her own voice and as part of her own tradition. An unbeliever could read both testaments simply as historical books, and a Jew could read the Jewish Scriptures as the record of his own faith, but the Christian will take both the Old and the New Testaments as integral parts of the record of what he believes are the saving acts God has performed in the world.

The Christian can read the Old Testament in two ways: (1) on its own terms, as the gradual education of the Jewish people in the worship of Yahweh, and (2) as the context for and anticipation of the New Covenant.

1. The Old Testament tells us about God and his actions, and it also shows how people should live and think if God is as he is presented to be. The Old Testament reveals a way of life as well as truths about God; it describes how we should act and understand ourselves if God is Yahweh and not the gods of the Gentiles. The Psalms are a good illustration of this pedagogy. They articulate the various human sentiments and thoughts we should have in response to the understanding of God that was being revealed when they were written. They sketch how we can think and feel when we address the God who creates both us and the world out of sheer generosity and independent power. It is not enough just to say, formally and abstractly, that God created the world and made a Covenant with his people; we have to draw various conclusions from and make various applications of this truth, and we must act, feel, and think accordingly. In the Psalms, many aspects of human life are expressed in response to what God is revealed to be and what he is revealed to have done.

Thus, the Psalmist says that he lies down to sleep and wakes again under Yahweh's protection; sleeping and waking, as well as the sleeplessness of those in distress, are interpreted as happening before God. The Psalmist is protected from evildoers and sinners, who are punished by God; he repents for his own sins and asks and hopes for forgiveness; he asks for deliverance from suffering and thanks God for restoration to health; he prays for the vindication of the poor and the oppressed; he complains about liars, perjurers, and flatterers and contrasts them with

God's fidelity; he describes what it is like to be in God's temple; he sees national victory and defeat, as well as the coronation of rulers and the exercise of justice, in the light of God's will. The Psalmist sees God's power in the sun, moon, and stars; in snow, rain, ice, frost, fire, the whirlwind, clouds, lightning and thunder, light and darkness, and wine and oil; in the ocean, ships, storms, and rivers; in trees, animals, mountains, and pastures; and he calls on all such things to praise God. Fraternal concord, peace among nations, fertility and children, and the human emotions of joy, fear, relief, worry, sorrow, anger, hope, and even hatred are seen in relation to the God who creates and knows his people. God is said to be everywhere, and the Psalmist is completely known by his Creator and could not run away from him; the Psalmist was known by God even before he was conceived in his mother's womb. The fugitive character of human life; the fragility of human treasure, which can be eaten up into nothing by moths; the sorrow caused by the betrayal of friends; the arrogance of the idolater and the proud; crimes done in secret; malice toward the weak and the sick, are all described as aspects of human life but seen as happening before the God who created everything and who entered into a Covenant with his people. How we should respond to all such human things in the light of revelation is disclosed to us.

It is true that the various Psalms must have been written in response to the situations they describe—coronation, justice, joy, malice, distress—but besides responding in faith to these situations, they also sketch a human possibility that is opened to us by the understanding of God that they help reveal: this is how we can take success, illness, defeat, or happiness, now that we believe that such things are part of what has been created by God; this is how we can hope and fear, rejoice and repent. These are possibilities, furthermore, not only for those who lived during the Old Covenant but also for us who continue to live in the revelation that occurred then. Also, the Psalms are not the only place in the Old Testament where this pedagogy of disclosure is found. Similar sketches of sentiments and responses are provided in the exhortations and the poetry of the prophets; the legal books of the Old Testament set down laws and practices that are to be followed in accordance with the biblical sense of God; and the historical narratives of the Bible give us illustrations of how individuals and groups reacted as God made himself known to his people.

In the New Testament, the Gospels and the Acts of the Apostles give us descriptions of how people reacted to Christ, both in his presence and in his absence, when he was proclaimed by the early Church, and the Epistles provide a description of various Christian sentiments provoked by diverse events and circumstances. However, because the New Testament was so concentrated and condensed in time and theme, it did not allow the proliferation of human situations and emotions that occurred through the centuries recorded in the Old Testament. The New Covenant occurred suddenly and sharply. The Old Testament, in contrast, contains a lavish range of human possibilities, of human phenomena, all related to the gradual disclosure of who and what Yahweh is and what he has done. As responses to this disclosure, they intensify and amplify the revelation itself. Just as Yahweh was distinguished from the "gods," so the proper human response to Yahweh was distinguished from the natural human religious sentiments that are felt in response to the "divine powers" encountered in the world. Reading the Psalms and the prophets is an exercise by which our spontaneous reverence for the divine is trained and adjusted into patterns appropriate to reverence for the biblical God. It was not only the ancient Israelites who needed this pedagogy; we also are ineluctably inclined to fall back into merely natural religion and we need the guidance of the prophets and the spirit of the Law to help us live up to biblical revelation.

2. Besides reading the Old Testament as the record of God's revelation and an education in religious sentiment, the Christian must also read it as an anticipation of the New Covenant. After sending his people deliverance, the Covenant, the Law, and the prophets, God sent his own Son as our Redeemer, and

when this final step was revealed, all the things that preceded it took on a new tone. Reciprocally, the last step itself, the Incarnation and the salvation given in Christ, can be correctly appreciated only *as* the last step, as preceded, prepared, and anticipated by what God did in the Old Covenant. When the Church and the Christian think about Christ, they think about him and his actions against the background of the Law, the Psalms, and the prophets. The fact that the Old Testament, and especially the Psalms, plays such a major role in the Church's prayer indicates that the Church even in its contemporary life recalls the New Covenant not just directly but also as anticipated by the Old, just as the Eucharist is celebrated not only on its own terms but also as anticipated by the Passover. Furthermore, much of the moral teaching of Christianity draws from the moral guidance that was given to the Jews in the Old Testament; the New Testament has relatively little to say about such important human things as the family, sexuality, property, social order, the responsibilities of people in public office, and political society. Christ and the early Christians largely accepted Jewish moral teaching in regard to such matters, introducing only a few corrections, such as the prohibition of divorce. The main task of the New Testament was the proclamation of the kingdom of God, not the establishment of a new social order.

The engagement of the Old Testament in the piety of the New is different from the involvement of natural religious experience in New Testament prayers. Natural religious sentiment must be mediated by the Old Testament before being incorporated into Christian prayer. We do not make use of pagan prayers or pagan hymns, such as the Stoic *Hymn to Zeus* or the songs of aboriginal religions, in our Christian prayer, but we do pray the Psalms. There is a break between pagan and Christian sacredness, but there is sameness between the Jewish God and the Christian, and there is continuity between the Jewish religious sentiment and the Christian, even though the Christian is understood to complete and intensify the Jewish. Furthermore, the Christian sentiment needs always to be read against

the Jewish, as resting on and yet differentiated from it. The fulfillment must always be stated as fulfillment and as anticipated.
The liturgy will never be without Advent, the Church's prayer
will never be without the Psalms. Christian faith did not arise as
a unique event without a context, nor did it use as its immediate context the sentiments and understanding of natural religion; it occurred within the setting of the Old Covenant, and we
in our remembrance must see it in that way. Without the memory of that context, our own grasp of Christian disclosure would
be distorted and our response to it would be out of key. Christian faith becomes gnostic when cut loose from its Jewish roots.

F

To conclude our study of disclosure in the Scriptures, we will
comment briefly on a special form of presentation that occurs in
the Gospel of St. John. This Gospel makes use of the literary
trope of ambiguity.[9] Ambiguity as a literary form does not mean
inexactness in expression; it does not imply that the author
failed to say clearly what he meant to say, that he unwittingly
used words that could be taken in ways different from the way
he intended. Rather, ambiguity as a trope is the deliberate expression of two meanings in one phrase. It is the use of one set
of words that can be taken in two senses, each of which manifests something in the thing being discussed. Moreover, each of
the senses is reinforced precisely by being placed against the
other within the single ambiguous phrase. A splendid example
of ambiguity is found in T. S. Eliot's lines in *Burnt Norton*:

> . . . as a Chinese jar still
> Moves perpetually in its stillness.

The word "still" is triply ambiguous and so is, therefore, the
entire phrase. "Still" can be taken as an adjective, an adverb, or

9. Joachim Gnilka, in *Neutestamentliche Theologie*, 129–30, speaks of ambiguity in
St. John's Gospel as both a stimulus to thought for the believer and a means of concealment before those who do not believe.

a conjunction. The phrase could say that the Chinese jar is motionless (still) and yet moves; it could say that the ancient jar moves even now (still); and it could say that despite its stillness the jar nevertheless (still) moves. It is the interplay of all these meanings that gives the lines their force.[10] A similar ambiguity, also based on the word "still," is found in a line from *East Coker*:

> We must be still and still moving.

In the Fourth Gospel, ambiguity is used in some of the remarks Jesus makes about his relationship to the Father. The first and most obvious meaning of these statements is about Christ as the one who has been sent by the Father; for example, when he says, "Just as the Father has life in himself, so also he gave to his Son the possession of life in himself" (5:26), the context shows that Jesus refers to the life that he gives to those who hear his voice and believe. It is the life he possesses and shares with us as our Redeemer, the life it is his mission to bring to us. However, we can without straining read in the phrase another sense. We can hear an overtone to the dominant meaning. The second sense would refer to the eternal life that the Son has from the Father within the Holy Trinity. The obvious "economic" sense of the statement is not without an allusion to the "immanent" trinitarian sense. It is not just the incarnate Word who receives life from the Father; he has this life from the Father as the eternal Son.

A similar ambiguity occurs in statements such as "The Father and I are one" (10:30), "Believe me, that I am in the Father and the Father is in me" (14:11), "Everything that the Father has is mine" (16:15), and "I made known to them your name and I will make it known, that the love with which you loved me may be in them and I in them" (17:26). In these sentences and in others like them, Christ speaks of himself as the one who was

10. A more amusing example of ambiguity, one that was obviously unintended, can be found in the newspaper headline that announced, "General MacArthur Flies Back to Front." The example was cited by Alastaire Fowler in a lecture given at The Catholic University of America.

sent into the world by the Father, but he also alludes to his eternal procession from the Father, and the allusion occurs in the same sentence in which he expresses his worldly mission. The redemptive mission is profiled against the eternal procession. If the life Christ brings us were not related to the life he has eternally from the Father, the sense of our Redemption would be incompletely expressed. The Fourth Gospel relates the two senses of life—it shows that they are two aspects of one life—by the literary trope of ambiguity, in which two meanings are embodied in one verbal whole. What the Fourth Gospel alludes to through this ambiguity in the words of Christ is, of course, stated explicitly and without ambiguity in the Prologue through the voice of the narrator when he says, "In the beginning was the Word, and the Word was with God, and the Word was God. He was in the beginning with God" (1:1–2). The Prologue goes on to say that this Word, which was with the Father in the beginning, was life and light, and that he shone in the darkness and was in the world and came to his own. These literal statements about the Logos in his preexistence and his Incarnation explicitly introduce the two dimensions within which the two senses of the ambiguous statements can occur.

The literary ambiguities in the Fourth Gospel are possible because of the play of presentational dimensions that occurs in Christian belief. The simply worldly can be taken just as it is, but it can also be seen in an iconic way, as a manifestation of a dimension that transcends it. A play of presentations also occurs in eucharistic celebration, which images the Last Supper (there is a provocative ambiguity as to which voice is speaking during the recitation of the words of institution); it also represents the sacrifice of Calvary, and then it images still further the eternal transcendence of God. Such hints and ambiguities are not deficiencies but disclosures, and the datives for them are we ourselves as participants in the ritual, and also the Father before whom the eucharistic celebration occurs. In such mirroring, interaction, and symbolism, Christian things are revealed to us in words, in conduct, and in ritual action.

I 2

❧

CHRISTIANITY AND NATURAL

RELIGION

CHRISTIAN REVELATION took place within the setting
of the Old Testament; the Old Covenant was in turn differentiated from the natural religion of the Gentiles. Both the
New and the Old Covenants were established through the
making of distinctions. The religion of the Gentiles, however, is
something like an outside boundary for biblical belief, not distinguished from any still wider human setting (although it may
be understood as a lapse from an earlier condition). If Christian
revelation is seen as the completion of God's word, pagan religion can be taken as a kind of beginning and widest context
for it. From the Christian point of view, the religion of the Gentiles, in all the forms it may assume, is identified primarily as the
religion outside the concentric circles of Jewish and Christian
faith. Natural religion is the religion that develops on its own
among men, without the revelation that occurred in the Bible.
It makes up the rim surrounding biblical religion. But both Jews
and Christians could easily imagine themselves as having been
born into that rim and having spent their lives in it. Natural religion is a human possibility latent, and perhaps even active in

various ways, in all men. What is the relation between natural religion and Christian belief, and between natural religious rituals and the Christian sacraments? What shifts in intentionality occur between these two modes of presentation?

To explore this question, (a) we will turn to St. Paul's remarks on Christ as surpassing the dichotomy between Jews and pagans, (b) we will speak about the pagan mysteries and their relation to the Christian mystery, and (c) we will show how the pagan religious use of water as lustration and of food as nourishment is fulfilled and transcended in the Christian sacraments of baptism and the Eucharist. Then, (d) we will close with a few comments on modern psychological interpretations of religious ritual.

A

It is true that paganism had to be mediated by the Old Covenant before an immediate context for Christian revelation could be provided. The New Testament could not have arisen under the aegis of Zeus or Vishnu. However, once the New Covenant is established, does it not appear to enjoy a new, more direct relationship to natural religion? St. Paul, when speaking to the Athenians in the Areopagus, could not say that he is there to tell them about the "true Zeus" or the "authentic Apollo," but he was able to proclaim to them the God for whom they had an altar but not yet a name (Acts 17:23). Christian revelation is a fulfillment of the revelation achieved in the Old Testament, but can it not also be seen as the fulfillment, in another way, of the search expressed in natural religion? Since St. Paul, Christianity has addressed the pagan world directly and claimed that it was able to identify the unknown God that the pagans try to honor.

It is commonly said that the Old Testament does not have a concept of nature, while nature is the central theme for Greek philosophy. Nature also plays a major role in Christian religious understanding and in Scholasticism. Are the concepts of nature and natural law a bequest of ancient paganism to Christianity? Does Christianity achieve a kind of affinity with the religion and the philosophy of the Gentiles that the Old Testament could not? Perhaps the divine pedagogy of the Old Covenant had to stress the distinction between the Jews and the pagans, between Yahweh and the gods; Jerusalem and Athens had to appear as polar opposites. St. Paul, in his letter to the Ephesians, speaks to the Gentiles as being "at that time without Christ, alienated from the community of Israel and strangers to the Covenants of the promise, without hope and without God in the world" (Ephesians 2:12). The Jews and the pagans were radically distinguished, and not simply because the pagans were somehow at fault; without this distinction, how could the Old Covenant achieve what it was destined to do? St. Paul goes on to say that these same Gentiles "who once were far off have become near by the blood of Christ. For he is our peace, he who made both one and broke down the dividing wall of enmity through his flesh" (Ephesians 2:13–14). The Gentiles then "are no longer strangers and sojourners, but . . . fellow citizens with the holy ones and members of the household of God, built upon the foundation of the apostles and the prophets, with Christ Jesus himself as the capstone" (Ephesians 2:19–20). Christ accomplished something that transcends both nature and the Law and makes possible a reconciliation that seemed impossible from the point of view of the Old Covenant alone. He brought about a new way of presenting God to the world, one that did not depend on the radical contrast between Israel and the Gentiles. This was achieved not only for the benefit of two groups of people, Jews and Gentiles, in the past, but also for the benefit of the moral, intellectual, and ontological traditions of both these people; the Law of the Jews and the nature of the Gentiles both come to fuller life in Christian belief.

B

At the end of the nineteenth century and the beginning of the twentieth, the relationship between Christianity and pagan religion was studied in the new science called the history of religions, *Religionsgeschichte*. One school of thought in this science, represented by such writers as Eichhorn, Lietzmann, Bousset, and Loisy, interpreted the sacramental dimension in Christianity as having been derived from the mystery religions of the Hellenistic world. In its most extreme form, this approach claimed that Jesus was essentially a Jewish moral teacher and that the Christian mysteries and sacraments were additions made to his teachings when Christianity spread beyond Palestine and came under the influence of pagan Greek and Oriental religions.[1] In this way of thinking, parallels between early Christianity and paganism were usually interpreted in a way that reduced the Christian to the pagan.

Other scholars countered this interpretation with various arguments.[2] First, the many Jewish elements in the Christian sacraments and mysteries were described, such as the Passover themes that remain in the Eucharist and the understanding of salvation that was developed in the Old Testament and found its fulfillment in Christ. Second, the great difference in meaning between pagan mystery rites and Christian sacraments was brought out. Pagan mysteries were rituals that expressed and celebrated the death and rebirth of cosmic divinities, the gods of generation and life. The rituals showed what happened to the gods, how they both suffered and were restored, how they were involved in the destinies of things. The rites enabled those who participated in them to attain an insight into the ultimate necessities and a reconciliation with them; the rites integrated the believing community into the cosmic whole. But the Eucharist

1. Concise surveys of the attempts to interpret the Eucharist in terms of pagan mysteries can be found in Klauck, *Herrenmahl und hellenistischer Kult*, 8–15, and Bouyer, *Liturgical Piety*, 86–114. Both authors discuss the important work of Dom Odo Casel, O.S.B.

2. Besides the works of Klauck and Bouyer cited in note 1, see: Prümm, *Der christliche Glaube und die altheidnische Welt*, and *Christentum als Neuheitserlebnis. Durchblick durch die Christlich-Antike Begegnung*; also Hugo Rahner, *Greek Myths and Christian Mystery*, and Bouyer, *The Christian Mystery. From Pagan Myth to Christian Mysticism*. One of the best studies of the relation of pagan ritual to the Christian sacraments is Bouyer's *Rite and Man*. Schmemann has some interesting remarks in his *Introduction to Liturgical Theology*, 43–45.

is different from this: it does not imitate simply natural energies and rhythms; the Eucharist reenacts a historical event that was accomplished by the God who transcends nature and who gave life through death in a manner that was not merely part of the ebb and flow of nature. God's action was not caught up in a continuous dialectic of life and death; it was a definitive victory by life, and by life of a kind different from that of the cycles of nature.[3] The Eucharist reenacts what was accomplished at a moment in time by Jesus, who was God as well as man; the Eucharist does not simply imitate and promote the permanent natural cycles of the world. History and nature were radically distinguished by God's saving action in the death and Resurrection of Jesus, as they had already been distinguished by God's actions in the Old Testament. It is interesting to note that in our own day, secular editorialists or commentators who want to speak positively, say, about the feast of Easter will often interpret it in terms of the rhythms of nature and the revival of life and hope at springtime, thus reducing the biblical mystery to human participation in the forces and necessities of nature. Third, the word "mystery" was shown to have had different meanings in the pagan mystery rites and the letters of St. Paul. For the pagans, the mysteries were the rites themselves, the rituals that were kept secret from the people and were known only to the clergy who were their custodians; for Christians, the mystery is not a ritual but the plan that God has to bring salvation to the world, the plan that is at the heart of both nature and history.[4]

Once it is made clear that the Christian sacraments were not simply derived from pagan rites, it becomes possible to appreciate the positive aspects of the relationship between the sacraments and pagan religion and ritual. There are affinities between them. As Hans-Josef Klauck writes, the Christian faith

3. Von Balthasar, "Mysterium Paschale," 163.
4. Bouyer, *Liturgical Piety*, 92–93. Although many scholars no longer accept the reduction of Christian belief and sacraments to natural religious phenomena, such reductions are often accepted on the level of *haute vulgarisation*, as witnessed, for example, by the popularity and influence of the television programs of Joseph Campbell.

would not have spread throughout the Hellenistic world had it not expressed something that could be understood by that world. Furthermore, this spread of the faith would quite naturally affect the beliefs and practices of Christianity: "Without a Hellenistic influence on many levels the sacramental understanding of the Lord's Supper would not have come about in early Christianity."[5] Klauck observes that the eucharistic ritual of the Last Supper, which was originally a part of an entire meal, gradually became a more stylized ceremony in which the bread and wine were withdrawn from their context in the meal and made into the substance of the rite.[6] The Eucharist, furthermore, was celebrated frequently, whereas the Passover liturgy took place only once a year. Klauck mentions other aspects of the Eucharist that have no parallels in the Old Testament, such as the contact achieved with the divine through eating.[7] The Passover by itself, Klauck observes, could not explain everything in the eucharistic liturgy.[8] He concludes that the Eucharist cannot be understood as simply the outcome of Jewish or pagan influences or both; it is a distinct and "underivable creative synthesis" that must be understood on its own terms and not reduced to anything else.[9]

Works like those of Hans-Josef Klauck are primarily historical studies of the relationship between the Christian sacraments and pagan mysteries and myths. Other works, while considering the historical information, try in addition to provide a theoretical clarification of how the Christian sacraments both draw on and fulfill pagan religious beliefs and practices. Louis Beirnaert, for example, in the essay "The Mythic Dimension in Christian Sacramentalism,"[10] discusses the sacrament of baptism, which of course incorporates the natural symbolism of water. Beirnaert shows that in the Bible and in the Fathers of the Church, the

5. Klauck, *Herrenmahl und hellenistischer Kult*, 372.
6. Ibid., 365.   7. Ibid., 374.
8. Ibid., 28–29.   9. Ibid., 374.
10. Beirnaert, "La dimension mythique dans le sacramentalisme chrétien," 255–86.

"waters" are taken to be a place of both danger and protection, of death and life, of dissolution and regeneration, just as they are in pagan mythology.[11] In pagan religion and myth, waters are taken to be the origin of things, and a descent into them is a return to origins, a dissolution of all form. The waters are both a danger and a protection, a tomb and yet the womb of life. They are the origin of cosmic being and order. In Christianity, however, the waters become a new kind of origin. Christ descends into them in his passion and death not to be regenerated but to triumph. The sacrament of baptism "is thus not the repetition of the birth of the cosmos and the birth of man, but the repetition of the redemptive event."[12] The waters of baptism do not simply express the ultimate aquatic powers, but symbolize the divine power of Christ triumphant over the elements of the world. Baptism is the new crossing of the Red Sea and a participation in the death and Resurrection of Jesus: "You were buried with him in baptism, in which you were also raised with him through faith in the power of God, who raised him from the dead" (Colossians 2:12). The Christian understanding of the sacred power of water is different from the pagan mythical understanding, but the Christian clearly draws on the pagan and elevates it: Beirnaert speaks of "the active presence of a mythical dimension inside the new dimension that subordinates the old to the new."[13]

Furthermore, the primeval waters of pagan myth are changed by Christ into the Church, the place in which baptism occurs, the place in which the disorder of sin is overcome and men are born into eternal life. Christ changes the waters from being the source of simply natural life to being the maternal womb from which the saints would be born in baptism. The femininity of water, Beirnaert says, becomes identified with the femininity of the believing community, the Church.[14] The Church is not sim-

---

11. A good example from the Bible is the story of Jonah, who was plunged into the water to be destroyed, but who was sheltered there by one of the monsters of the deep and came forth from the water with new life.

12. Beirnaert, "La dimension mythique," 260.

13. Ibid., 270.   14. Ibid., 282.

ply part of cosmic rhythms, nor is she coextensive with the cosmos, nor is she the source of the cosmos as such; she is rather a part of the cosmos, an enclave within the whole, the selected place through which all of creation becomes renewed by God's redemptive action. The Church is the location and the custodian of the sanctified water of baptism.

All these shifts of meaning, this transposition of water from expressing elemental power to being an image of the power of God, become possible because of the new sense of divine transcendence introduced in biblical belief. The biblical God is not subject to the forces of the cosmos and is not caught up in the rhythms of the cosmic ultimates. He would exist even if the world did not, and so his power is not subordinated to his Creation. The sacraments, as they change the meaning of pagan myth and ritual, reflect and recall this new understanding of the divine.

C

The redemptive action of Christ is, for the Christian, the new ultimate event, the point of Creation. The sacrament of baptism and the sacrament of the Eucharist both allow us to participate in this one action, in the death and Resurrection of Christ, but they do so in different ways. Baptism is the beginning; it allows us to enter for the first time into the mystery achieved by God in Christ. We can enter only once, so we are baptized only once. The sacrament is not repeated. Once we are baptized and have entered, the essential has been done; there is no further new step to take, nothing more for us to do except to grow in the holiness that has been granted to us by our entrance into grace.[15] The growth that we are to achieve, however, is nourished by the Eucharist. The Eucharist is not a beginning but a continuation. The Eucharist cannot be received until after we have been baptized, but then it can be repeated over and over again. There is only one baptism for each of us but there are

15. Ibid., 279.

many Eucharists, and yet both baptism and Eucharist reenact one and the same event, the death and Resurrection of Christ: as Vonier writes, "Baptism . . . is not any kind of cleansing of the soul, but it is a cleansing of the soul which is a burial with Christ and which is a resurrection with Christ. Baptism is not only the present, but also the past and the future."[16]

In the sacraments we are united with Christ through the mediation of material elements. We as bodily creatures either can be absorbed by the elements of the cosmos or can absorb the elements into ourselves. Thus, in death we return to the earth from which we came; in eating and drinking we take the fruits of the earth into ourselves. The themes of pagan myth and ritual express our double dependence on the material cosmos. The rituals and myths of water speak about our origins, death, and regeneration, while the rituals and myths connected with eating speak about our nourishment by the natural world. We as living organisms, as inquirers and knowers, and as sources of action and centers of feeling emerge from nature and return to it, and we sustain ourselves, for the short time we remain an identifiable part of nature, by taking what she offers, preparing it, and assimilating it into ourselves. The nourishment we take from nature, furthermore, furnishes us with more than mere survival: it enables us to carry out the activities for which we emerged from nature. Eating allows more than mere subsistence; it gives us strength and allows action and thinking to take place. Thus, in our human condition we come out of nature and ultimately return to it, and so long as we live and act we draw our life from nature by taking her elements into ourselves. The act of assimilating the elements of nature into ourselves has been elevated into a religious action: "Mankind . . . has always realized the naturally mysterious character of eating and drinking (as essential communion with the cosmos and, through it, with divinity) and has consequently assigned a cultic form to this sign."[17]

16. Vonier, A Key to the Doctrine of the Eucharist, 22.
17. Von Balthasar, The Glory of The Lord, 1:571. As Klauck has said, "The phe-

The rhythm between us and nature, the rhythm of absorbing and being absorbed, is reflected in the Eucharist and in baptism. In baptism we enter into the waters of rebirth; in the Eucharist we consume bread and wine. In baptism we enter into the sanctified natural elements; in the Eucharist the elements enter into us. We are immersed into the baptismal water, but we do not drink it; we eat the bread and drink the wine, but we do not enter into them. Each sacrament establishes a different mode of presentation—one is an entrance, the other an assimilation; one is performed only once, the other repeatedly—but both relate us to the death and Resurrection of Christ.

Baptism deals with water; the Eucharist deals with earth, or rather with the fruits of the earth. The water of baptism is nature taken in its pristine condition, whereas the bread and wine of the Eucharist have been transformed by man: we offer the bread "which earth has given and human hands have made," and the wine that is "fruit of the vine and work of human hands." In the Eucharist we do not offer just wheat and grapes, but bread and wine. If we merely ate food as we found it, we would in this respect be no different from the animals; the Eucharist involves specifically human eating, the consumption of what we have domesticated and prepared, and not simply organic replenishment. It further involves eating taken as an icon, not eating as satisfaction; hence only a little food is consumed in the sacrament, just enough to serve as a vehicle for what it represents. Baptism, in contrast, expresses a more elementary activity than does the Eucharist; it represents the transition through death to life, so it is appropriate that it draw on an element of nature that has not been transformed by human art. In baptism we come in contact with our origins, where there is no room for something made, tended, or changed by man. In the sacramental death and rebirth in the waters of baptism, we come into contact with nature as it simply is, but again even this simple nature is taken as an icon.

---

nomenon of the sacred meal is one of those religious universals that know no boundaries, whether cultural or temporal." *Herrenmahl und hellenistischer Kult*, 31.

D

In his article on the mythical dimension in the Christian sacraments, Louis Beirnaert first shows how the cosmic elements described in pagan myths and rituals are transformed in biblical faith and in the patristic theology of the sacraments. He then goes on to discuss the same themes from the point of view of Jungian psychology. He shows how the archetypes described by Jung, the "psychic representations" that arise at critical stages in the development of the self, are similar to the symbols used in myth, ritual, and religion.[18] Beirnaert compares the symbolic descent into water with the descent into the unconscious, into the dark part of us in which form is dissolved and the primitive terrors lurk that are symbolically expressed as the serpents, dragons, and demons of myth.[19] He goes on to say that the coming of Christ transforms not only the cosmic elements of pagan mythology but the unconscious as well; he speaks about an "évangélisation des profondeurs." Salvation reaches into the depths of the psyche: "Christ and the Church have taken over the great images of the sun, the moon, wood, water, mother, and the like; this signifies an evangelisation of the affective powers represented by them."[20]

It is interesting that Beirnaert supplements his analysis of the mythic expression of nature by an appeal to the psychology of Jung. He develops the two in parallel and does not try to reduce the mythical to the psychological, but many thinkers in our day would be inclined to perform such a reduction. We are generally inclined to think that the only "scientific" role left for myth is in regard to the science of the mind. We might be willing to concede that myth and its symbols can provide us clues in the science of psychology and psychiatry, but we would be very sus-

18. Beirnaert, "La dimension mythique," 271.

19. For a similar psychological interpretation of religion, see Loewald, *Psychoanalysis and the History of the Individual*, chapter 3: "Comments on Religious Experience," 53–77, and *Papers on Psychoanalysis*, 7–10, 100. For a response to Loewald's work, see Sokolowski, "Religion and Psychoanalysis: Some Phenomenological Contributions."

20. Beirnaert, "La dimension mythique," 285.

picious of any help that myth might try to offer in regard to the science of nature. In investigating nature, we believe we must appeal only to the rigorous methods of experimental and mathematical science.

But perhaps we ought to reassess this conviction, at least in regard to the very basic distinctions and dimensions in nature; the ancient, prescientific myths may still be able to shed some light on them. The myths cannot help us in mapping the genome of a biological species or in working out the quantum-theoretical features of a particular molecule, but they may be able to illuminate things like life and death, male and female, beginning and end, threat and preservation. Such things are not merely projections made by our collective unconscious. They are basic features of nature itself, and our unconscious, whether personal or collective, can in its basic symbolizations be reflecting what is "out there" when it expresses them in mythical form. It need not be merely projecting things it has fashioned or inherited within itself. And while it is good to think of the sacraments as bringing a Gospel light to our own affective depths, it is also important to see them as transforming nature and its powers into icons. The sacraments do not merely occur in our isolated consciousness, but take place in the natural material world, parts of which they sanctify and elevate into being both vehicles and representations of grace.

Of course, if Christianity elevates human affectivity and the elements of nature into a higher service by making them part of sacramental actions, it also runs the risk of reductive abuse; whenever a lower is raised to a higher, it becomes possible for the lower to resist this elevation and to threaten to topple what supervenes. This occurs in a theoretical way when thinkers claim that the higher is in fact nothing but the lower, and it occurs in a practical way when the higher is shaken by the lower in its actual execution. Thus, on the theoretical side, some schools in the history of religions have interpreted the sacraments as essentially the same as the mysteries of Hellenistic paganism, and some theological positions have taken the sacraments to be just commemorations of historical events and not reenactments of the work of our salvation. In both these reductions, a natural foundation is taken as the substance of a sacramental form. On the practical side, some liturgical abuses may effectively change the sacramental rituals from being icons of God's action to being expressions of sentimentality, whether Dionysian or maudlin.

Such theoretical and practical reductions are always a possibility whenever a lower is in the service of a higher. They occur even on the purely natural level: human thinking and action risk being reduced to mere biological states or compulsive forces, life itself risks being reduced to mere molecular chemistry, art might be reduced to mere affectivity. The danger of reduction is even greater when the "higher" in question is as exalted as the transcendence involved in Christian faith. The transcendence presented to us in Christian belief does not intrude on us obviously, with an affective and perceptual insistence of its own; it is present in faith and through hearing. Christian transcendence is therefore especially vulnerable to reductionism. It is difficult to sustain in both theory and practice. There is always the danger that the Christian sense of God will be reduced to that of a cosmic deity, that providence will be reduced to fate, that Christ will be taken as merely a good and wise man, that grace will be taken as mere inspiration; Newman accused Milman of just such a reduction when he said that Milman "will make the message of the Gospel relate mainly to moral improvement, not to forgiveness of sins."[21] Christian transcendence must be sustained through the teaching and discipline of the Church, as well as through the efforts of theological reflection, one of the most important tasks of which is to preserve Christian things as they truly are, to prevent them from being confused with other things from which they must be distinguished, and to prevent them from being reduced to that which they use as their material and affective instruments.

21. Newman, "Milman's View of Christianity," 203.

Natural religion and its ritual provide the widest setting for biblical belief and the sacraments. They provide an anticipation and a terminology that prepare men for the Gospel of salvation presented in Christian faith. It is not just that paganism gives us nature (in its fallen and hence confused state) and that Christianity brings grace; Christianity brings not just grace but the combination of nature and grace, the restoration of nature and the gift of the supernatural. As Peter Wust has said, "Belief in the supernatural mysteries of revelation . . . transformed the naturally religious attitude of the ancients toward immanent being into a piety that was in the strictest sense at once natural and supernatural."[22] Christ was man as well as God, and the Christian reality completes and heals nature even as it elevates it into the condition of grace. Nature and grace, reason and faith are not at odds with one another in Christian belief. What people look for in pagan myths and rituals is both found and transformed in the Church, the Bible, and the sacraments.

22. Wust, "Crisis in the West," 106.

13

⁂

THE THEOLOGY OF

DISCLOSURE

THIS BOOK, as we have said at the beginning, is written
with two purposes in mind: as a theological reflection on the
Eucharist, and as an example of a kind of thinking that can be
called a theology of disclosure. After introducing the concept of
this form of theology in Chapter 1, we have explored various
dimensions of the mystery of the Eucharist, and from time to
time we have made comments about the nature of our theological reflection. In this chapter we will again speak more directly
about the kind of theological thinking we have been carrying
on. In this chapter our mode of speech will be metatheological,
not simply theological. We will try to clarify what is meant by
the theology of disclosure, the form of theological thinking that
can be derived from the philosophical tradition known as phenomenology.

At the outset we must admit that the name "theology of disclosure" is not very satisfactory, but it is hard to find a more suitable term. "Theology of manifestation" is no better and "phenomenological theology" is far worse. The problem lies with the
word "phenomenology." It is clumsy as a noun and almost

impossible as an adjective in English. When the adjective is joined to a noun, especially a noun like "theology," whose vowels are so similar to those in the adjective, the result is a term that chokes every sentence in which it appears. Therefore, because of a lack of alternatives, we will continue to use the term "theology of disclosure," along with some synonyms, despite its awkwardness.

In this chapter, (a) we will claim that the differences brought to light by a theology of disclosure are genuine and objective and not merely psychological. Then we will show that the theology of disclosure is (b) an appropriate response to issues raised by modern philosophy and that it is also (c) a form of thinking that responds to cultural and moral problems related to appearance in contemporary life. We will then (d) turn to the fundamental epistemological issue raised by modernity and show how phenomenology comes to terms with it. This will allow us (e) to examine four important themes in phenomenology, those of absence, the world, the making of distinctions, and symbolism, and we will show how these themes surface in the theology of disclosure. We will also examine (f) what it is to disclose a dimension of presentation and will show how such a mode of presence functions in Christian belief. Finally, (g) we will discuss work of Hans Urs von Balthasar as an example of theological reflection directed toward the theme of manifestation.

A

It may seem uninformative to say that the theology of disclosure examines the way theological things appear. The statement is so general that it seems practically empty; what, concretely, does it mean to analyze the way things appear? We can become more specific in describing the nature of this sort of theology if we turn to some actual contributions made by the theology of disclosure. Consider, for example, the analysis of the words and actions used in the eucharistic consecration. We have observed that in the Eucharist the priest's words and actions are quotational and not pictorial. What the priest says and does are not to be taken as a theatrical depiction of what Christ said and did at the Last Supper, but as a quotation of the words and actions of Christ. The difference between picturing and quoting is a phenomenological difference, a difference in appearance or in the manner of presentation. It is with differences such as this that the theology of disclosure is concerned.

Furthermore, these are real differences. It is not the case that the difference between picturing and quoting is only a matter of the intention of the celebrant or the participants. No matter what the celebrant intends, and no matter whether he is aware of it or not, he is quoting and not depicting when he pronounces the words of consecration and performs the gestures. The difference between quoting and depicting is not a mere psychological distinction, not something that arises "in the mind alone." It is not subject to our arbitrary will. Even if the celebrant were to become as overtly dramatic as an actor on a stage, he would still be quoting and not depicting; his behavior would simply be at odds with what he is doing.[1] It is the nature of the rite that determines what he does, not any purpose he might have in mind. Phenomenological differences are genuine, "objective" differences in the presentation of things.

As another example, consider the observation that the Eucharist reenacts the sacrifice of Calvary not directly but through the mediation of the Last Supper: the Eucharist does not simply represent the sacrificial death of Jesus, but represents it as it had been anticipated by Jesus himself at the Last Supper. This is a claim made about the manner in which the sacrifice of Christ is presented in the Eucharist. The sacramental presence of the sacrifice of the Lord is more complex than it would be if we were dealing with a direct representation.

---

1. For an example of behavior that is at odds with what one is doing, imagine that a clerk at a checkout counter were to sing out, like a performer in an opera, the amount of money that the customer owes. He would be doing his job, he would be conveying the required information, he would be clerking; but he would be doing it in an inappropriate way, through a manner of disclosure that belongs to another setting.

Although an ontological theology would be most concerned with the reality of the eucharistic sacrifice, with the fact that the sacrifice of the Mass is the same as the sacrifice on Calvary even though the "species," the appearances of what is offered, are different, the theology of disclosure turns its attention to the appearances of the sacrifice and tries to bring out their structure and theological sense.

The theology of disclosure would, of course, not deny that the same sacrifice is enacted in the two ways of being offered, first as a natural sacrifice and later as a sacramental one. Indeed, if identically the same sacrifice were not being offered in the two ways, there would be no need for a theology that reflected on the special kinds of appearance that allow one and the same sacrifice to take place. It is only because there is just one sacrifice that is historically achieved and sacramentally reenacted that there is an issue calling for a theological clarification of its disclosure. The theology of manifestation adds to the insistence on the sameness of the sacrifice an exploration of the manifold of appearances through which the one sacrifice occurs.

Furthermore, the theology of manifestation does not only observe that the celebrant quotes and does not depict; it does not only observe that the Eucharist represents the sacrifice through the mediation of the perspective offered on it by the Last Supper; besides doing these two things, it also describes the wider contexts within which the sacramental reenactment of the one sacrifice of Christ can happen: it speaks of the nature of the God whom Christians worship, the God who could be even if the world were not, the God who is not part of the temporality of the world but exists in eternal actuality. It points out that only against the background of such an understanding of God could there be a sacramental reenactment of an event that occurred at one moment in history. All these issues, and many others as well, are issues of appearance, to be examined by a theology of manifestation.

The theology of disclosure serves as a complement to the ontological theology of the Scholastics. Speculative, Scholastic theology presents Christian things by starting from what is first in itself and moving on to what is derived. It discusses the being of God as preceding Creation; then it discusses Creation, the Incarnation, Redemption, Resurrection, and finally the Eucharist. But from the perspective of disclosure, the logic moves in the opposite direction. The Eucharist, celebrated in our moment of time, reveals to us the truth of the Resurrection, showing us that Christ did not just rise from the dead but that he shares his glorified life with us now; the disciples at Emmaus recognized the risen Lord in the breaking of bread (Luke 24:35). The Resurrection in turn reveals what the passion and death of Christ were, the triumph of divine life over sin and death. The Redemption in its turn shows what the Incarnation was: not just God becoming part of his creation, but God the Son assuming in humility the fallen condition of man in all respects except sin, and even, at the end, accepting the condition of the sinner.[2] The Incarnation in turn reveals the Godhead: it reveals that God lives as Father, Son, and Spirit and that he is so transcendent to the world that he can become part of it without diminishing his divinity. This revelation of the divine nature is at the same time a disclosure of the nonultimacy, the contingency of the world. Thus the Eucharist perpetually reminds us of the transcendence of God and of the difference between the Christian God and the divinities of nonbiblical religion. Because the Eucharist is different from the Passover, it also sheds light on the development that occurred between the Old and the New Testaments.

Finally, the theology of disclosure serves as a complement to positive theology, and it helps such theology defend itself against the danger of historicism. The theology of disclosure helps to show, in an explicit and systematic way, how the biblical sense of the divine is disclosed throughout the events and circumstances involved in the history of salvation. These events and circumstances are not to be taken as mere historical facts, but as

2. See von Balthasar, "Mysterium Paschale," 145.

elements in the gradual and then the definitive manifestation of the God who could be, in undiminished goodness and greatness, even without creatures, the God who has acted to redeem us in Christ. The sacraments, the Church, Mary the Mother of God, and all the other essential elements in Christian belief are related to this central revelation as responding to it and being derived from it. Positive theology explores historical fact, but the facts are to be taken as involved in the activity of disclosure, in a kind of disclosure that has no parallel in the natural order. By providing this service to positive theology, the theology of disclosure mediates between historical study on the one hand and both faith and speculative theology on the other. Faith is seen as an acknowledgment and acceptance of the transcendent God who is manifested in history, and speculative theology is no longer seen as simply conjoined, in a brusque and perhaps uneasy way, with historical theology, but as an attempt to articulate more clearly the sense of the divine that has come to light in revelation.

Von Balthasar has pointed out the serious challenge to Christian faith that a "historico-critical" approach has brought about: "Christian thought today has been uprooted and split right down to its foundations," between an approach that accepts the received articles of faith as principles beyond which one cannot go, and an approach that tries to adjudicate these articles by rational investigation and to interpret their content in a manner that is "anthropologically" acceptable.[3] Von Balthasar goes on to say that in this approach the interventions of ecclesiastical authorities are themselves historically-critically interpreted and the authorities are asked to demonstrate the warrant under which they claim to be empowered to act. He claims that this mentality has been presented as a form of aggiornamento and an essential precondition for the "evangelization of the contemporary world." This historicist and critical mentality has come about, he claims, under the influence of the Enlightenment, and

3. Von Balthasar, *Theodramatik*, 3:429; see also pp. 427–33.

it has spread throughout the educational system of the Church, with very harmful effects: "The Enlightenment in all its forms is so mortally dangerous in the Church because, starting with 'the learned and the clever' it has gradually, through catechesis, preaching, and the mass media, spread throughout the people and shaken the faith of 'the simple'."[4] This judgment of von Balthasar is echoed by the remarks of Alexander Schmemann, who criticizes historicist treatments of the liturgy as leading to a loss of sacred transcendence: "By 'dissolving' worship into history in the first place, they supplied the means for its dissolution in contemporary life today."[5] The theology of disclosure, through its concern with appearance, helps to show the special character of what is revealed in the history of salvation; in doing so it provides a bridge between positive and speculative theology, and helps preserve the integrity of the Christian act of faith.

B

A theology of disclosure is an appropriate form of theology for our time. It provides us with a way of theologically appropriating modernity and not just trying to evade it. The modern era began with the political philosophy of Machiavelli and Hobbes; with the natural science of Galileo, Descartes, and Newton; and with the epistemology, anthropology, and metaphysics that lay behind these political and scientific traditions. These modern

4. Ibid., 433.

5. Schmemann, *The Eucharist*, 198. Schmemann criticizes both rationalism and historicism from an Orthodox perspective. In *The Eucharist* he writes: "The basic defect of school theology consists in that, in its treatment of the sacraments, it proceeds not from the living experience of the Church, not from the concrete liturgical tradition that has been preserved by the Church, but from its own a priori and abstract categories and definitions" (p. 13). But after this critique of "theological rationalism" (p. 116), which he equates with Scholasticism, he also writes, "Now that historical investigation has helped free us from the *scholastic* reduction, we are now threatened with a new, this time *historical* reduction" (p. 197). Schmemann considers both extremes to be rooted in the introduction of purely rational categories into faith during the Middle Ages. We would agree with his critique of both historicism and rationalism but would differ with his interpretation of Scholasticism as a form of rationalism. Scholasticism has a profound appreciation of Christian faith and mystery.

developments have been very productive, but they have also brought with them difficulties for human understanding in general and for theology in particular.

Modernity isolates the individual human being from the rest of the world: the individual is taken to be an enclosed consciousness, a thinking thing, and "the outside" is taken to be a mechanical system of material elements. The self and the world seem to stand in opposition to each other. Furthermore, the ideas in the mind of the isolated thinking subject seem to be the direct object of our conscious awareness, and we think that we must somehow infer from these ideas what the real world must be like; the world is not directly given to us. Furthermore, in modernity reason seems to be radically distinguished, almost separated, from emotion and inclination. In addition, for modernity nature seems to be bereft of any species or forms; there is only extended matter and energy arranging itself into various combinations. Natural teleology seems lost; the only teleology that seems to survive is the kind that we ourselves insert into nature when we set goals and purposes of our own; there seem to be no ends given in the natural world. As far as human society is concerned, we are said to enter into society and political life not as ends that our nature endows us with, but only as a refuge from the isolation and mutual danger that are part of an original uncivilized condition; we, the isolated and autonomous individuals, become social and political only by contract, not by nature. Finally, in modernity the freedom and spontaneity of individual human beings are considered to be absolute. Since we as thinking things are not embedded in larger wholes, and since the natures of things are not manifested to us, there are no limits prescribed for our conduct. Any limitations on our actions are self-imposed. We are to act autonomously, not heteronomously; we ourselves draw the borders of our actions. Instead of being a part and a child of nature, man strives to be its master. Even the constraints that society puts on us are ultimately things that we ourselves will; they are implied in the contract we freely make when we enter society.

Religion and theology find little support in these trends. The desacralized world shows no sign of having been created, and it is hard to see how a purely mechanical world can become a sacramental icon. The individual in this world takes himself as merely the outcome of random evolutionary processes, not someone chosen to be by the providential God who not only created but also redeemed him. Christian theology has reacted to modernity in various ways. One of its strategies has been to go back to a period before modernity, to the medieval speculative theologies or to patristic thought. Another strategy has been to seek a safe haven within the self, searching for God in imma-nence and in the subject's own freedom, leaving the mechanical world to run on according to its inexorable laws. A third strat-egy of Christian theology has been to ally itself with one or other of the great figures of modernity, such as Descartes, Kant, or Hegel, and to try to reconcile the thought of that figure with Christian belief. Thus, much of eighteenth-century Scholasti-cism had a decidedly Cartesian flavor, transcendental Thomism accepted many of the premises of Kantian philosophy, and liber-ation theologians followed in the tracks of Hegel and Marx.

The theology of disclosure is different from such attempts to deal with modernity. It does not try to evade modernity by turning to a premodern form of thought, it does not turn away from the world into privacy and immanence, nor does it try to be reconciled with modernity by adopting the thought of one or another of its heroes. The theology of disclosure takes advantage of resources found in the thought of Edmund Husserl, who broke through the axioms of modernity and was not restricted by them.[6] Husserl's work enables us to accept the valid dimen-sions introduced by modernity without falling prey to the distor-tions that have accompanied them. Husserl claims to have built on the insights of Descartes, but he also claims to have radically transformed Descartes' thought. He calls his own phenomenol-

6. An excellent discussion of the relation of Husserl to modernity can be found in Cobb-Stevens, *Husserl and Analytic Philosophy*, especially 123–203.

ogy a type of idealism, but he sharply distinguishes it from the traditional idealisms of modernity.[7] He accomplishes this adjustment of modernity through his new understanding of intentionality; he makes it possible for us to think of the mind as public, not as confined inside what John Locke has called its own "cabinet."[8] Husserl helps us to see that the mind is "outside" from the start and that the world itself presents itself to man. Through his understanding of intentionality, Husserl makes it possible for us to speak about the forms of things; we can recognize forms as substantial in their own right and irreducible to the material elements out of which they are made. He also makes it possible for us to overcome the alienation of reason from sensibility; his analyses show how the propositions achieved by reason are built upon a perceptual basis.[9]

Phenomenology makes it possible for us to recover many of the themes of classical philosophy that were lost in modernity—forms, perceptual intuition, publicness of mind, teleology in nature—but to recover them in a postmodern way, with due regard being paid to the contributions of modernity. The main philosophical contribution that we can take from modernity is a more explicit and positive philosophical concern with appearance or manifestation or disclosure. The very suspicion that modernity casts on appearances can be turned to our advantage; just as Plato's philosophy arose in response to the challenge of the Sophists, so a positive and deeper understanding of appearances can arise in response to the misunderstanding of appearance that stands at the root of modernity.

Appearance, manifestation, disclosure were appreciated in antiquity; the very term *eidos*, which was central to the thought of

---

7. See Husserl, *Ideas*, Book 1, §55. Also *Cartesian Meditations*, 1: "One might also call transcendental phenomenology a neo-Cartesianism, even though it is obliged—and precisely by its radical development of Cartesian motifs—to reject nearly all the well-known doctrinal content of the Cartesian philosophy."

8. Locke, *An Essay Concerning Human Understanding*, 1:48: "The senses at first let in particular ideas, and furnish the yet empty cabinet." See Cobb-Stevens, *Husserl and Analytic Philosophy*, 23.

9. Cobb-Stevens, *Husserl and Analytic Philosophy*, 147–54.

THEOLOGY OF DISCLOSURE 183

Plato and Aristotle, implies presentation. *Eidos* primarily means the "look" or the "view" that things present to us. In modernity, the *eidos* of a thing, instead of being a disclosure, becomes merely the subjective impact the thing makes on us or the idea we ourselves fabricate of an unknown thing. The *eidos* of classical philosophy is replaced by the "idea" of modernity. Ideas exist in the self-enclosed mind and they are immediately present to it.[10] Ideas come between us and things. We have to get around them and outwit them if we are to reach the things themselves. To do so, we form hypotheses and build models in our minds, and we try to determine, by experiment, which of these hypotheses and models are false and which can be at least provisionally confirmed. In this way we hope to get beyond appearances to the things themselves, to the things that always remain absent and hidden from us.

This suspicion of appearances and this postulation of ideas as mental entities came about partly under the influence of scientific developments at the start of modernity. The mathematical turn given to physics by Galileo, Descartes, and Newton led to an understanding of material things as bereft of any "primary qualities," as being just extended bits of matter and points of force. Since the world was found by science to be so different from what we experience it to be, it was concluded that the appearances we have of the world are deceptive; they do not directly reveal the way things are; they are only our subjective reactions to the effect things have on us. They are just subjective entities or events, just "ideas." This reduction of appearances to mere ideas was reinforced by discoveries in the physiology of perception. Vision, for example, was found to be caused by light rays that strike the retina and give rise to neural stimulations that are transmitted through the optic nerves to the visual cortex. With all these physical processes going on between us and the things we are supposed to be seeing, what else could percep-

10. See Hanna, "How Ideas Became Meanings: Locke and the Foundations of Semantic Theory," 777–79.

tion be but the brain experiencing its own internal states, its own neural reactions, which appear to it, and hence to us, as images or ideas?

Another assault on the validity of appearance came from modern innovations in political thought. Machiavelli's dismissal of ideal republics and principalities as normative for politics, his rejection of "imaginary" kingdoms as unsuitable distractions for the realistic, effective statesman, is essentially a modern move in the metaphysics of appearance.[11] Indeed, Machiavelli provides the moral and political background for the understanding of appearances that was introduced along with the new scientific methods of Galileo, Descartes, and Newton. "The way things seem" was already under suspicion for moral and political reasons when the great scientific revolution of the seventeenth century took place.[12] Thomas Hobbes' criticism of general political opinion and his desire to turn politics into a rigorous science similar to geometry constitute a dramatic codification of the moral and political attitude toward appearance taken by modern thought.[13]

The suspicion of appearance in modernity has made manifestation the central issue in the philosophy of the last five centuries. Appearances are the metaphysical problem of modernity. Phenomenology takes up the challenge to give a better account of appearances and it succeeds in doing so. It thus comes to

11. See Strauss, *Thoughts on Machiavelli*, 295. Strauss says that Machiavelli does not acknowledge the suprapolitical order. "The consequence is an enormous simplification and, above all, the appearance of the discovery of a hitherto wholly unsuspected whole continent. In fact, however, Machiavelli does not bring to light a single political phenomenon of any fundamental importance which was not fully known to the classics. His seeming discovery is only the reverse side of the oblivion of the most important: all things necessarily appear in a new light if they are seen for the first time in a specifically dimmed light. A stupendous contraction of the horizon appears to Machiavelli and his successors as a wondrous enlargement of the horizon."

12. See Strauss, *The Political Philosophy of Hobbes*, 1–29. See also Lewis, *The Abolition of Man*, 89: "It might be going too far to say that the modern scientific movement was tainted from its birth: but I think it would be true to say that it was born in an unhealthy neighborhood and at an inauspicious hour."

13. See Hobbes's epistle dedicatory to *De Cive*, 25.

terms with modernity, and the theology of disclosure tries to draw some of the benefits of phenomenology's success.

Husserl's overcoming of the modern understanding of appearances is an original philosophical move. He does not merely work within the context set by Descartes, Hume, or Kant. He marks a new beginning. Another radical beginning for philosophy occurred in the work of one of Husserl's contemporaries, Gottlob Frege. Frege set the context for what has become known as analytical philosophy. The basic problems he raised and the definitions he established became the setting for mathematical logic, for computer languages, and also for the epistemological issues in twentieth-century Anglo-American philosophy. Frege, like Husserl, also cannot be reduced to his immediate predecessors. The difference between Husserl and Frege, however, is that Frege never fully frees himself from the grip of modernity.[14] He does not resolve the issue of appearances. He also does not bridge the gap between reason and sensibility. He fails to show how propositions can be achieved and stated by speakers without being dissolved into the psychological activities of those speakers; Frege wants to avoid psychologism, but he does not know how to do so.[15] The differences and conflicts between Husserl and Frege are a version in miniature of the differences and conflicts between phenomenology and analytical philosophy, between the Continental and the Anglo-American traditions of thought that have dominated the philosophy of the twentieth century. In this contest, Husserl handles the issues of

14. See Cobb-Stevens, *Husserl and Analytic Philosophy*, 22–23.

15. Frege's weakness is revealed in his inability to explain how "thoughts" (or propositions) are "grasped" by us. In an essay published posthumously he writes as follows concerning our ability to grasp the law of gravitation: "But still the grasping of this law is a mental process! . . . For in grasping the law something comes into view whose nature is no longer mental in the proper sense, namely the thought; and this process is the most mysterious of all. . . . It is enough for us that we can grasp thoughts and recognize them to be true; how this takes place is a question in its own right." In a footnote he adds: "I should say that this question is still far from being grasped in all its difficulty" ("Logic," 145). It is precisely where Frege stands astonished that Husserl begins his work. What Frege calls psychologism in Husserl is the latter's attempt to deal with the problem recognized in the passage we have quoted.

modernity more adequately than Frege. Husserl faces and re-
solves the problem of the ontology of appearances in ways that
Frege is not able to comprehend.

C

An attention to appearances is appropriate in our day and age
not only because of the philosophical concerns of modernity, but
also because in our time appearances have become a predominant cultural and moral issue. Because of new technologies,
images and words have proliferated in television, radio, visual
and audial tapes and disks, computers, and printing; this expan-
sion has served the dissemination of information and the growth
of science, it has made people less restricted to their immediate
context, and it has enhanced recreation and the enjoyment of
the arts. At the same time, it has served advertising and propaganda and has greatly influenced moral education. Images and
words have always been part of the human scene, but now they
are artificially fabricated on an enormous scale, and they fill so
much of our lives that some people have been inclined to think
that there is nothing else besides them. The literary and philosophical movements called structuralism and deconstructionism
claim that words and images refer only to other words and
images: there are only texts that refer to other texts, codes that
become reinterpreted into other codes; there is no center, nothing beyond the merely apparent to which our words, images, and
consciousness can be related. The absolute freedom and spontaneity of the individual become expanded into the freedom to
create our own world. We not only claim that we can do what
we want to do; we also think we can make the world as we want
it to be. What is often called the relativism of the contemporary
self-understanding is a form of the voluntarism of modernity.

If there is indeed nothing beyond the text and the picture,
and if people think that the world can be changed by changing
the way we speak about things and the way we picture them,
then the text and image become the center of great struggles for

power, as people try to push forward the appearances they want as the standards of public life and general education. Each group that has access to the public media will fight to have its view of the good prevail. The community described by Locke, the community of minds all enclosed each in its own cabinet, is now modified by the new technologies of images and words. We no longer have to deal just with the wandering Sophists and with the written word, but must cope with the daily visits of commentators whom we do not know, with political figures that are glimpsed intermittently for a few seconds every few hours, with people telling us that this or that will be exactly what we truly want, and with words and pictures that are stored on disks and appear fleetingly on a screen. Our moral attitudes are no longer influenced primarily by people whose character we can come to know for ourselves, by our parents, friends, neighbors, pastors, and teachers; our moral attitudes now come under the influence of a few dozen script writers who live thousands of miles away from us and whom we do not know personally. We are not familiar with the characters, actions, and lives out of which their ethical judgments and moral displays arise.

Through the technologies of appearance, we have ventured onto a new, open sea, one that is truly "our" sea because we can do so much to shape the appearances it takes on for us.[16] This moral and political situation is only in its early stages. The radio was invented within the century that is now drawing to a close and photography was introduced only a few decades earlier. In the present century, the artificial fabrication of appearances has taken hold on an unprecedented scale. Before this time there were pictures and spoken and written words, but there were no means of shaping and storing appearances mechanically or electronically. Now we have many ways of reproducing images and words; what developments will occur in future centuries in the handling of appearance? What will be the effect of this proliferation of appearance on our way of being?

16. Nietzsche, *The Gay Science*, 280.

We must remember that underlying all the public and artifactual treatments of appearance is the human power of imagination, that mental space in which each of us has his own store of manifestations, the memories and images that make up so much of our private selves. Our imagination seemed resilient enough when it had to deal with simple pictures and spoken or written words, but what will it do in the face of global networks and large industries that fabricate appearances? The whole point of all these industries is to get into our imaginations, to fill up the repositories of mental space. The purpose of these industries is not just to deliver an image to a screen, but to make the image reverberate in the imagination of people; that is why the image is a rhetorical device. Can our imagination hold up under these new conditions, or will we be turned inside out by them? What sort of upbringing will be possible, and what sort of agency will we be capable of? How will our emotions be shaped? Eva Brann, in a recent book on the imagination, states the view that once "food and shelter are assured, nothing matters to feeling and intellect, to private happiness and well being, as do well-stocked memories."[17] We do indeed dwell with the things we dwell on, and we can become corrupted if we store depraved things within ourselves; we are morally obliged to store our imagination with things worthy of contemplation. But how much choice will people have in the future about what they store within themselves, and what sort of strength will we need to be able to shape our own imagination, as well as the imaginations of those who depend on us, with forms that are worthy of human life and thought?

Some of these comments might seem alarmist. One might respond to them by saying that no one really thinks that there are only words or images; no one would think his hunger could be assuaged by a picture of a sandwich or a speech about food. But

17. Brann, *The World of the Imagination*, 5. Brann presents herself as an advocate for the imaginative life (p. 791) and speaks of the imagination as "a home within" (p. 796). She says that "the proper memorial participation of the imagination in action is not in the mode of nostalgia but of renascence" (p. 797).

certainly there is a widespread belief that we can redefine what a family is, or what men and women are, or what education or politics is, by refashioning our grammar and changing the way we speak. And hours of watching television every week will certainly influence the understanding people have of human emotion and action. On a more formal level, simply being exposed to a computer terminal for a large part of one's life will incline at least some people to think that things really happen there; as John Perry Barlow said about his computer, "It was the one place I found I could really manipulate reality."[18] If we begin to spend more time in artificial perception than we do in responding to things themselves, both our imaginations and our characters will show the effect.

In this moral and political situation, thinking about appearances is of more than merely academic interest. It is necessary to show philosophically that appearances are not all there is. It is necessary to show that in the many appearances that occur to us, beings are manifested; there are not just appearances, there are things that appear in them. These things have forms and natures, which appear to us when we think about what we perceive. Until now, the modern quest to master nature has been satisfied to work with technological improvements on nature itself: we have been able to make light and heat available where there were darkness and cold, we have been able to make it easy to move quickly from one place to another, we have been able to heal disease when the body could not manage to do so by itself. But now, with our informational and imaging technologies, with artificial viewing and artificial hearing and artificial intelligence, we may like to think that we can master nature on a deeper, more subtle level; we may become exhilarated by the thought that we can change the way the world is simply by changing our words and images. But sooner or later nature will assert itself against our attempt to say and image what it should be, just as it asserts itself from time to time against our engineer-

---

18. Quoted in Bromberg, "In Defense of Hackers," 48.

ing and medicine. Nature's way of reasserting itself, moreover, is not always gentle. As a scientist once put it in another context, "Mother Nature is a mean bastard. She always collects. The only question is who pays and when. She always collects."[19]

D

We have described several features of modernity: human beings are understood as self-conscious thinking things isolated from the world and from one another, mind is isolated from body and reason from sensation, and our individual freedom and spontaneity have fewer and fewer limitations. It is hard to decide which of the ideas in this network come first and which are derived. The ideas that make up an understanding of the whole come as a package, and it is difficult to determine logical priorities among them: do we assert our unrestricted individual freedom because we understand ourselves to be isolated from nature and the world, or do we understand ourselves as so isolated because we want to assert our freedom? Does the epistemology depend on the voluntarism or the voluntarism on the epistemology? It is hard to say. Furthermore, it is possible that the ideas that we explicitly formulate are themselves derived from other ideas that are hidden from us. But whether or not we can map the logical derivation of these understandings, we can see that one of the central thoughts in this network is the conviction that each of us exists as an isolated consciousness, that we do not begin with a common world. This is the point at which the phenomenological critique of modernity is made.

How is this central issue of modernity, this "egocentric predicament," to be resolved? Once we get into the isolated consciousness, how do we get out of it? At first glance, it might seem that we should boldly accept the challenge of modernity on its own terms. We should manfully take on the problem of the external world: we should concede that first and foremost

19. Quoted in Rosenthal, *At the Heart of the Bomb*, 215.

we know our ideas, then we should prove that through these ideas we do in fact reach the real world. But such a head-on strategy is doomed to failure. Once we lock ourselves into a mental cabinet we can never get out of it. There is no way we can prove that we can reach "the external world." The very problem is meaningless and terms like "the external world" and "extramental reality" are incoherences. What is the opposite to "the external world"? What sort of "internal world" is the external one distinguished from? The "problem of the real world" is not a problem at all. If there is a real problem here, it is the question of how the problem could have arisen in the first place: that is, it is not a problem about the real world, but a problem about the problem of the real world.

Instead of trying to face "the problem of the real world" head-on, what we can do to resolve this issue is to make a series of distinctions in how we talk about the world and the things in it. We must distinguish three points of view: (1) We first experience things and begin to speak about them directly, articulating things and features and relationships. This discourse is our naive, world-directed discourse. (2) We then reflect on the things and features and relationships we have identified; we distinguish the substantial from the accidental, the essential from the contingent, the stable from the moving, and the like. This form of speaking is ontological speech. It is reflective discourse. (3) Finally, we can speak about things *insofar as they are experienced and spoken about*, that is, insofar as they present themselves to us or are intended by us in the various modes achieved in (1) and (2). This third form of discourse is phenomenological. In it we describe the various ways things can be intended in their presence and in their absence; the various ways they can be perceived, identified, articulated, imaged, remembered, and scientifically explained; the way stability and change are given, the way the essential and the coincidental are distinguished, and the like. Now, one of the ways in which things can be intended is as merely supposed, as merely proposed by a speaker. When things are so intended, they are taken as ideas or as concepts or as propositions. To formulate concepts or to have ideas or to grasp propositions is one way of being in the world, one way of intending things, one way of allowing things to present themselves to us.[20] It is not to have an image or substitute or representation for the world immediately given to us in privacy and immanence.

What occurs in the epistemology of modernity is that the way things are proposed to be is taken to be a kind of internal mental representation of the things. The things that are referred to and articulated by speakers are projected as such into the mind or into the brain as intermediary entities. What was one of the ways of "being outside" is made to exist "inside" us. Then the problem arises as to how we can get through these substantialized internal entities and reach the "real" world. But the internal entities are just postulated in the mind through a philosophical confusion; they are not discovered there. They are the result of a highly artificial, constructed way of thinking about things. They are never *given*, they are only posited. The epistemological dilemmas of modernity are the result of self-deception, not a problem given to us by nature or experience. The full unraveling of the modern way of ideas would require that we work through many distinctions in regard to perception, thinking, speech, imaging, remembering, and the other forms of intentionality or presentation that occur when things are given to us. It would involve a careful treatment of the many ways in which things can be absent to us and yet intended, in their absence, as the same things that can also be present to us. Carrying out such analyses will gradually help us realize that the "problem of the real world" or "the egocentric predicament" is not a problem or a predicament at all, only a difficulty we had talked ourselves into having. The "problem" is not solved but dissolved.

In classical philosophy, the distinction between what we have marked out as (2) ontological discourse and what we have marked out as (3) phenomenological discourse may not have been drawn very clearly. The two enterprises were treated together: the study of the being of things was generally also the study of their manifestation; the ambiguity of the word *eidos* is an indication of this failure to distinguish. The word means the substantial form of things (a principle in ontology) and also the appearance, the "look" of things (a factor in phenomenology). One of the benefits we can draw from modernity is a sharper distinction between these two forms of reflective thought.

The main purpose of phenomenology, however, is not the negative and tedious task of dealing with the misguided epistemology of modernity. Its task is much more positive: it is to clarify the various forms of appearance, to show how various things can manifest themselves to us, to examine what we must be and what we must do to allow manifestation to occur, to show how reason and logic arise out of perception, to examine how speech and communication occur and what images and memories are, and the like. It is illuminating and gratifying to know such things. By knowing them we come to a deeper appreciation of being and to a deeper understanding of ourselves both as datives of manifestation and as agents in a shared world.

E

The theology of disclosure should also be seen as a positive reflective activity. There are many themes that can be explored by this way of thinking: the way language functions in both Scripture and the sacraments, the way both words and grammar are adjusted in Christian discourse to allow for analogy, the manner in which Christian religious action differs from simply ethical conduct. All the particular issues in theology depend, however, on a central issue of disclosure, on the new perspective on the world that is introduced in Christianity. All the particular issues presuppose the Christian distinction between the world and God, the new understanding of the divine that is introduced in biblical belief. They all presuppose this background belief, but they each also add nuances and dimensions to it. All these issues are, of course, also studied in ontological theology, but they can be clarified in another way by phenomenological reflection. The examination of how they come to light helps to bring out their nature and helps make clear what they are.

A topic that has been especially prominent in phenomenology has been the theme of absence. Philosophers have always been aware of the dimension of absence, but phenomenology provides a more systematic analysis of it than had been achieved in the past. Absence is a particularly important theme in the understanding of human existence and in thinking about being. The fact that we can hold the absent in mind is one of the central factors in human intelligence: speaking about absent objects, remembering what was past, anticipating the future, are all central to our constitution as human beings. It is particularly important to note that our ability to identify things (and hence to name them) is the ability to deal with things as both present and absent to us: we recognize that an object can be both present and absent, and yet remain the same; in this way, the object's identity is given to us. Furthermore, such specifically human dispositions as anxiety, regret, hope, and nostalgia depend on our ability to deal with the absent. The power to deal with universals is another form of dealing with the absent. A universal is something that is absent as far as sensible experience goes; it surpasses any individual that is perceptually given to us. Furthermore, the very notion of transcendence is related to absence: to transcend means to go beyond, and this involves some sort of absence. Finally, absence is not just a subjective, merely human issue: it is also a theme in the philosophy of being. Being can be both present and absent to us; being is found in the interplay between presence and absence. When we discuss the absent, we are thinking about being and not just about ourselves.

There are many different kinds of absence: spatial absence, the absence of the past and that of the future, the absence of the minds and emotions of other people, the absence of what we are trying to remember, the absence of what we are trying to learn, the absence of the meaning of an enciphered message or of something written in language we cannot read, the absence that our own emotions can have to us. Each kind of absence is correlated with a distinctive kind of presence and has its own way of being transformed into presence. One of the forms of absence is what we could call the absence of the sacred. The divine has always been understood, even in paganism, to transcend any presentation it makes to us; it is always more than what we can see or possess, and it is more in a way different from the way other things can be more than we perceive at any moment or the manner in which, say, our joy or anger can be more than what we experience in a given episode. This natural absence of the divine is intensified in biblical revelation; the biblical God is radically absent from the world, so much so that he could be if there were no world, but this deep absence enables him as Creator to be even more immanent, through his creative and providential action, to all things, places, times, and events in the world. The interplay of absence and presence is enhanced and transformed in biblical belief, and we who have been chosen to be the datives of this presence and absence, those to whom the identity of this God has been revealed, are exposed to a kind of absence and transcendence beyond those we encounter in our worldly involvements. We ourselves are changed by this transposition of presence and absence. We are stretched into a new context. A new kind of absence (an absence in faith), an expectation of a new kind of presence (in hope), and a new possibility of identification (in charity) are made possible; they are only analogous to the absences, presences, and identifications that occur in our dealings in the world. Christian presence, absence, and identity are subjects for the theology of disclosure, and so are their differentiation from the forms of presentation that occur within the world. They are among the positive issues for us to think about as faith seeks an understanding appropriate for our day and age.

Still another theme that is prominent in phenomenology is the issue of the whole. Husserl referred to this topic as the issue of the world or the world-horizon. The correlate to the world as a phenomenon is what he calls fundamental belief (*Urglaube* or *Urdoxa*), the basic attitude we have toward the whole as such. This attitude is not just one opinion or one particular conviction among others, just as the world is not just one object among others. All particular cognitions are embedded as partial opinions and partial understandings within the whole, but the "belief" about the whole cannot be like any partial belief. It has special features that must be brought to light, and the whole has features that are different from those of any part of the whole. They too must be brought to light in a philosophical analysis.

It is in the context of the whole and its presentation to us that the issue of Creation arises, as well as the sense of the divinity that creates the whole. Even in pagan religion, the divine is related to the whole. The divine is not just one thing we encounter; it is the preeminent part, the part that calls up a concern with the whole. The divine is the most favored part of the whole.[21] As human beings we have a sense of the whole and take a stance toward it, and whatever we call "divine" awakens that stance within us. Biblical revelation adjusts our understanding of and our stance toward the whole, and it does so in a way that surpasses anything that our own powers could have achieved. It "breaks" the whole. It asserts that the whole that is given to us need not have been, and that the divine, which is no longer a mere part of the world, not even the most awesome or excellent part, could have been even without the whole. Such a revelation comes through hearing and not through perceptions.

All these themes concerning the whole and how it is presented to us, including the theme of the special form of presence and absence at work in regard to the whole, as well as the special form of presence and absence at work in the biblical revelation concerning the world and God, are themes for the theology of disclosure. How these things manifest themselves to us,

21. The phrase "the most favored part of the whole" is from the essay by Patzig, "Theology and Ontology in Aristotle's *Metaphysics*," 40–41.

how our language has to be adjusted to accommodate them, how we experience, believe, understand, hope, and act in response to them, are all issues for this form of theological reflection.

A word might be said about the method used in our analysis of appearance. One of the central forms of thinking used in phenomenology is the activity of making distinctions. Working with distinctions is a much more strategic part of philosophy than is usually recognized. It is not just that we declare that one thing is not another—perception is not intellection; emotion is not action—but that we dwell on such distinctions: we belabor them, we work them out, we make them clearer and more vivid. When we make and work with distinctions, we do something that is more basic than giving proofs, because proofs depend on premises. Making distinctions is the procedure that yields premises. It gets at the fundamentals of argument by working one thing off against another and showing that necessarily this one thing is not that other. Distinctions are the tools of the philosophical trade. To work out, for example, the truth that action is not the same as production and also not the same as labor, that the political life is not the same as the economic life, that responsible action is not the same as compelled behavior, that choice is not chance—to work out all such things is to disclose each of them and to make them clear in their nature and their necessity. This is the kind of thinking and speaking or writing that is proper to philosophy; philosophy does contain argument, but primarily it is concerned with working out distinctions, not with proving conclusions on the basis of premises.

Moreover, besides being fundamental, the activity of making distinctions is always energetic. It is never routine. We do not just repeat statements. When we work out how *this* is not *that*, we are always overcoming a confusion and bringing something to light. There is a kind of built-in resistance to boredom in the making of distinctions, provided the listener or reader is able and willing to put himself into the state of perplexity that calls for the distinction, provided one gets the point of the issue that is at hand.

The theology of disclosure also works with distinctions. Because it tries to get to ultimate religious issues, theology must work with distinctions; it tries to get to the point where one must work out the elementary fact that *this* is not *that*. It tries to preserve the integrity of things like the Incarnation, grace, the Bible, the sacraments, the Church, by preventing them from being simply identified with things that are like them and with which they run the danger of being confused: gods taking on human form, inspiration, religious writings, worldly signs and symbols, human communities. Behind all these more particular distinctions, the theology of disclosure is especially concerned with the Christian distinction between the world and God, the distinction that establishes the religious and theological space within which all the other Christian distinctions can come to light. This preeminent Christian distinction must strive to prevent the Christian sense of divinity from being confused with natural senses of the divine, and it must also prevent the Christian sense of the world from being confused with the sense of the world as the ultimate matrix of things. This Christian distinction is always energetic and always needs to be worked out and worked through, because we have a permanent propensity to take the whole as ultimate and to see the divine as part of the whole. Revelation was needed to bring the Christian distinction to light, and grace and a continued response to grace are continuously necessary to keep it alive for us. Although it is the central theme for theological thinking, the Christian distinction between the world and God must first be lived in faith before it can be reflected on theologically. Theology confirms and protects the distinction; it does not engender it.

A final issue in which phenomenology can be of help in theological discussion can be found in the treatment of the symbolic character of the Eucharist. Many recent writers on the Eucharist observe that an important change in the concept of symbolism occurred in the transition between the Patristic period and the Middle Ages. For the Fathers of the Church and for the ancient world generally, a symbol did not only signify something; it also was thought to participate in that thing and to make it concretely present. The symbolic was not contrasted with the real. This symbolic realism is said to have been especially characteristic of Platonism and Neoplatonism. In the Middle Ages, however, the symbolic is said to have become distinguished from and even separated from the real; if something were taken as symbolic, it was considered to be merely symbolic and not real. The difficulties in the eucharistic theology of Berengarius of Tours, for example, are said to have followed from this separation. From that point on to the present day, we have been left with an unfortunate alternative: either a symbolic or a real presence.[22]

In this issue, the core problem is how the world is presented to us and how we are datives for its manifestation. It is the problem of intentionality and presentation. For modernity, not only the symbolic but even the perceived needs to be restored; it is not only symbolism that is deprived of any real presence, but perception as well.[23] Only when the notion of form in nature has been recovered can the symbolic be understood in a more positive sense. Furthermore, a historical analysis of the problem is not sufficient; it is not enough simply to record what the ancients or the Fathers thought about symbolism and to point out the difference between us and them, since such a historical study would simply leave us with the fact that we think differently than they did. A philosophical resolution is necessary; the ancient sense of the symbolic cannot be taken seriously again so

22. These considerations have been presented in Rahner, "The Theology of the Symbol," 243, 251; Shmemann, The Eucharist, 223; O'Neill, Sacramental Realism, 97–101; Léon-Dufour, Sharing the Eucharistic Bread, 10, 128, 289–95; Congar, in his introduction to Marliangeas, Clés pour une théologie du ministère, 6–7. The issue is extensively developed in Crockett, Eucharist: Symbol of Transformation, 80–89, 107–17, 232–34. Crockett, Congar, and many others refer to Harnack in making this point about ancient and modern symbolism; see Dix, The Shape of the Liturgy, 256. Crockett, toward the end of his book (pp. 236–51), describes some elements of a "recovery of the symbolic" in contemporary thinking. He uses many authors, such as Cassirer, Langer, Ricoeur, Eliade, Weber, Durkheim, Marx, Bellah, and Gilkey, as well as many approaches, such as the philosophical, psychological, and sociological, in addition to the theological.

23. For a lively discussion of this modern dilemma in regard to literature, art, and culture generally, see Steiner, Real Presences.

long as the only things we think we have present to us are signs referring to other signs.

Moreover, the modern move into a purely formal sense of the symbolic is not only a loss of something important; it is also a development of a powerful new type of intentionality without which modern science would not be possible. Any recovery of a richer sense of religious symbolism would have to acknowledge the value of purely formal signs.

F

When we speak of disclosure, we generally think that it is the disclosure of some thing or some sort of thing. For example, dinosaurs, electrical currents, politics, Leif Ericson or George Bush, the city of Chicago are all things or kinds of things that are disclosed to us in their various ways. But besides such disclosures of things, there is also a disclosure of dimensions, the disclosure of formal modes of presentation. Such disclosures are more subtle and more strategic than the manifestation of any particular sort of thing. Suppose, for instance, that we had never encountered the sense of being a picture, and then picturing were suddenly disclosed to us. It is not that we come across some new thing; rather, a form of presentation arises for us and consequently the whole world, and everything in it, begins to look different. It opens a prospect. Some things can now be taken as pictures of others, and, more universally, practically all things now become picturable. It is not just that there are now pictures among the things we know; it is that everything takes on the capacity to be pictured. The introduction of the new dimension changes the way everything seems. It bestows a bonus on everything we can experience.

There is a dramatic record of the disclosure of a dimension in the well-known story of Helen Keller's discovery of what words are. Stricken by an illness eighteen months after her birth, Helen Keller became deaf, blind, and apparently unable to speak. She grew to the age of seven "unable to utter a word," as

Van Wyck Brooks writes, "unable even to comprehend that words were related to things or that words existed."[24] In response to her parents' appeals, a teacher was selected for her, Anne Sullivan, a young woman who had worked at the Perkins Institution in Boston, a training school for the blind. As part of her teaching, Anne tried to spell words into Helen's hand, but Helen could not appreciate them as words. Finally there occurred the famous incident "when Anne held Helen's hand under the spout in the pump-house [and] she connected the word 'water' with the cool stream, realizing for the first time that things had names and that the manual alphabet was the key to them all."[25] It dawned on Helen that Anne's fingers moving in her hand made a sign of the water; it was not just a touch, but a touch with meaning and reference. She also realized immediately that there were signs or names for everything, and that everything was signable or nameable. Everything, including all the things she had already known, could be named. This was the disclosure of a dimension, not just the manifestation of a new thing.

There are many such presentational dimensions in being.[26] Naming and the nameable, viewing and the viewable, picturing and the picturable, remembering and the rememberable, articulation and the articulatable, predication and the predicable are only some of the dimensions of intentionality and the pre-

24. Brooks, Helen Keller. Sketch for a Portrait, 11. See also Keller, The Story of My Life, 21–24, and see the letters of Anne Sullivan describing Helen's insight into words and her account of the word-play that had gone on before. The need for a personal relationship and for teaching and listening as prior conditions for the emergence of words is worthy of note. For a more recent account of these incidents, see Lash, Helen and Teacher. The Story of Helen Keller and Anne Sullivan Macy.

25. Brooks, Helen Keller, 14.

26. The concept of a presentational dimension can be illustrated as follows. When we claim that the institutional narrative in the Eucharist quotes the words of Christ, someone might object that different versions of the words of Christ are to be found in the various synoptic, Pauline, and liturgical traditions; which of these, if any, are the words we ought to quote? Such an objection would miss the point. It is not so much the exact content as the form of quotation that is at issue. Even if I were to be inexact or incorrect when I quote someone, I am still engaged in quotation as such. The diversity of verbal traditions does not destroy the form or dimension of quotation, which is what the theology of disclosure is interested in.

sentability and representability of things. These forms of presentation are the focus of phenomenological reflection. When we say that in phenomenology we examine the structures of intentionality, we mean that such presentational dimensions become the theme of our interest.

The Christian disclosure of God as Creator is also a disclosure of a dimension. It is not simply the manifestation of something that had been unknown and hidden; it is also the introduction of a new mode of presentation. We will try to clarify this disclosure, and we will do so by working with analogies from our worldly experience.

One dimension of disclosure in the world is that of "intersubjective experience." As we experience things, we realize, with greater and greater finesse, that the things we experience are also given to other datives of manifestation, other centers of awareness. We gradually differentiate between our view on things and the views others have. It is not that we just become aware of other cognitive beings and differentiate ourselves from them; it is that the things we know take on a new dimension as we see them as also seeable by others. The child does not only recognize its mother; it also becomes aware that the things it sees are also seen by the mother. Things become enhanced in their viewability, in the manifold of ways in which they can be manifested. Their identity also becomes enhanced, since there is more identity to them when they are known to be seen from viewpoints other than the one we have. We come to see this dimension of intersubjective presentability in them.

The natural belief in the gods adds a new dimension analogous to that of worldly intersubjectivity. In the naturally religious attitude we take the world and the things in it as not only presented to and known by human beings, but also presented to and known by the gods. We appreciate things as being seen from that special detached point of view that the poets and ancient theologians, those who told stories about the gods, attributed to the divine spectators and agents. We also take ourselves as presented to these divine beings; we think of ourselves and others as subject to their choices and judgments. The gods see things in a way we do not; they take in things that are hidden from us and they see without the distortions that always keep us blinded in some degree. As Agamemnon says in an attempt to defend himself against Achilleus:

> Yet what could I do? It is the god who accomplishes all things.
> Delusion is the elder daughter of Zeus, the accursed
> who deludes all; her feet are delicate and they step not
> on the firm earth, but she walks the air above men's heads
> and leads them astray. She has entangled others before me.[27]

But being finite and only part of the world, even the gods can be hindered in what they know. Agamemnon continues:

> Yes, for once Zeus even was deluded, though men say
> he is the highest one of gods and mortals.[28]

The Christian understanding of God is not merely the acceptance of the pagan dimension of divine presentation, not merely the introduction of a new divinity in the place of the older gods. It is a transformation of the pagan religious viewpoint, the introduction of a new dimension beyond that of the pagans. Christianity is different from paganism not just because it believes in a deeper sense of divinity, but also because this deeper sense of divinity entails a kind of presentational dimension in the world that is different from the dimension correlated with the pagan gods. As Creator, the biblical God is more detached from the world than are the pagan gods, but he is also more immanent to it, since the world could not be except through his creative and concurrent power. What sort of "intuition" of things does God have? He does not perceive in any way that is familiar to us, and yet as Creator of all things he knows them not only in their universal form but also in their individuality. He knows them as the cause of their being, and he is, as St. Au-

27. *Iliad*, 19 lines 90–94. Taken from *The Iliad of Homer*, translated by Richard Lattimore.

28. *Iliad*, 19 lines 95–96. See Prufer, "Providence and Imitation: Sophocles's *Oedipus* and Aristotle's *Poetics*," on the analogies between the viewpoint of the gods and the viewpoints of the writer and the spectator of drama.

gustine says, *interior intimo meo*: more intimate to me than my own inwardness.[29] Appreciating things and ourselves in this way is made possible not simply by the belief in a being that had been hidden and unknown, but by the introduction of a new presentational possibility. The being of the Christian God brings with it a new presentational mode. The world and everything in it are now understood as capable of being seen from a new point of view, that of the transcendent Creator.

If the intersubjective dimension enhances the identity and being of things, how much more does this divine perspective strengthen them in our eyes? The world and the things in it are now seen as being known and chosen to be by the Creator. We ourselves cannot, of course, adopt the divine point of view, but in faith we can formulate something of what it is, and we can see the world as subject to it. The theology of disclosure strives to bring out the special features of this dimension, this form of presentation, which is one of the constitutive elements in the theological virtues of faith, hope, and charity. Reflection on the act of faith, for example, must take into account how the God we believe in is presented or represented to us, and also how we understand the world and ourselves to be presented to him.

We should also observe that the revelation of this new dimension is often at work as a kind of subtext or overtone in many passages in Scripture. Very often we will read that some particular event is being described or some course of action is being exhorted, but besides this explicit content, something implicit is being conveyed. For example, in I Corinthians 4:1–5, St. Paul says that he is not concerned about being judged by any human tribunal and that he does not even judge himself; he will be judged only by the Lord. The direct sense of this text is Paul's independence of human judgment and his desire to be judged favorably by God. It is an edifying text. But the subtext or implicit message is that God does indeed judge, that God knows and judges his creatures and his elect, and that we *can* be judged by

29. St. Augustine, *Confessiones*, Book 3, §5.

him alone, even beyond any human judgment. This more meta-physical implication is also part of what is stated in the text, and such implicit teachings about God and his nature run through the entire Bible, even when the text is speaking about other things. When the Scriptures tell us about the *magnalia Dei*, the great interventions of God, the deepest part of this revelation is not simply that God has done these things, but that he exists and that he is of such a nature that he can do them. When they tell us that we should put our faith and hope in God, they im-plicitly reveal that he is such that we *can* believe and hope in him and love him in this unqualified way. The possibilities that the Scripture disclose are even more important than the facts that they report and the commandments they enjoin.

G

Since the issue of appearances has been so prominent in modern thought, it is not surprising that many theologians have addressed it in various ways. For example, Étienne Gilson has claimed that Newman's *Grammar of Assent* is "a first sketch of what philosophers would today call a phenomenology of religious belief," and Karl Rahner has called for a "theology of symbols," which would of course involve reflection on the mode of presen-tation of theological things.[30] At the end of this chapter on the theology of disclosure, we will discuss briefly the work of a con-temporary theologian, Hans Urs von Balthasar, whose writings we have often cited in this book. We turn to him as an example of someone who has made the issue of appearance a predominant theological concern.

Von Balthasar's major work is a multivolume series made up of three parts, entitled, respectively, *Herrlichkeit*, *Theodramatik*, and *Theologik*. The first part has been translated into English as *The*

---

30. Gilson, "Introduction" to Newman's *Grammar of Assent*, 20; see also page 21. Karl Rahner, "The Theology of the Symbol." Bouyer mentions the importance of phenomenology for the theological work of Edith Stein, Sister Teresa-Benedict of the Cross; see his trenchant remarks in *The Christian Mystery*, 258–59, 266.

Glory of the Lord. Its subtitle is *A Theological Aesthetic.*[31] The word "aesthetic" is meant to be taken in the sense of the Greek *aisthēsis*, perception or experience. *Aisthēsis* does not mean brute sense experience; it does not mean having sequences of sounds and color patches flash before us, as suggested by some epistemological theories. An *aisthēsis* is something larger and more identifiable. For example, when a person visits Budapest he can be said to have an *aisthēsis* of that city; it is the way he takes in the city, the way the city shows itself to him, and the way he lets the city appear to him. When someone is involved in an angry exchange with another person, he can be said to have had an *aisthēsis* of that-person-as-angry, or perhaps of anger as such. The theological "aesthetic" that von Balthasar writes about is an account of how the divine is manifested, how it presents itself to us. Von Balthasar is primarily concerned with the manifestation of the biblical God, but in *Herrlichkeit* he also speaks about how the divine was manifested in nonbiblical times and places and he uses this presentation as a contrast with biblical revelation. The study of how the divine is manifested comes before or is prior to the study of its more conceptual expression in "speculative" theology.

The German word *Herrlichkeit* is translated as "glory" in English. It is a modern term used to convey the meaning of the Greek word *doxa*, which was used in the Bible to translate the Hebrew *kabod*, the manifestation of God to the world and to his people. But the divine glory is not merely a supreme version of worldly beauty.[32] God's glory is a beauty that is awesome and majestic and close to terrifying. God's grandeur is at times present in his actions for his people, but it also conceals itself with a kind of absence that is like no other deprivation: the presence of God makes the loss of God possible; grace brings the possibility of refusal. The abandonment of Christ on the cross is the extreme form of this divine hiddenness.

---

31. Von Balthasar, *The Glory of the Lord. A Theological Aesthetic.* This work has been translated into English in 7 volumes.

32. See the remark on distinguishing "between the beauty of the world and the divine glory" in von Balthasar, "The Grandeur of the Liturgy," 349, n. 2.

Von Balthasar says that theology should be approached from the viewpoint of the "third transcendental," beauty. Without the presence of beauty the other two transcendentals—truth and goodness—as well as being itself are destabilized. "In a world without beauty" truth loses its power to convince ("the very conclusions are no longer conclusive") and the good loses its power to attract ("For this too is a possibility, and even the more exciting one: why not investigate Satan's depths?").[33] The deepest "motivations" to be good are the attraction of the beautiful or the noble, in which we participate when we are good, and the repulsion of the ugly and the ignoble, which attaches itself to vice; these are stronger motives for virtuous action as such than are any rewards or punishments or consequences that might follow upon what we do. The beautiful is not the "merely aesthetic": it is the admirable, and it completes the good and the true.[34] The admirable does not exist except in display; it involves both perception and enchantment, so the theme of disclosure is built into it.

In his meditations on the grandeur of God, von Balthasar makes use of categories that are usually not found in theological treatises; in one of the volumes of *Theodramatik*, for example, he develops an extended comparison between the dramatic art and the action of God. The concept of person is related to the roles played by actors, the functions of playwright and producer are used to illuminate the divine plan and its execution, the role of the audience and the public character of drama are taken into account, and so on.[35] These would all be just so many brilliant metaphors if they were to be taken in a strictly ontological theology, but if theology is to consider the way things manifest themselves, the use of such categories from the domain of the theater can become analogies and not mere metaphors. All such categories work in the element of display, presentation, representation, and concealment, and if theology

33. Von Balthasar, *The Glory of the Lord*, 1:19.
34. On the admirable see Sokolowski, *Moral Action*, 186–89.
35. Von Balthasar, *Theodramatik*, 1:230–449.

begins to focus on the manner in which the divine reveals itself in biblical faith and in the actions and events associated with that faith, the use of these terms can become more than simple rhetorical tropes. Theology can find resources in dimensions of the world it has too long neglected.[36]

36. Thus, in *Theodramatik*, 1:17, von Balthasar says that the theater, with the light it sheds on human existence, provides "an instrumentarium (Instrumentar) that has heretofore been hardly noticed by theology." See also p. 230. *Theodramatik* is made up of 4 volumes: *Prolegomena, Die Personen des Spiels* (which could be translated *Dramatis Personae*), *Die Handlung* (*The Action* or *The Plot*), and *Das Endspiel* (*The Final Act* or *Endgame*). Studies of manifestation abound throughout von Balthasar's works, not only in his theological writings but in his sermons as well. For a particularly good example, see his sermon on the Transfiguration, "What Is Required in Witnesses," in *You Crown the Year with Your Goodness*, 58–64, where he speaks of believers who will simply contemplate the divine goodness, witnessing to the divine display or *doxa*: "The 'one thing necessary' is for people to bear witness to the glory of God's love for the world, witnessing through adoration and adoring through witness" (p. 63).

14

⁂

CONCLUDING REFLECTIONS

IN THIS final chapter we will review some of the salient aspects of Christian eucharistic faith. We will try to bring out the understanding of ourselves and of being that is proposed by such faith, particularly in contrast with the secular understanding found in our contemporary world. We will discuss (a) how the Eucharist is involved in time and (b) how its embodiment in bread and wine calls forth an appropriate response from us. We will then consider the deeper context that underlies eucharistic faith. As a step toward this deeper context, (c) we will first describe three nonbiblical attitudes human beings can have toward themselves and toward the whole of things. Using these three as foils, (d) we will describe the Christian understanding of ourselves and the world. Finally, (e) we will close with some remarks about the Eucharist and the theological virtues of faith, hope, and charity.

A

The Eucharist brings to the fore the temporal character of human existence. It engages the various dimensions of time. It stresses the distance between present and past by recalling events that, in their worldly sense, are now completed and absent: the death of Jesus, the Last Supper, the Exodus, the Passover. The Eucharist makes these events present to us in their respective manners: the death of Christ is reenacted, its anticipation at the Last Supper is quoted, its prefigurement in the Exodus and Passover is implied. The Eucharist makes these events present to us, but it also brings their pastness, their temporal distance from us, to the fore. We know that they occurred originally at other times and in other places, not in our time and place. The Eucharist, as a sacramental sign, represents temporal contexts that are not our own. It draws us into those contexts and takes us out of the time and place in which we live. The distance between those contexts and ours is an essential feature of eucharistic representation. The reality of time and the density of the differences that time introduces are conditions for eucharistic action. If it did not bridge a temporal span, the Eucharist would not be a sacramental sign.

But the Eucharist activates the dimensions of time in a still deeper way. Besides displacing us into the past, it also turns us toward the end of time and to its beginning. It anticipates the final coming of the kingdom of God and it recalls the act of Creation, the first of the saving actions of God. In calling up these more remote limits of time, the Eucharist displaces us into contexts that are even more foreign to our own than are the irretrievably past contexts of Calvary, the Last Supper, the Passover, and the Exodus. These, although far from us in time, took place in the flow of time in which we exist, but the contexts of the end and the beginning of time have little in common with the settings in which we live. What such an end and beginning might mean is opaque to us: every event we can imagine is a successor and predecessor to some other event. We can imagine only events that take place in the course of time. Acts that mark the beginning and the end of time are beyond our experience.

Indeed, the contexts of the beginning and the end of time call forth for us the context in which there is no time, the context of the eternal life of God, who could be and live in undiminished goodness and greatness even if there were no time, and nothing at all in time. Only against this context of eternity can the idea of the beginning and the end of time make sense. Time and the world can begin and end only as profiled against the timeless being of God. In calling to mind the act of Creation and the final coming of God's kingdom, the Eucharist also represents the eternally active life of God, the life that is beyond time, the life of the Holy Trinity, within which the redemptive action of the death and Resurrection of Jesus was decided upon as "a plan for the fullness of times" (Ephesians 1:10). It is a life that was imaged in the world by the filial obedience of Jesus, the Son of God, and it is imaged again in the sacramental pledge or earnest of eternal glory.

It was only after the Resurrection and Ascension of Jesus that the disciples appreciated fully who and what he was. Although his divinity was present to them during his lifetime, it was fully recognized as such only in his absence, when the Holy Spirit enlightened their minds to understand what they had experienced. Jesus had promised them, "The Advocate, the holy Spirit that the Father will send in my name—he will teach you everything and remind you of all that [I] told you" (John 14:26). The Holy Spirit taught and reminded them of these things in the absence of Christ, when his presence had become past; a deeper grasp of the truth of Christ became possible when he was no longer with those who believed in him. As St. Leo the Great says in his magnificent sermons on the Ascension, "The visible presence of our Redeemer has passed over into sacraments; and that faith might be more excellent and more firm, vision has given way to doctrine."[1] He continues, "Then, dearly beloved, the Son of Man was more perfectly and more sacredly revealed as the Son of God when he returned to the glory of his Father's majesty, and in a mysterious way he began to be more present in his divinity as he became more distant in his humanity." Faith and Christian

---

1. St. Leo the Great, "Sermon II on the Ascension," in Migne, *Patrologia Latina*, 54:398.

understanding increased as perception ended: "Then faith gained greater insight and by a leap of the mind began to reach out to the Son as equal to the Father, and no longer needed contact with Christ's bodily substance, by which he is less than the Father." These same thoughts were expressed earlier by St. Ignatius of Antioch: "Our God Jesus Christ is within the Father, and so he appears all the more clearly."[2] It would seem that the full revelation of the divinity of Christ, of his equality with the Father, required his bodily absence, and required that his incarnate presence be given as past. Although the first concern of our Christian reflection is the truth that Christ in his divine nature is the equal of the Father, a further theme for our theological reflection can be the manner in which this equality is disclosed to us, in its mixture of presence and absence.

The interplay of mental presence and bodily absence, and of temporal present and past, occurs in a different way in the Eucharist. The Mass involves both words and actions. The liturgy of the word, in the reading of Scripture, calls to mind the past actions of God, while the liturgy of the Eucharist makes the past action of God present again: what had been reported in words can now be registered in its sacramental presence.[3] The liturgy of the Eucharist endows the action of God with a bodily presence, but with a presence that is sacramental, not natural. Thus, although the Eucharist bodily reenacts the culminating action of God, the death and Resurrection of Jesus, it does so with a kind of distance, the kind that occurs as the event is reenacted under the appearances of bread and wine.

This sacramental embodiment does more than to materialize God's saving action; precisely by materializing God's action, the Eucharist brings his action into the present. Although the primary focus of the sacramental action is away from the present, toward the past death and Resurrection of Christ and toward the

2. St. Ignatius of Antioch, "Letter to the Romans," in Migne, *Patrologia Graeca*, 5:689–90.
3. On the concepts of registration and report, see Sokolowski, *Presence and Absence*, 7–17.

eternal life of God, and although the Eucharist primarily draws us toward these other contexts, the sacramental action also highlights the present moment and the place in which it occurs. The Eucharist embodies and reenacts God's action here and now; it does not get lost in sheer absence and mere symbolism. It engages all the dimensions of time including the present. As Bouyer writes, "The Christian religion is not simply a doctrine, it is a deed, an action; and not an action of the past, but an action of the present in which the past is restored and the future appears."[4]

The Eucharist is able to reenact the past in the present only because it is staged against the context of the eternal life of God, who is the ultimate agent in the sacrament. If worldly time were not transcended by the ever-active moment of eternity, and if Redemption were not an action of the eternal God, the Eucharist would not be able to make the death and Resurrection of Christ truly present again. Only through such eternal life is time sacramentally overcome. Thus the Eucharist is a perpetually renewed reminder not only of the death and Resurrection of Jesus, but also of the transcendence of God. In reenacting our Redemption, the Eucharist calls to mind the horizon within which that Redemption must be understood. If God were not as distinct from the world and its temporality as biblical faith declares him to be, the Eucharist could not be the sacramental sign that we believe it is.

The Eucharist draws us into the new contexts of past, future, and eternity. Our proper place is within the space and time of the world. We are born into time and we know it goes on when we drop out of it. We cannot get away from being here and now, even if we know that there are other points of view, other here-and-nows enjoyed by others like us, and even if we know that there were and will be points of view very distant from ours in time and space: how did things look to some human being dwelling in time some twenty thousand years ago, and how will things look to someone living twenty thousand years

4. Bouyer, Le mystère paschal, 9–10.

hence (assuming that the human race continues that long)? We can transcend our situation and displace ourselves, in imagination and in thought, into other here-and-nows, both near and far, but whenever we do so we never relinquish the grip we have on our privileged here and now (or perhaps we should say we never escape the grip it has on us). Any displacement also retains the placement we have; when displaced, we also stay where we are.

Likewise, when we are displaced by faith and sacramental action into the context of the eternal life of God, we again do not lose the placement we have here and now; we in our current position are made to consider the "position" that has no before or after and that could be, with no lessening of goodness or greatness, even if there had never been a world or time. We are made not only to look up to that context of eternal life, but also to appreciate our own temporal situation, our here-and-now, as it might seem to the eternal God who knows it and acts in it. We and our situation are to be taken by us as presented to a new "point of view." We are to appreciate ourselves as viewed not only from distant reaches of time and space but from eternity. Time-bound as we are, we appreciate this new context and its perspective through the words of faith rather than through our imagination, which provides resources, minimal as they may be, only for sympathy with other moments in time.

Some writers have claimed that mystical experience gives us a sense of such timelessness, and others have said that such experience can be interpreted psychologically: it is a contact we have with the primary process that precedes and underlies the distinctions that generate past, present, and future, as well as subject and object, for us.[5] But if such mystical experience puts us in touch with a kind of timelessness, it is not yet the kind we speak of in regard to the biblical God and the Creator of time. His eternity does not appear as one of the phenomena of the world, not even as the prepredicative basis for all articulation

5. See Loewald, *Psychoanalysis and the History of the Individual*, 53–77; also *Papers on Psychoanalysis*, 138–46.

and thought. At best such worldly appearances can serve as icons of his life.

B

In its bodily form, the Eucharist is so small a thing that it makes an extremely great demand on those who take part in it. In rituals in which the sacrificial action is physically striking, the rite may exercise such a powerful impact on its participants that they may overlook the role they themselves should be playing in it. If bulls are slaughtered as a sacrifice to the gods, the spectacle itself can easily be taken as the substance of the rite; what importance could our own dispositions have in comparison with the scene we witness? The physical event draws all the attention to itself, and the dispositions of those who make the offering seem to pale in comparison. In this regard, the death of Jesus was already a transformation: as the letter to the Hebrews says, Christ "entered once for all into the sanctuary, not with the blood of goats and calves but with his own blood, thus obtaining eternal Redemption" (Hebrews 9:12). It was not that Christ just substituted one kind of bodily sacrifice for another, that he substituted his own blood for that of animals; rather, the blood became more of a vehicle for something beyond itself, for the obedience Jesus showed to the Father. There was shedding of blood in the sacrifice of Christ, but it was the expression of something that went far beyond any simple bodily exchange and physical offering; the shedding of one's own blood, which is the offering of one's own life, cannot be a mere external token as the shedding of an animal's blood might be. As the letter to the Hebrews continues, "For if the blood of goats and bulls and the sprinkling of a heifer's ashes can sanctify those who are defiled so that their flesh is cleansed, how much more will the blood of Christ, who through the eternal spirit offered himself unblemished to God, cleanse our consciences from dead works to worship the living God" (Hebrews 9:13–14). The offering that Christ made of himself is what elevated the shedding of his

blood beyond other sacrifices and made it be the single, definitive sacrifice to the Father.

The eucharistic sacrifice offered by the Church continues this
trajectory from the material of the sacrifice to the obedience of
the one who sacrifices. In the Eucharist, the shedding of the
blood of Christ is replaced by the offering and consumption of
bread and wine. To the bodily eye, the bread and wine are mere
tokens; what material value do they have in comparison with a
fattened calf or the first fruits of a harvest? All the more, in
their triviality, do they call forth the obedience of those who
participate in the sacrifice, the dedication of their lives in union
with the dedication of Christ. If the offering were more spec-
tacular, we could offer less of ourselves.

Furthermore, the response of the Christian to the Eucharist
occurs not only during the moment of the eucharistic celebration itself, but throughout one's life. Jesus, in his passion and
death, was obedient to the will of his Father: he understood
himself as having been sent by the Father, and the configuration
of his mission became clearer to him as his life moved toward its
climax. The redemptive action of Christ revealed to us the
meaning of the transcendence of God: only in the light of the
Incarnation and Redemption did the full biblical sense of God's
transcendence appear. Furthermore, only in that light do we see,
retrospectively, what Creation itself fully means: that it is an act
of sheer generosity, done not out of any need or imperfection, by
the God who could be in undiminished goodness and greatness
even if he had not created. The generosity of the Redemption
sheds light on the generosity of Creation. This is part of the
logic of disclosure in Christian faith.

But if God creates the world and us in this way, then our lives
are led under the providence of God. God's providence was revealed in the history of the people elected in the Old Covenant;
it was fully expressed in the life, death, and Resurrection of Jesus
and further confirmed in the history of the Church. Our own
lives then can be led in obedience to divine providence. It is
shown to us that we can take ourselves as guided by the will of

God, that we can see what occurs to us not merely as the outcome of necessity, chance, and human design, but also as what God has chosen us for. The events of our lives become for us an opportunity before God. Our response to what occurs to us must then involve an element of acceptance, of obedience to God's will. This does not mean that we stop our own deliberation and choice, but it does mean that our own human situation and the actions it calls forth are all to be profiled against the setting of divine providence. To say that we are to obey the will of God is not so much an injunction as a revelation. A new dimension is opened by our understanding of the providential transcendence of God.

The Eucharist expresses this understanding of God and calls forth our obedience to his providence. By reenacting the perfect obedience of the Son, the Eucharist reminds us that we can and should see our own lives as the will of the Father. This eucharistic expression of the acceptance of God's will is further echoed in the evangelical vow of obedience taken by religious, who embody their acceptance of the will of the Father in their obedience to the superiors of their community. For both religious and lay Christians, eucharistic faith is thus expressed in Christian life.

C

The Eucharist presents to us the deeper context of the eternal life of God, but it does so not just as a matter for contemplation. It does not serve simply as an illustration of speculative truth. The Eucharist, embedded in Christian faith, proclaims not just ultimate necessities and final truths, but also salvation. It expresses the redemptive action of God, the Creator of the world. The truth that it manifests is not just the inescapable destiny of things; it expresses what God has done, first by bringing things into being and then by redeeming the most conspicuous part of those things, *hoc genus humanum*, the human race. Finally and more specifically, the Eucharist, when it is celebrated here and now, proclaims the salvation of those who participate in it at that moment. The Eucharist expresses the salvation accomplished by the God who created the world, but in expressing this salvation it also brings to mind the nature of the God who saves. The Eucharist reflects our faith; it implicitly declares how God must be if he is to have created and redeemed in the manner that the Eucharist represents.

Let us dwell for a while on the Christian attitude toward salvation and toward the whole of things. We will compare this Christian attitude with three other attitudes that can be adopted toward salvation and toward the whole: (1) the simply secular attitude; (2) the religious attitude that acknowledges divine agency, but as part of the whole; and (3) the attitude that recognizes a divine principle in the world but philosophically demythologizes it. We have briefly discussed these three understandings in Chapter 10, where they were related to the concept of person and the sense of mission; here they are treated, more fully and in a different order, in regard to salvation.

1. The secular attitude does not recognize divine agency. It is atheistic. For this attitude, the world is simply there, governed by its own internal and natural forces. We as human beings have emerged in this world as effects of its natural elements and powers. Through our scientific exploration we may be able, gradually, to shed light on how we came about and how we depend on the laws of nature for our life and activity. We may, for example, be able to shed light on how genetic structures allow the evolution of more and more complex forms of life and how they have permitted the development of the human organism; we may be able to show how chemical and electrical forces work in our neural systems to permit human behavior, thought, and action. It is likely that we will never know all we would like to know about these matters, but even if we do not find out everything, we can—according to this attitude—continue to believe that the elements and laws of nature suffice to account for our being. We, the human race, are a small clan living together on the earth, placed within an overwhelmingly large universe that

moves along on its mechanical ways with no knowledge or concern regarding us. We are a small and mortal part of this great whole, but despite our size and fragility we are a significant part, one that embodies knowledge and choice and thus surpasses in complexity and dignity all the rest. Even though we are the effect of natural causes, we rise above these causes in our thinking and acting; although natural causes have brought us about, the causes themselves are blind and anonymous. They recognize neither ends nor means, but we establish among ourselves a domain in which we must treat one another as ends and not as means, with respect and with recognition of the dignity we deserve.

In this secular understanding of the world and of ourselves, "salvation" means doing the best we can to become most fully what we are. We save ourselves because there is nothing beyond us that can save. We are here through the forces of nature and the contingencies of evolution, but once here we can in some degree take responsibility for what we become. We can introduce more and more thinking into our lives: instead of rummaging for food we can plant things; instead of being exposed to the elements and to animals that prey on us we can set up shelters in which to live; instead of merely responding to things as they happen we can think ahead and prepare for what might occur. More intimately still, instead of simply following our impulses we can act in such a way that our impulses become shaped according to the way we should be. We are helped in this by the forms of action that have been achieved by those who went before us and who have shown us how we can act. We are helped even more as parental guidance and custom develop into law, and as familial and tribal life give way to political society. Much depends on chance in such developments, but chance is not everything: our thoughtfulness slowly asserts itself in the face of natural forces and the recurrent insistence of impulse; it reasserts itself after the inevitable onslaught and ruin; and it makes a human space in which we can live and flourish and respect one another as best we can. We know that in the end, sooner or later, the light that was struck in us will be spent—*mortal' cosa son io, natura humana*—but our deliberations and choices do not have to range to that extreme. They have enough to do within the space that has been cleared, at least for a time, for us.

Furthermore, our salvation, in this secular attitude, does not only involve the preservation of our life and the performance of action; it also is achieved, perhaps in its most exalted form, in our activity of watching the stars move and the grass grow, and of understanding why such things happen as they do. The life of understanding and insight is for human beings an even higher life than the economic and political lives. It is, more than they, the reason why we are here: it expresses most simply what we are and what we can do. The lives of economics and politics have their human dignity because they share in reason, but the theoretical life is the activity of reason in as pure a form as we are able to achieve it.

For this atheistic understanding of the whole, there is no point in addressing anything in the world outside the human race (or perhaps, in a derivative manner, some of the other animals). It makes no sense to ask for help or salvation from anything besides ourselves and other human beings. There is nothing to which we can pray. Any address directed toward nature and its forces is merely literary, an apostrophe and not a prayer. We must reconcile ourselves to what is possible, we must overcome resentment at the fact of our limitation and mortality, we must accept the conditions under which life was given to us—or rather, since the word "given" implies a giver of some sort, the conditions under which we have happened to come to be. Within these limitations, we can shape ourselves to some extent, and precisely to that extent our lives and characters are most truly our own. Within these limitations we can be happy; we can even, to use Aristotle's term, be blessed (*makarioi*), but in a measure appropriate to what we are: blessed, but only as men.[6]

2. The second understanding of ourselves and of the world is quite the contrary of the one we have just examined. In this sec-

6. Aristotle, *Nicomachean Ethics* I 8, 1101a19–21.

ond understanding, there are divine agents in great number in the world. We can be affected by what they do and it makes sense for us to address them and to ask for their protection and favor. Expressions of this understanding can be found in the legends and myths of aboriginal people and primitive societies, but the most developed literary expression of it comes from the religious writings of the ancients, the writers that Aristotle referred to as the theologians. The poems of Homer, Hesiod, and Virgil; the myths and epics of the Near Eastern peoples; the Teutonic myths and the legends of Asia all describe the gods as endowed with knowledge and choice and as acting in the world. The gods intervene in worldly and in human affairs. There are gods of the earth, the oceans, and the winds; gods of volcanoes and weather; gods of birth and death; gods of sexuality; gods of crafts, arts, and sciences; gods of cities and peoples. The things that happen are not just the outcome of natural necessity and chance; things happen as they do partly because the gods want them to happen. Even the order of things can be seen, in this view, as the achievement of the gods. These gods know the world and the events in it. They are far superior to us, but they know who we are and what we do. They may favor some of us and not others, they may change their minds, they may be indifferent to us, but it is appropriate and even necessary for us to pray to them. They can bring us a kind of salvation: defense against enemies, good fortune, preservation or restoration of health, success in business, inspiration and enlightenment, even elevation into their company. Both chance and the necessities of nature are not anonymous and automatic, but are to a large degree chosen to be what they are by the gods.

We may be inclined to think that this polytheistic understanding of the world belongs to an early stage in human development, that it is appropriate only for people who have not reached cultural, intellectual, and emotional maturity. It is, we may think, a view of things that prevailed before the advent of biblical religion and philosophy, before the Enlightenment, and before the development of science. We might like to think that we have gone beyond this alienation of our hopes into the powers of nature, that we have learned to trust in ourselves. But if we were to think this way, we would be overlooking many manifestations of polytheistic or animistic belief in our contemporary world. The understanding of the "gods" we have sketched does not belong only to antiquity or to primitive peoples. There are many ways in which the polytheistic or the animistic understanding of the divine continues to exist among us: in superstitious behavior; in doing things that are supposed to ward off bad fortune or bring us good luck; in using religious rituals primarily as a guarantee of good health, financial success, or national achievements; in belief in reincarnation, astrology, charms, and witchcraft. Such behaviors exist and reflect a permanent disposition in man to recognize his subjection to what St. Paul called "the principalities and powers" of the world (Colossians 2:15).

The gods of such polytheistic religion are obviously part of the world and could not exist independently of the world. They are subject to destiny and may have to struggle to achieve their plans. They quarrel among themselves. The partiality of these gods poses a problem for us mortals, because in invoking one of them we run the risk of offending another, but this is one of the baleful limitations of the human estate.

3. There is a third attitude toward the whole that must be distinguished from the two that we have described. It is theistic, but in a philosophically critical way. One of the most vivid examples of this third understanding can be found in Aristotle, who acknowledged the being of a divine principle (and hence differed from the atheists) but criticized the anthropomorphic theology of the poets (and hence differed from the polytheists).[7]

For Aristotle, the divine encompasses and orders the world but does not know the world. The divine is the self-thinking thought and the prime mover of the processes and actualities of the world, but it works its effect in the world simply by being the highest and best entity and thus the exemplar for the actu-

7. On Aristotle's critique of theological anthropomorphism, see *Metaphysics* XII 8, 1074a38–b14.

ality and activity of all other things. This divine principle is reached through philosophical reflection; the poets only hint at it, and they have added many human features to the divine as a way of inspiring and regulating the multitude of men, who are not capable of philosophical reflection. Aristotle philosophically purifies and demythologizes the divine principle of the poets; he trims away the unworthy aspects the poets have added to it and makes it acceptable to the more critical thinker.

When he does this, he takes away from the divine principle any possibility of intervening in the world. Aristotle's god is not capable of what von Balthasar has called *Theodramatik*. The god does not act or choose; not because he is impotent, but because action and choice would be unworthy of him. To act is to be immersed in contingency and to choose is to make one selection among many possibilities, leaving many things undone. Aristotle's god is beyond contingency and risk. He dwells in eternal necessity, in which there are no surprises and no limitations. But although so noble and impassive, this god is still only part of the world. He is the best and most perfect part, but it would make no sense to claim that this god could be without the world. Although the world depends on his causation, he and the world form a whole that is larger and better than either of its parts taken by itself. God is for Aristotle the most favored part of the whole, the part to which all the other things in the whole must ultimately be referred, but he could not be without the rest of the whole, even though he is ignorant of anything beyond himself.

This way of understanding the divine and the whole is, again, not merely a philosophical position that was entertained by a Greek thinker some two thousand years ago. It is not merely an anecdote in the history of ideas. It expresses a permanent human possibility. Just as the polytheistic or animistic understanding of the gods is always there as one of the ways in which we can and do look at the whole, so the demythologized, philosophical understanding of the divine is always there as another. In our day, one of the forms that this demythologized understanding of the divine and the whole has assumed is the form known as process theology or process philosophy.[8] The god of process theology is the way the divine principle is understood when time and evolution—and perhaps also mathematical science—have been taken into account.

Aristotle's universe was permanent. He considered the form of the heavens and even the species of living things to be eternal. We, in contrast, now think of the universe as expanding and developing, and we think of life as evolving over time; we thus consider the time at which things occur to have a more significant ontological role than it did in the physics of Aristotle. The first principle, the god of such a developing universe, will have some features that are different from the first principle of an Aristotelian universe, but the two "divinities" will also have much in common. They will have in common the fact that they are both reached through a purification of common beliefs about the divine. They will have in common the fact that they are understood in the light of the most advanced scientific knowledge we have of the world. They will have in common the fact that as principles they are both only part—even though the most favored part—of the whole. Finally, they will have in common the fact that they do not act in the universe in the way the gods of popular belief do. They are exemplars for the being of things, not agents that intervene in what happens. The philosophically purified divine principle can appear at one time as Aristotle's prime mover and self-thinking thought, at another as the god of process philosophy, and at others in still other forms: it can be the divine spirit of the Stoics, the carefree divinities of the Epicureans, the dialectical spirit of Hegel, the object of the ultimate concern described by Tillich, the benevolent divinity described by John Findlay. This sort of divinity is meant to be a credible god, one that the intellectuals of the age can accept, one that is purified of the credulities of polytheism. It is the di-

8. Another important author whose work expresses a purely philosophical theology is John N. Findlay. See, for example, his "Religion and Its Three Paradigmatic Instances."

vinity of the intellectually sophisticated, in contrast to the divinities of popular folklore. It is a formulation of the divine that allows us to be both religious and critically thoughtful.

Salvation before this divinity does not mean being saved by the god, because the god does not act toward us. We exist through the necessities of nature and so does the god, but he exists in a manner far superior to ours. We are the lesser lights; he is the light at the center. We can admire him and can do our best to be like him in his perfection. His image brings out the best in us. We salute him, but we do not and cannot pray to him; he is not the kind of god to whom one prays. In this understanding, salvation is rather like an exalted and energetic resignation, an acceptance of our being and his, a willingness to let things occur as they must occur according to the necessities of things, and an effort to conform ourselves to the way we ought to be.

We have distinguished three nonbiblical ways of understanding the whole and our salvation within it: the secular, the popularly religious, and the philosophically religious. Before turning our attention to the Christian understanding, let us reflect briefly on these three and compare them with one another.

All three take the world or the whole of things as simply there. Even the two religious forms of understanding, the popular and the philosophical, accept the world as simply there; the divine brings order into things but does not create them out of nothing. Both these religious understandings avoid the question of how the world came to be in the first place; such a question would seem to them to be meaningless—as it would, a fortiori, to the secular understanding—because it would imply that something could come out of nothing. For these understandings, the divine is part of the whole, so any question about the origin of things would have to include in its scope the origin of the gods as well. Both the divine and the profane would have to arise from nonbeing. Any question about how this could happen would lack sense. Meaningful questions can be raised only within the context of being; they cannot address the advent of being itself.

As we have already mentioned, the three understandings should not be taken as mere facts of intellectual history. They are not simply three opinions that have arisen in the course of Western thinking. They also are not just beliefs that have arisen successively at appropriate moments in the development of Western thinking, as stages in the maturation of human reason. Rather, they represent three long-term and rather stable alternatives for the mind. They are three basic ways in which human beings can take a stance toward the whole. We can be atheists, we can see the world as peopled by gods, we can purify popular belief and reach a critical understanding of the divine. The shape that these possibilities take on will change and will reflect the culture of the time—the atheism of Thucydides will be different from that of Hobbes or that of a logical positivist—but the three remain as a permanent set of alternatives.

Furthermore, it need not be the case that we can easily and clearly place every thinker or every human being in one or other of these categories. In our analysis, we have discussed these categories in their pure and rather abstract form, but they actually exist, as do all philosophical forms, in mixed ways. This or that person may be inclined toward this or that form, but may not be without some element of one or both of the others as well. A person may be philosophically religious, but may at one time or another have a sense of the gods as present in various immanent ways in the world; Aristotle, after all, confessed that the older he got the more he began to love the myths.[9] A person may be atheistic and yet suspect the presence of the divine; another person may be animistic in his understanding of the world, but may also glimpse the possibility of a single divine principle underlying all the others. He may also at times harbor the thought that there may be no divinity in the universe at all. In the common opinion of people, in the kind of vague understanding that is measured by surveys asking questions about religious attitudes, the "belief in God" that is usually recorded may

9. See Jaeger, *Aristotle*, 321.

well be just a kind of vague religiosity, an amalgam of the popular belief in many immanent gods and the more sophisticated insight into a single divine principle.

Finally, another thing common to the three forms of belief is that they all make a distinction within the world between the necessary and the contingent. For the religious attitudes, the necessary is the domain of the divine: it is the domain of the gods, of the eternal and changeless, of the controlling and dominant forces, while the contingent is the domain of the mortal, the changing, the unpredictable, the domain of choice and chance, the world in which we live. Even the atheistic position recognizes this difference and formulates it as the difference between the permanent laws of nature, the laws that govern and explain the rest of things, and the world of actual phenomena, which are mixed, changeable, and chancy. The first domain is the object of scientific inquiry, the second of direct experience. In all three of the ways people can be related to the whole, the world is taken to be simply there as the final context for everything, and it is divided into the domains of the necessary and the contingent.

D

Now we turn to the Christian understanding of the whole and of our place and our salvation in the whole. The Christian understanding is different from the three forms we have described, but it is not just one more option, a fourth human possibility, ranged alongside the others. It is radically different. It is different because it is believed to have been revealed by divine intervention. It comes from without in a way that the other three do not: they stem from the possibilities of human nature; it comes because of a choice made by God. But the difference between the Christian and the other viewpoints can be specified more exactly. It is different from the others not just because it comes from another source, but also because its content is radically different from that of the others.

The new perspective offered by Christian belief is that the whole is no longer seen as ultimate and ontologically dense, as simply there, enclosing the divine and the profane. The whole itself is now understood as not having had to be. The ontological density of the whole is questioned. Its ultimacy as the context for everything is no longer taken for granted. The understanding is now proposed that the whole that is given to us as the context for everything might in fact not have existed. The whole is there because of a choice, a choice made by God the Creator. God is now understood not just as the most favored part of the whole, but as capable of being even without the whole. Furthermore, the manner in which God could be apart from the whole is distinctive; God could be in undiminished goodness and greatness even without the world. It is not the case that God before Creation was somehow less divine; if this were the case, then God would ultimately be only part of the whole, because his own full perfection would require the being of the rest of the whole. For God to be truly distinguished from the whole, he must be capable of being in undiminished perfection even without the whole. God does not need to create in order to be God, in order to be what he is: "God's life does not depend on his being the Creator. Creation is not his life; it is but a gratuitous expression of that life."[10]

This shift in thinking does not just introduce a new sense of the divine. It also introduces a new sense of the world, which is now seen as capable of not being, and a new sense of ourselves, who are seen to have been created through the personal knowledge and choice of God. Instead of seeing ourselves as embedded in a world that is simply there, we see ourselves as existing through divine action. Everything looks different. Salvation is now understood as being achieved by a divine action that has no parallel in the interventions of the gods described in polytheistic religions. We are saved by the redemptive action of God in Christ, an action that was anticipated by the providential and

10. Bouyer, *The Eternal Son*, 322.

saving acts of the Old Covenant, an action that sheds light even on the act of Creation, which is now seen as the first of the saving acts of God. The redemptive action of God in Christ is then reenacted in the Eucharists that allow it to permeate, like leaven, the life of the human race spread over all the earth. The saving action is then further reflected in the lives of confessors and martyrs, in the life of the Church and the saints.

This Christian understanding transposes the natural distinction between the necessary and the contingent. The Christian understanding continues to recognize the difference between the necessary and the contingent as the basic distinction within the world. Like the nonbiblical viewpoints, it draws a contrast between the two domains. As von Balthasar observes, the Bible itself recognizes a difference between the heavens and the earth. However, whereas the pagans thought that the heavens were either divine or at least coeternal with the divine, the Bible sees both the heavens and the earth as created by God.[11] For the Bible, the heavens are the place where God dwells, but they are not co-eternal with him, nor are they a principle somehow equal to him. The heavens are as much subject to his creative power as is the domain of the contingent and the changeable. Thus, the worldly necessary and contingent, which provide the ultimate context in nonbiblical thinking, now both together become contingent in a new way. Their contingency is not the same as the contingency that is found as part of the whole. Likewise, the necessity by which the biblical God exists is a different kind of necessity from that partial necessity found in the heavens, among the gods, in the immanent divine principle, or in the laws of nature.

The Christian understanding of the divine goes beyond the three nonbiblical attitudes we have distinguished. By purifying the sense of the divine, by condensing what von Balthasar has called the diffuse religious sense of god ("der überall diffus vorhandene Gott der Religion")[12] into the transcendent sense of

---

11. See von Balthasar, Theodramatik, 2/1:155–69; Theodramatik, 3:21.
12. Von Balthasar, Theodramatik, 3:60. On p. 58 von Balthasar refers to "eine art

God as Creator and Redeemer, incarnate in Christ himself, biblical revelation has desacralized the world and eliminated the animistic and polytheistic divinities that had populated it. But in this transformation, the sense of local and intermediate sacredness was not entirely lost; it was transformed into the presence of shrines and saints, which are now taken not as independent divine powers but as points of contact and intercessors with the one true God. These places and persons are sacred in a new way, one compatible with the transcendence of the Creator. Their holiness depends on his and participates in it. Likewise, the various worldly concerns that were attached to the particular gods—government, health, art—are also respected in Christian belief. The human concern with suffering, for example, was directly addressed by Jesus in the cures he performed, and it is also dealt with at places such as Lourdes and Fatima and in the prayers we request of the Blessed Virgin and the saints: but once again, these remedies of human ills are seen as signs of the power and grace of God, not as things that are bargained for, and a Christian prayer for help in suffering is always also a prayer of resignation to the will of God.

Christian faith transcends popular belief in the gods, but it equally transcends the philosophically critical religious belief. The most favored part of the world, the first principle of philosophical theology, gives way to the divine principle that could be even without the world. In this transformation, our attitude toward the first principle is changed. The effort of speculation is transposed into the obedience of faith, but this faith retains a glimpse of understanding. The piety of thinking is not extinguished. Christian faith is not a leap into sheer darkness and ignorance; it is a faith mediated by the Logos. The Spirit that enlivens our faith proceeds not only from the Father but also from the Son, the Logos, and hence the Divine Reason expressed in

---

verworrener Theodramatik" to speak of the divine activity described by pagan mythology.

the Logos leaves an imprint on our faith.[13] Christian faith could not be reached by philosophy, but once it is revealed to us it elevates human reason, in both its speculative and practical capacities, and makes it possible for human reason to take the whole and its principles in a new way. The first principle of philosophical theology can then be seen as an anticipation of the biblical sense of God.

E

In Christian faith and understanding, the world is taken to exist as the outcome of a choice. The choice found in Creation, however, is only analogous to the choices that we experience in human affairs. The domain of necessity that is within the world does not have room for choice, not because it is too feeble ontologically to sustain choices, but because it is too noble and perfect; there are no contingencies, no capacity for things to be other than they are, in the domain of the necessary. Worldly choice can exist only in the domain of the contingent, the domain in which things can be determined to be either this way or that, and in which such determination depends on the deliberations of an agent. Every choice made in this domain is a restriction; if we select one option among several, the other options are left undone. Choice is both the outcome and the source of limitation.

In biblical understanding, God exists in a new kind of necessity, not the kind that is part of the natural world. In biblical understanding, the world as a whole exists in a new kind of contingency, not the kind that is part of the natural world. The contingency by which the world exists is the kind that comes from a choice. However, the choice in question is not the kind that belongs in the contingent domain found within the world, but the kind that is compatible with the eternal necessity of the

13. This interpretation of the debate concerning "Filioque" was expressed by Professor Andrzej Grib of St. Petersburg during a meeting at the Pontifical Academy of Theology at Cracow, Poland, in May 1991.

biblical God. When God chooses to create, his choice does not limit him; he does not choose one among many options laid out before him, leaving the others undone and leaving himself restricted in his being; when he chooses to create, he is not constricted to only one form of being as opposed to another; he is no more perfect or less perfect after the choice than he was before it was made.[14]

It is by the God who chooses in this way that we are saved. The divine decision to redeem is also not a constricting choice, not one that limits God to being only this way and not that. It is only analogous to human decisions and choices. What we respond to when we respond to our salvation is not anything like the finite human interventions we are familiar with; it is a sovereign choice, made out of a perfection and generosity that we cannot imagine. We can speak about it more by the language of negation and eminence than by strict description. How can we respond to such a choice to redeem? Only by what we call the theological virtues, the dispositions of faith, hope, and charity. Faith is the recognition of who God is and what he has done, hope is the expectation that his saving action will reach its fulfillment, and charity is the form of conduct, indicated by Christ, in which we allow God's choice to function in our love of God and in our actions toward other men. Faith, hope, and charity are not the civic virtues that equip us to act well within the horizon of the natural world; they are not equivalent to justice, prudence, temperance, courage, and the other natural virtues; they are the dispositions that enable us to respond to the divine choice made in the context which is not embedded within the whole given to natural experience and thought. They are the vir-

14. Some valuable remarks on the concept of the Creator as artisan of the world can be found in Burrell, *Knowing the Unknowable God*, particularly in chapter 6, where Burrell discusses the "alternatives" left uncreated by God. He shows that such a category is inappropriate, as is the notion that God is faced with a series of possible worlds and that he chooses among them. The focus should be on what is actually created and on its mode of being, not on what else might have been done.

tues that enable us to act—and here even the word "act" is used analogously—toward the God who could be all that there is, in undiminished goodness and greatness, even if there were no world: the God who created the world and redeemed us through the Incarnation, death, and Resurrection of his Son.

The virtues of faith, hope, and charity are to be exercised in all spheres of life, but they are exercised in a concentrated way in the celebration of the Eucharist. The Eucharist does more than merely symbolize and remind us of the saving action of God. It makes that action present again through the quoted words and gestures of Christ, the words and gestures he used when he anticipated and accepted the death by which we were saved. It is in faith, hope, and charity that we take part in the eucharistic celebration, as we see beyond the looks of bread and wine and acknowledge the presence of the God who created us and who could be, in undiminished goodness and greatness, even without the world; we recognize his presence not just as the eternal God, but as the God who acts in the sacrament to bring about our Redemption.

Theological reflection can help deepen our understanding of what faith presents in the Eucharist. To appreciate the Redemption that is given sacramentally to us, we must realize who is acting in the sacrament; consequently, the theological reflection that strives to make more distinct the Christian understanding of God is of no small value even for the moment of our eucharistic action. Thinking about the necessity by which God exists and about the contingency of the world is not simply metaphysical speculation but an attempt to help us accept the Eucharist for what it is. It helps us to see the difference between the Eucharist and the signs and symbols of our worldly way of being. The theology of disclosure does not only help us clarify the teachings that are given in Christian belief; it also helps us receive the sacramental signs in faith and to accept them for what they truly are as they present themselves to us in the liturgical life of the Church.

WORKS CITED

Anselm, St. *Proslogion*. Translated and introduced by M. J. Charlesworth. Notre Dame: University of Notre Dame Press, 1979.

Aquinas, St. Thomas. *In duodecim libros metaphysicorum Aristotelis expositio*, edited by M. R. Cathala, O.P., and R. M. Spiazzi, O.P. Rome: Marietti, 1950.

———. *Quaestiones disputatae de malo*. Leonine Edition, vol. 23. Paris: Vrin, 1982.

———. *Quaestiones disputatae de potentia dei*. In *Quaestiones disputatae*, vol. 2, edited by P. Bazzi et al. Rome: Marietti, 1953.

———. *Summa theologiae*. Blackfriars edition and translation. Vols. 58, 59, and 60. New York: McGraw-Hill, 1965, 1975, and 1966.

Arendt, Hannah. *The Human Condition*. Chicago: The University of Chicago Press, 1958.

Arsac, Jacques. *Jacques Arsac. Un Informaticien. Entretien avec Jacques Vauthier*. Collection scientifiques et croyants, no. 1. Paris: Beauchesne, 1989.

———. *La science informatique*. Paris: Dunod, 1970.

Athanasius, St. "On the Incarnation of the Word." In *A Select Library of Nicene and Post-Nicene Fathers of the Church*, vol. 4, *St. Athanasius*, 36–67. Reprint. Grand Rapids, Mich.: Eerdmans, 1980.

Augustine, St. *Confessiones Libri XIII*. Edited by Lucas Verheijen, O.S.A. Corpus Christianorum Series Latina, vol. 27. Turnhout: Brepols, 1981.

Austin, Gerard, O.P. "Is an Ecumenical Understanding of the Eucharist Possible Today?" *The Jurist* 48 (1988): 668–91.

Balthasar, Hans Urs von. *The Glory of the Lord*, vol. 1. Translated by Erasmo Leiva-Merikakis. San Francisco: Ignatius Press, 1982.

———. "The Grandeur of the Liturgy." *Communio* 5 (1978): 344–51.

———. *Licht des Wortes*. Trier: Paulinus Verlag, 1987.

———. "Mysterium Paschale." In *Mysterium Salutis*, vol. 3, part 2, *Das Christusereignis*, edited by Johannes Feiner and Magnus Löhrer, 133–512. Einsiedeln: Benzinger Verlag, 1969.

———. *Theodramatik*, vol. 1, *Prolegomena*. Einsiedeln: Johannes Verlag, 1973.

———. *Theodramatik*, vol. 2, *Die Personen des Spiels*, part 1, *Der Mensch in Gott*. Einsiedeln: Johannes Verlag, 1976.

———. *Theodramatik*, vol. 2, *Die Personen des Spiels*, part 2, *Die Personen in Christus*. Einsiedeln: Johannes Verlag, 1978.

———. *Theodramatik*, vol. 3, *Die Handlung*. Einsiedeln: Johannes Verlag, 1980.

———. *You Crown the Year with Your Goodness. Sermons throughout the Liturgical Year*. Translated by Graham Harrison. San Francisco: Ignatius Press, 1989.

Barden, William, O.P. "The Metaphysics of the Eucharist." Appendix 3 in St. Thomas Aquinas, *Summa theologiae*, vol. 58, *The Eucharistic Presence*, 207–14. Blackfriars edition. New York: McGraw-Hill, 1965.

Beirnaert, Louis. "La dimension mythique dans le sacramentalisme chrétien." *1949 Eranos Jahrbuch*, 255–86. Zurich: Rhein Verlag, 1950.

Besançon, Alain. *The Rise of the Gulag. Intellectual Origins of Leninism*. Translated by Sarah Matthews. New York: Continuum, 1981.

Bouyer, Louis. *The Christian Mystery. From Pagan Myth to Christian Mysticism*. Translated by Illtyd Trethowan. Edinburgh: T. and T. Clark, 1990.

———. *The Eternal Son*. Translated by Sr. Simone Inkel, S.L., and John F. Laughlin. Huntington, Ind.: Our Sunday Visitor Press, 1978.

———. *Eucharist. Theology and Spirituality of the Eucharistic Prayer*. Translated by Charles Underhill Quinn. Notre Dame: University of Notre Dame Press, 1968.

———. *Liturgical Piety*. Notre Dame: University of Notre Dame Press, 1955.

———. *Le mystère paschal*. Paris: Les Éditions du Cerf, 1947.

———. *Rite and Man*. Notre Dame: University of Notre Dame Press, 1963.

Brann, Eva T. H. *The World of the Imagination. Sum and Substance*. Savage, Md.: Rowman and Littlefield, 1991.

Bromberg, Craig. "In Defense of Hackers." *The New York Times Magazine*. 21 April 1991.

Brooks, Van Wyck. *Helen Keller. Sketch for a Portrait*. New York: E. P. Dutton, 1956.

Brown, Raymond E., S.S., and Sandra M. Schneiders, I.H.M., "Hermeneutics." Chapter 71 in *The New Jerome Biblical Commentary*, edited by Raymond E. Brown, S.S., Joseph A. Fitzmyer, S.J., and Roland E. Murphy, O.Carm. Englewood Cliffs, N.J.: Prentice-Hall, 1990.

Burrell, David, C.S.C. *Knowing the Unknowable God. Ibn-Sina, Maimonides, Aquinas*. Notre Dame: University of Notre Dame Press, 1986.

Cajetan, Thomas de Vio, O.P. Commentary on the First Part of the *Summa Theologiae* of St. Thomas. In Thomas Aquinas, *Summa Theologiae, Prima Pars*. Leonine Edition, vol. 4. Rome: Sancta Congregatio de Propaganda Fide, 1888.

Clark, Francis, S.J. *Eucharistic Sacrifice and the Reformation*. 2d ed. Oxford: Blackwell, 1967.

Cobb-Stevens, Richard. *Husserl and Analytic Philosophy*. Phaenomeno-
logica, no. 116. Dordrecht: Kluwer, 1990.

Congar, Yves M. J., O.P. "L'ecclesia' ou communauté chrétienne, sujet
intégral de l'action liturgique." In *La liturgie après Vatican II.
Bilans, études, prospective*, edited by J. P. Jossua, O.P. and Y. Congar, O.P.,
241–82. Paris: Les éditions du Cerf, 1967.

"Constitution on the Sacred Liturgy," *The Documents of Vatican II*, edited
by Walter M. Abbott, S.J., 137–78. New York: America Press, 1966.

Crockett, William R. *Eucharist: Symbol of Transformation*. New York: Pueblo, 1989.

Dix, Dom Gregory. *The Shape of the Liturgy*. Westminster: The Dacre Press,
1947.

Findlay, John N. "Religion and Its Three Paradigmatic Instances." *Religious
Studies* 11 (1975): 215–27.

Frege, Gottlob. "Logic." In *Posthumous Writings*, edited by Hans Hermes,
Friedrich Kambartel, and Friedrich Kaulbach; translated by Peter Long
and Roger White, 126–51. Chicago: University of Chicago Press, 1979.

Gadamer, Hans-Georg. *Wahrheit und Methode. Grundzüge einer philosophis-
chen Hermeneutik*. 2d ed. Tübingen: J.C.B. Mohr, 1965.

Giraudo, Cesare, S.J. "The Eucharist as Re-Presentation." *Religious Studies
Bulletin* 4 (1984): 154–59.

———. *La struttura letteraria della preghiera eucaristica*. Analecta Biblica 92.
Rome: Biblical Institute, 1981.

Gnilka, Joachim. *Neutestamentliche Theologie*. Würzburg: Echter Verlag,
1989.

Haag, Herbert. *Vom alten zum neuen Pascha*. Stuttgart: Katholisches Bibel-
werk Verlag, 1971.

Hänggi, Anton, and Irmgard Pahl, eds. *Prex Eucharistica. Textus e variis
liturgiis antiquioribus selecti*. Spicilegium Friburgense, no. 12. Fribourg:
Éditions universitaires Fribourg Suisse, 1968.

Hanna, Robert. "How Ideas Became Meanings: Locke and the Foundations
of Semantic Theory." *Review of Metaphysics* 44 (1991): 775–805.

Hobbes, Thomas. *De Cive*. Edited by Howard Warrender. Oxford: At the
Clarendon Press, 1983.

Holenstein, Elmar. "Eine Maschine im Geist. Husserlsche Begründung und
Begrenzung künstlicher Intelligenz." *Phänomenologische Forschungen* 21
(1988): 82–113.

Homer. *The Iliad*. Translated by Richard Lattimore. Chicago: The University of Chicago Press, 1951.

Husserl, Edmund. *Cartesian Meditations*. Translated by Dorion Cairns. The
Hague: Nijhoff, 1960.

———. *Ideas Pertaining to a Pure Phenomenology and to a Phenomenological
Philosophy. First Book*. Translated by F. Kersten. The Hague: Nijhoff, 1982.

———. *Ideen zu einer reinen Phänomenologie und phänomenologischen Philoso-
phie. Drittes Buch*, edited by Marly Biemel. The Hague: Nijhoff, 1952.

Ignatius of Antioch, St. "Letter to Polycarp." In Migne, *Patrologia Graeca*,
5:717–28.

————. "Letter to the Romans." In Migne, *Patrologia Graeca*, 5:686–95.

Jaeger, Werner. *Aristotle. Fundamentals of the History of His Development.* Translated by Richard Robinson. Oxford: Oxford University Press, 1934.

Jasper, R.C.D., and Cuming, G.J. *Prayers of the Eucharist: Early and Reformed.* 3d ed. Collegeville, Minn.: The Liturgical Press, 1992.

John Paul II, Pope. "The Lord's Supper. *Dominicae Coenae.*" *The Pope Speaks* 25 (1980): 139–64.

————. "Lord and Giver of Life. *Dominum et Vivificantem.*" Fifth Encyclical Letter. Washington, D.C.: United States Catholic Conference, 1986.

Journet, Charles. *La Messe. Présence du sacrifice de la croix.* Paris: Desclée de Brouwer, 1957.

Jungmann, Josef. *The Eucharistic Prayer.* Translated by Robert L. Batley. Wheathampstead: Anthony Clarke, 1978.

————. *The Mass of the Roman Rite. Its Origins and Development.* Translated by Francis A. Brunner, C.SS.R. 2 vols. New York: Benzinger, 1951.

Keller, Helen. *The Story of My Life.* New York: Grosset and Dunlap, 1905.

King, Archdale A. *Eucharistic Reservation in the Western Church.* New York: Sheed and Ward, 1965.

Klauck, Hans-Josef. *Herrenmahl und hellenistischer Kult.* Münster: Aschendorff, 1982.

Kodell, Jerome, O.S.B. *The Eucharist in the New Testament.* Wilmington, Del.: Michael Glazier, 1988.

Lash, Joseph P. *Helen and Teacher. The Story of Helen Keller and Anne Sullivan Macy.* New York: Delacorte Press, 1980.

Leo the Great, Pope St. "Sermon II on the Ascension." In Migne, *Patrologia Latina*, 54:396–400.

————. "Sermon XII on the Passion." In Migne, *Patrologia Latina*, 54:355–57.

Léon-Dufour, Xavier, S.J. *Sharing the Eucharistic Bread.* Translated by Matthew J. O'Connell. New York: Paulist Press, 1987.

Lewis, C. S. *The Abolition of Man.* New York: Macmillan, 1974.

————. *Mere Christianity.* New York: Macmillan, 1943.

Ligier, Louis, S.J. "From the Last Supper to the Eucharist." In *The New Liturgy*, edited by L. Sheppard, 113–50. London: Darton, Longman, & Todd, 1970.

————. "The Origins of the Eucharistic Prayer: From the Last Supper to the Eucharist." *Studia Liturgica* 9 (1973): 161–85.

Locke, John. *An Essay Concerning Human Understanding.* 2 vols. Edited by Alexander Campbell Fraser. New York: Dover, 1959.

Loewald, Hans. W. *Papers on Psychoanalysis.* New Haven: Yale University Press, 1980.

————. *Psychoanalysis and the History of the Individual.* New Haven: Yale University Press, 1978.

Maritain, Jacques. *The Person and the Common Good.* Translated by John J. Fitzgerald. Notre Dame: University of Notre Dame Press, 1966.

Marliangeas, Bernard Dominique. *Clés pour une théologie du ministère. In persona Christi, in persona ecclesiae.* Paris: Éditions Beauchesne, 1978.

————. "'In persona Christi,' 'In persona ecclesiae.' Notes sur les origines et
le développement de l'usage de ces expressions dans la théologie latine."
In *La liturgie après Vatican II. Bilans, études, prospective*, edited by J. P.
Jossua, O.P., and Y. Congar, O.P., 283–88. Paris: Les éditions du Cerf,
1967.

Masure, Eugene. *The Christian Sacrifice*. New York: P. J. Kenedy and Sons,
1943.

Mazza, Enrico. *The Eucharistic Prayers of the Roman Rite*. Translated by Matthew J. O'Connell. New York: Pueblo Publishing Co., 1986.

McKenzie, John J. "Aspects of Old Testament Thought." Chapter 77 in
The New Jerome Biblical Commentary, edited by Raymond E. Brown, S.S.,
Joseph A. Fitzmyer, S.J., and Roland E. Murphy, O. Carm. Englewood
Cliffs, N.J.: Prentice-Hall, 1990.

Mitchell, Nathan, O.S.B. *Cult and Controversy. The Worship of the Eucharist outside Mass*. New York: Pueblo, 1982.

The New Testament of the New American Bible. New York: Catholic Book
Publishing Co., 1986.

Newman, John Henry. *A Grammar of Assent*. New York: Doubleday, 1955.

————. "Milman's View of Christianity." Chapter 12 in *Essays Critical and
Historical*, vol. 2. New York: Longmans, Green and Co., 1907.

Nietzsche, Friedrich. *The Gay Science*. Translated by Walter Kaufmann.
New York: Random House, 1974.

Oakeshott, Michael. *On Human Conduct*. Oxford: At the Clarendon Press,
1975.

O'Connor, James T. *The Hidden Manna. A Theology of the Eucharist*. San
Francisco: Ignatius Press, 1988.

O'Neill, Colman E., O.P. *Meeting Christ in the Sacraments*. 2d ed., edited by
R. Cessario, O.P. New York: Alba House, 1991.

————. *Sacramental Realism. A General Theory of the Sacraments*. Wilmington, Del.: Michael Glazier, 1983.

Ott, Ludwig. *Fundamentals of Catholic Dogma*, edited by James Bastible and
translated by Patrick Lynch. Cork: The Mercier Press, 1955.

Patzig, Gunther. "Theology and Ontology in Aristotle's *Metaphysics*." In
Articles on Aristotle, vol. 3, *Metaphysics*, edited by Jonathan Barnes, M.
Schonfield, and Richard Sorabji, 33–49. New York: St. Martin's Press,
1979.

Pius XII, Pope. *Mediator Dei. Encyclical Letter of Pope Pius XII on the Sacred
Liturgy*. Washington, D.C.: National Catholic Welfare Conference, 1947.

Power, David N., O.M.I. *The Sacrifice We Offer. The Tridentine Dogma and
Its Reinterpretation*. New York: Crossroad, 1987.

Prufer, Thomas. "Juxtapositions: Aristotle, Aquinas, Strauss." In *Leo
Strauss's Thought. Toward a Critical Engagement*, edited by Alan Udoff,
115–21. Boulder, Colo.: Lynne Rienner Publishers, 1991. Reprinted in
Prufer, *Recapitulations. Essays in Philosophy*, 35–42. Washington, D.C.:
The Catholic University of America Press, 1993.

————. "Providence and Imitation: Sophocles's *Oedipus* and Aristotle's
Poetics." In *Philosophy and Art*, edited by Daniel Dahlstrom, 1–10. Wash-

ington, D.C.: The Catholic University of America Press, 1991. Reprinted in *Recapitulations. Essays in Philosophy*, 12–21.

Prümm, Karl, S.J. *Christentum als Neuheitserlebnis. Durchblick durch die Christlich-Antike Begegnung*. Freiburg: Herder, 1939.

―――. *Der christliche Glaube und die altheidnische Welt*. 2 vols. Leipzig: Verlag Jakob Hegner, 1935.

Rahner, Hugo, S.J. *Greek Myths and Christian Mystery*. Translated by E. O. James. New York: Harper and Row, 1963.

Rahner, Karl, S.J. "The Theology of the Symbol." In *Theological Investigations*, 4:221–52. Translated by Kevin Smyth. Baltimore: Helicon Press, 1966.

―――. "The Word and the Eucharist." In *Theological Investigations*, 4:253–86.

Rosenthal, Debra. *At the Heart of the Bomb. The Dangerous Allure of Weapons Work*. New York: Addison-Wesley, 1990.

Schmemann, Alexander. *The Eucharist. Sacrament of the Kingdom*. Translated by Paul Kachur. Crestwood, N.Y.: St. Vladimir's Seminary Press, 1988.

―――. *Introduction to Liturgical Theology*. Translated by Asheleigh E. Moorhouse. Bangor, Me.: The Orthodox Press, 1966.

Schmitz, Kenneth. *The Gift: Creation*. Milwaukee: Marquette University Press, 1982.

Simon, Yves. *A General Theory of Authority*. Notre Dame: University of Notre Dame Press, 1962.

Sokolowski, Robert. "Creation and Christian Understanding." In *God and Creation. An Ecumenical Symposium*, edited by David B. Burrell, C.S.C., and Bernard McGinn, 179–92. Notre Dame: University of Notre Dame Press, 1990.

―――. *The God of Faith and Reason. Foundations of Christian Theology*. Notre Dame: University of Notre Dame Press, 1982.

―――. *Husserlian Meditations. How Words Present Things*. Evanston, Ill.: Northwestern University Press, 1974.

―――. *Moral Action. A Phenomenological Study*. Bloomington: Indiana University Press, 1985.

―――. *Pictures, Quotations, and Distinctions. Fourteen Essays in Phenomenology*. Notre Dame: University of Notre Dame Press, 1992.

―――. *Presence and Absence. A Phenomenological Investigation of Language and Being*. Bloomington: Indiana University Press, 1978.

―――. "Religion and Psychoanalysis. Some Phenomenological Contributions." In *Psychoanalysis and Religion*, edited by Joseph E. Smith and Susan A. Handelman, 1–17. Baltimore: The Johns Hopkins University Press, 1990.

Steiner, George. *Real Presences*. Chicago: The University of Chicago Press, 1989.

Stevenson, Kenneth. *Eucharist and Offering*. New York: Pueblo, 1986.

Strauss, Leo. *The Political Philosophy of Hobbes. Its Basis and Its Genesis*. Translated by Elsa M. Sinclair. Chicago: University of Chicago Press, 1952.

————. *Thoughts on Machiavelli*. Seattle: Washington University Press, 1958.

————. "What Is Political Philosophy?" In *What Is Political Philosophy? and Other Studies*, 9–55. New York: The Free Press, 1959.

Strawson, Peter. "Freedom and Resentment." In *Freedom and Resentment and Other Essays*, 1–25. London: Methuen, 1974.

Talley, Thomas J. "From *Berakah* to *Eucharistia*: A Reopening Question." *Worship* 50 (1976): 115–37.

————. "The Literary Structure of the Eucharistic Prayer." *Worship* 58 (1984): 404–20.

Van de Pol, Willem H. *The Christian Dilemma*. Translated by G. Van Hall. London: J. M. Dent and Sons, 1952.

Vonier, Anscar, O.S.B. *A Key to the Doctrine of the Eucharist*. Westminster, Md.: The Newman Bookshop, 1946.

Wust, Peter. "Crisis in the West." In *Essays in Order*, edited by Jacques Maritain, Peter Wust, and Christopher Dawson, 95–152. New York: Sheed and Ward, 1940.

INDEX

Eucharistic Presence: A Study in the Theology of Disclosure
was composed in Goudy Old Style by Books International, Norcross,
Georgia; printed on 60-pound Glatfelter Supple Opaque Recycled paper
and bound by Thomson-Shore, Inc., Dexter Michigan; and
designed and produced by Kachergis Book Design,
Pittsboro, North Carolina.